D1616137

THE THOMAS BOOK

NEAR DEATH, A QUEST AND
A NEW GOSPEL BY THE
TWIN BROTHER OF JESUS

BRUCE FRASER MACDONALD, PHD

Eloquent Books

Eloquent Books
An imprint of Strategic Book Group
P.O.Box 333
Durham, CT 06422

www.StrategicBookGroup.com

ISBN: 978-1-60860-819-5

Printed in the United States of America

In memory of my parents — Rev. Peter Stuart MacDonald (1915–2007), minister in The United Church of Canada in Nova Scotia, Bermuda and India, and Edna Jean (Lesbirel) MacDonald (1916–2007), faithful companion and worker.

CONTENTS

Acknowledgements

I WOULD LIKE TO THANK THE EDITORS AND DESIGNERS AT Eloquent Books for taking on this project and for producing this attractive volume. I would like to thank Dr. William Wynn who has given me the opportunity to speak to many of his classes about my experiences and to all the other groups who have invited me to share with them. I thank Marilyn and Leigh and the Nova Scotia groups for their experience and observations. I am grateful to the members of my family who have provided a home where I could grow and learn of the dynamics of family — of security and loss, of conflict and resolution, of unity and separation, of anger and love. And I especially thank my wife, Olive, who has been with me for almost forty-four years now, through so many of the joys, love and difficulties, so many of the changes and challenges, through travels and search and the building of our own family, in this and other lives — you have been faithful, loving and supportive through it all, and I thank you more deeply than you realize.

To contact the author please write to:
TheThomasBook@gmail.com

INTRODUCTION

I DISCOVERED THE GOSPEL WHICH IS IN PART TWO OF THIS BOOK in the early 1980s. The text was privately circulated in 1985, but the whole story, including an account of the search for and discovery of the document, as well as important parts of the narrative, were not completed until 2009.

Part One describes a spiritual quest no less taxing than the adventures of the knights of King Arthur's court and their search for the Holy Grail. I sought my own Grail, starting with a childhood in India, a Near Death Experience after a broken back in Canada in 1966, a PhD from the University of Leeds in England, a university teaching and research career stretching from North America, through the West Indies, India and into other parts of the world, followed in 1991 by mosquito borne encephalitis in Western Canada with its resulting brain damage and almost complete loss of memory and ego.

It seems strange that finding a new Gospel would include a broken back and a severe case of viral encephalitis, but the Spirit works in mysterious ways. I discovered that the process of spiritual education is not just a simple matter of looking in books or sitting quietly in monasteries. I thought *The Thomas Book* would be just a new Gospel text independent of my daily experience. That was before I discovered that this is a "living text," both for me and for others. Expect it to have profound effects on every aspect of your life.

One of the biggest discoveries, which turned my whole world on its head, came in 2007, after I had submitted this book and *The Prayer of Silence* (a book on a new kind of meditation based on the awareness which my Near Death Experience opened to me) to a publisher. It was then that I found how profoundly we are affected by reincarnation; by the rebirth of the people we have been in the past and by meeting others with whom we have had relations in other lives. Not all discoveries of this sort are welcomed. There are several people who would prefer I had not discovered who they were in the past and who they pretend to be in the present.

Before I could truly come to terms with who I had been in the past, and why I was the one who found this Gospel, I had to work my way through the intrigue of a spiritual identity theft which stretched over 2000 years, and the concerted effort of a number of people to keep that stolen identity hidden. The drama of two millennia finds its conclusion in this book at the beginning of the twenty-first century.

The Gospel I discovered in the early 1980s did not have a nativity story. However, in 2007, a strange new nativity story was not merely written (this is also in Part One) but was actually lived out in a surprising way in my own life. This new account brings into question many of the cherished doctrines of the churches and may be one of the most controversial parts of the whole story — and perhaps one of the most liberating.

Who is telling this story? Who is this Thomas who gives us such a radical new view of events surrounding the life, death and resurrection of Jesus? How was he able to reach through the centuries and write his story in such a different age from that in which it took place? Why was I the scribe who wrote it? You will find the answers to these questions in the whole book, since they are interwoven in the present and past and the mysterious connections between the two in the ever-present now of human consciousness.

Whether you start with Part One or Part Two, then, you will be thrown into the middle of a surprising new vision of the life and message of Jesus, the Christ. The book will give you a panoramic view of life over centuries, since it presents a dynamic adventure of how human spiritual consciousness grows and changes over thousands of years. It feels as if the first century was yesterday, as if we lived all our lives at the same time, molding and shaping them into a work of living art which spans millennia.

This is the story of Judas Thomas, Jesus and the other disciples. But it is also about me — a university professor who happened to write a Gospel — and my search, deep into the realms of the spirit, for information which may be able to liberate at least a few people from their bonds. My search for patterns of thought and reaction add to the efforts now underway to save our planet and help humanity in its growth to spiritual maturity.

Many people are extremely concerned about the future of our earth. I am one of those. And I believe that the solutions to our potentially catastrophic situation must be found in an understanding of the "things of the spirit." Religion, politics and science have only compounded our human propensity for mutual self-destruction. A spiritual vision, which shows our fundamental oneness over vast distances of time and space, may be able to help us in our attempts to overcome the forces of division and conflict with which we now have to deal.

This is a radically new vision of the events surrounding Jesus in the first century. It is also a radically new vision of how human consciousness functions. I hope you find it compelling, because our survival may depend on it and others like it. It is one of a growing number of voices which is calling for change, from the roots up, in the way we treat each other and the planet we share.

PART ONE

THE QUEST

CHAPTER ONE

~

NEAR DEATH AND THE LOST GOSPEL

So I say to you, ask and it will be given to you:
Seek and you will find:
Knock and it will be opened to you.
(Luke 11:9)

WHEN I CAME BACK FROM THE DEAD IN THE SUMMER OF 1966, I knew there was something terribly wrong with the Gospel stories in the Bible. I didn't know what the problem was, but I knew without a doubt that something had been badly distorted in the retelling of the events of Jesus' life and death. I also knew that part of the reason I came back to life was to solve this mystery.

But it wasn't just the Gospels. My experience of death propelled me on a spiritual quest to understand in greater depth the life to which I had returned. If I could die and return to life, the world was much larger than I had ever imagined. There was a vast spiritual potential I wanted to explore.

In death I had entered the sacred mystery central to all human spiritual quests. The mystery is that death is not death — it is merely a shift of consciousness, like birth. In birth we make a body for ourselves; we continue making the body from day to day during our life; and then in death we leave it behind to continue our life in a different state of awareness.

Jesus is central to this story. It is, after all, a Gospel in the tradition of the four canonical Gospels in the Bible. His experience and teaching about death and resurrection came sharply into focus for me when I realized that I had also died and risen, fulfilling his words that "Unless a seed fall into the earth and die, it will not attain eternal life."

In death I had planted the seed. The rest of my life involved tending, pruning and watering the young plant until it grew strong. This book about my "Jesus quest" is part of the harvest from that seed planted in a Near Death Experience (NDE) in 1966. Later I refer to this as a "Death Experience," because I believe I actually went through the whole process of dying before coming back to life. I was, therefore, not merely "near" death.

June 3, 1966, was a chilly, wet day. It was my third day on the job, employed as a laborer on the early stages of a new retail complex in downtown Regina, Saskatchewan, Canada. We worked in the mud that day, cleaning up used lumber. I lifted up a piece of muddy plywood, stepped ahead with it and fell feet first into an unmarked piling shaft, plummeting thirty-seven feet into the dark depths of the earth. The shock, as my heels hit bottom, was like a pile driver sending shock waves up my back, shattering one of my vertebrae, crushing it to half size, and badly fracturing two others. My internal organs were ripped out of place by the impact.

I survived for a few days, then my body stopped working and, as one nurse told me later, "We thought we had lost you. We did everything we could to bring you back, and when we were just about ready to give up, suddenly you were there again."

Death was the most interesting experience I have ever had. As my physical system became unable to support life, I found myself looking at the body from just about two feet above my left shoulder. But I was no longer a body. I was a centre of consciousness which was connected with everything in the body by a kind of comprehensive awareness, all at the same time. I was aware of all the cells, all the memories and all the life forces of the person, "Bruce," who had used that body as his home for a few, short years.

Then I began to realize that, really, I was not this Bruce. I sensed that the "glue" that held the cells together and made it possible for what I had thought was "Bruce" to function as a coherent personality, was coming apart. From that time on I knew I was not my ego, that part of us we tend to identify with in this life. I knew that I was something much bigger and much more mysterious.

I thought to myself, with some excitement, "Wow! This is what it is like to die." There was no fear or pain, just an amazing sense of recognition, as if I had been in this state before and had forgotten.

Then "I," as this centre of awareness, observed but also participated in extracting the memories from all the cells in the body where they had been progressively stored as Bruce grew and experienced the world. Once the memories were removed, this new "I" withdrew the energy field that held the cells together. Whatever this disembodied "I" was, it was not just a passive observer of events. I was active in the process of the death of the body and seemed to be harvesting a whole range of memories and energies from it.

Removing the memories and the life force from the person who had been Bruce MacDonald took some time. Once that part of the process of dying was complete, I shifted instantly into a different dimension of being. The world of bodies disappeared and I found myself in a self-luminous grey "time-landscape," almost like clouds. Here, it seemed that the farther away from me I looked the farther back in time I was seeing.

This part of the process reminded me of an experience I had as a child of about six years in the mountains of North India where I grew up. I was standing on a path not far from the town of Mussoorie, looking down through a gap in the mountains to the Dun Valley far below. Suddenly I found myself above my body, watching this young Bruce as he looked at the valley. I had somehow moved out of the child's consciousness and knew that this experience of looking at the valley was similar to one I had before birth. Then, before entering life, I had looked down on the "Valley of Time" much as the child looked on the Dun Valley.

I knew, from the perspective of the before-birth consciousness, that I could have been born up the Valley of Time to the right, in the future, or down to the left, in the past. But I had chosen to be born in the present, in the spot visible between the mountains. In the Time Landscape, the moment of birth had been about six years earlier, on December 8, 1944, while war raged in Europe and the Pacific — in the time of the ushering in of the nuclear age.

Time, I realized as a child, could exist apart from the world of material objects which we think of as the only reality. In the Death Experience of 1966, I had a similar sense of being in time and apart from the physical world, only this time I was in the moment after the life of Bruce had ended. I was not above the Time Landscape, however, but still immersed in it. In fact, I was in a transitional dimension of time which had some strange properties.

There were three men standing in this Time Landscape. For many years after coming back, my earth mind would not accept who they were, but in my spiritual state I had no surprise at meeting Yeshua (Jesus), Elijah and Moses, each receding into the Time Landscape. Yeshua was a bit in front of me, but to the left: Elijah was to my right, but farther away: and Moses was in the middle, but farther back in time.

Also to the left, over Yeshua's shoulder but higher up, as if in a different dimension above time, was the tunnel of light which has become so familiar from research into NDEs. It seemed to lead outside of time, into a most attractive realm. This was 1966, a full ten years before the first books on NDE's had been published, but although I had not read anything about this tunnel, I knew what the tunnel was for, as if I had already experienced it in the past.

In fact, there was a familiarity about this experience which was a bit surprising. I knew, if I wanted, I could go up into the amazing love and light I sensed in the dimension where the tunnel led. Then

I would be outside of time and its limitations. I also knew that if I did go there, I would never want to return to the broken body back in the hospital which was in the realm of space-time.

We four discussed a "project" that we were all part of, a project which extended through the vast reaches of time, change and growth of human consciousness. It involved a great many people and extended into the past, well before Moses had been called by the Burning Bush to be part of it. The Bruce MacDonald who had just died had been preparing to play his role in the ever expanding project. We discussed how to proceed now that he was dead.

After a while, we brought our deliberations to a close. There were decisions to be made.

Yeshua turned to me. "You can go back, or you can stay here," he said, "But be aware that it will not be easy to heal your broken body."

I could move into the light or I could go back to the body. My role in the project depended on what I decided at that moment.

At first I was noncommittal, as I thought about my options. Then I said I felt I should return to the life which had been Bruce.

Yeshua warned me, "You don't have to. We can do this a different way. But if you do, remember the body is very badly smashed up and it will be hard to get it going."

I said I was sure I should go back. I felt my role in the project was important to carry on through the body of Bruce because he had established the experiences and relationships which would be important in fulfilling the project.

Yeshua warned me a third time, almost severely this time, "You don't have to go back. We can do this in another way. The old machine is really badly smashed up. It will take a long time to get it going again. You don't have to go back!"

I knew then that what I was proposing was going to be very difficult. But at that point I knew also that the best way to achieve our goals was to return. So I said, "I will go back."

The return was instant. We did not say farewell and there was no transition. I returned instantly to my body. But for a moment there was a terrible realization — I could not get into the body. It was dead. I had removed the memories and the life-force from it. The unifying consciousness, which had made it possible to live, had been withdrawn. As I looked around I also realized I could not return to the spiritual state I had been in before. For a little while I was at a loss what to do.

Then it came to me. I realized that I had to will the memories back into the cells and then I had to draw the cells together into a living whole by putting a magnetic field, a life field, around them with my Spiritual Will.

I don't know how long this process took, but it was the afternoon of the next day when I came to consciousness in a badly damaged body.

Yeshua was right. It took seven months of surgery, therapy and wheelchairs just to get the old machine going well enough to walk out of the hospital into a new life with braces on my back and leg and with crutches to keep me from falling over.

With my death, I had been immersed in the greatest mystery of the human condition. But I had also taken on an assignment. And what an assignment! It seemed like an impossible task, to track down what was wrong with the Gospels and to discover how my experience of death related to the spiritual longing of humanity. How was I to discover anything about the project which was the focus of our discussion?

I didn't bring any secrets back with me. When I returned I was merely an ignorant young man with a broken body in a hospital bed without any idea of how to proceed.

And, to make matters worse, I had lost my brief connection with Yeshua and, often, in my pain, felt that even God had abandoned me. The phrase which Yeshua is quoted as having said on the cross came to me often, "My God, my God, why have you forsaken me?" It was as if I had crossed a wall of forgetfulness when I returned to the body. In the years ahead I often felt terribly abandoned and pleaded in some of the darkest moments to be taken back into the light.

I did not understand why someone who had met Jesus and who was involved in this profound spiritual project could be treated in this way.

Now I understand. I had to struggle, like everyone, to find the way back to that state of spiritual consciousness we all seek. If I had been zapped with special powers of perception and didn't have to enter again into the limited human consciousness, I would not be able to teach others because my experience would have been so different from that of other people. I had no special favors. I was on my own. I had to conduct my own search, looking for clues wherever I could find them, just like everyone else. That was the best, even if hardest, way for me to learn and then to teach.

I describe this process of returning to life in more detail in the book called *The Prayer of Silence.* There I teach a meditative prayer based on what I discovered as a result of my search. I provide not only theory but the practical means to achieve a profound shift into spiritual consciousness. You don't need to die first! You can experience dimensions beyond the body and ways to transform your life in the body in amazing and powerful ways. And if you have already had a Near Death Experience, this *Prayer of Silence* will help you to integrate your experience into life.

I finally got the old machine going, even if only to a creaky start. However, when I was discharged from the hospital, the real work of solving the riddles began. What was wrong with the Gospels? What did this Death Experience have to do with the growth of human consciousness? What was my role in all of this?

Since I didn't know what I had to learn or where I would find solutions to the mysteries I carried with me, I decided to study everything. I had been studying philosophy and theology in preparation for the Christian ministry, but I now knew that path was far too narrow for my purposes.

In a sense I "fell into" studying literature, since in January of 1967, when I left the hospital, I couldn't get into any other classes. Many times in my life after that, I seemed to fall into a lot of things, experiencing over and over what many people on the spiritual path experience—what Carl Jung called "synchronicities"—which provide us with the experiences we need at a particular time in our quest.

Perhaps finding this book has been a synchronicity for you. I have had phone calls from people who have had this book literally fall off a shelf into their hands.

In order to understand literature, I also had to understand the creative processes which produce novels and poetry and plays, seemingly out of nothing. So I read whatever I could on psychology, sociology, history, philosophy, religious studies, science, anthropology and any subject which helped clarify this whole area of the creative potential of humanity.

But creativity is a worldwide phenomenon, so I found myself studying literature, culture and history from all over the world — finally completing a BA in English and Philosophy from Mount Allison University, an MA in English Literature from the University of New Brunswick, both in Canada, and a PhD from the University of Leeds in England, in "World Literature Written in English," with classes in African, Australian, Canadian, English, Indian and West Indian literature and a dissertation on the effects of the colonial experience in the fiction of Africa and the West Indies.

I also held teaching positions at Acadia University, the University of New Brunswick and the University of Leeds before synchronicity brought me back to Regina exactly ten years after the accident, to a position teaching Canadian and Commonwealth Literature at the university where I had re-started my studies after the accident. Then, as if to remind me that my first priority was really to solve the puzzle of the Gospels, the texts which underlie Christianity, I got a job at Luther College, a Lutheran federated college of the University of Regina.

As you can see, I immersed myself in learning. I needed to find out what other cultures and civilizations had to say about creativity, spiritual experience, religion and human consciousness.

I had thought that perhaps in this world-wide emphasis in my searching I would find some obvious clues to the puzzle. But none emerged. While teaching at Acadia University, a Baptist related institution in Nova Scotia, I even purchased the Bible Society tract versions of the Gospels and cut them up, pasting them into a note-book, trying to see if there was anything I could find that way. But that didn't give me any clues.

The Dead Sea Scrolls looked like they would provide some answers, but the Roman Catholic scholars who controlled the research on those would not release any of their findings until a scandal and international pressure forced their publication in the 1990s, well after I had actually found the solution to the Gospel mystery.

The *Nag Hammadi Library*, discovered in 1945 and published in 1977 (General ed., James M. Robinson, HarperSanFrancisco), pro-vided some examples of early Gospels. However, many of them arise from the concerns of small Gnostic sects and are written in obscure, symbolic, mythological terms. That obscurity makes it dif-ficult to pick up clues about what a new Gospel might look like.

The most important text in the collection, *The Gospel of Thomas*, preserved almost undamaged, records a number of sayings of Jesus. Some of them are quite similar to sayings in the four canonical Gospels and it is likely one of the earliest collections of Jesus' say-ings in existence. It is obviously very important, but for my pur-poses, it was far too sketchy. (It did however, have profound implications in establishing my first century identity, many years after I had written the Gospel which follows here. I will explain that shortly.)

A lot of research has been done by scholars exploring the devel-opment of the Jesus tradition and how that is reflected in the Gos-pels. But again, I found very little in the scholarly literature which was helpful in solving my particular puzzle.

I was trained as a scholar and enjoyed working in archives and searching through old manuscripts. I found a couple of important, dusty and almost forgotten books in the Research Library in Post of Spain, Trinidad. I also discovered some important aspects of a couple of 19th century Canadian writers by rummaging through archival materials. But although that added to knowledge in my academic field, it did not help with the Gospel mystery. I had hoped that the solution would be as simple as finding a whole new Gospel somewhere on a forgotten, dusty shelf, or in a hidden jar or, like Morton Smith, in the binding of another book altogether.

Finally, I did not find what I was looking for in archives or any other obvious place. I found the Gospel by exploring the mysteries of consciousness through meditation and art.

I knew from my research that creativity is a strange process. I wanted to know where artistic inspiration comes from. Writers often make strange claims for the source of their inspiration. The American novelist, William Faulkner, said that he wrote when the voices spoke to him and stopped when they stopped. Margaret Laurence, a Canadian novelist, said that it was the characters in her novels who wrote her books. William Blake claimed supernatural authorship for many of his poems and art.

Even Carl Jung, the "father of spiritual psychology," channeled a short work, *Septum Sermones ad Mortuos* ("Seven Sermons to the Dead,") as if possessed by the consciousness of a Gnostic writer from the first century. His experience was preceded by ghostly presences in his house, which made it impossible for the family to breathe freely, by a wildly ringing doorbell, when nobody was there, and by a group of ghostly voices intoning, "We have come back from Jerusalem where we found not what we sought."

In all of this, it became obvious that there are mysteries of consciousness which most people are not familiar with. Creativity, I discovered, often puts people in touch with some very strange phenomena.

Many people will be familiar with *A Course in Miracles*. Dr. Helen Schucman, a psychiatrist working in the United States, started hearing a voice telling her to write in the evenings after work. She wrote three long, inspired volumes which came from some mysterious dimension of consciousness. I found it difficult to put myself in the ranks of people like her, or in the company of Edgar Cayce with his readings or with Jane Roberts and the Seth Books, although I was to find that Cayce and *A Course in Miracles* would become a surprising part of my adventure.

I was a rational scholar, I thought, and it was with reason that I would find the solution to the mystery of the Gospels. However, I gradually realized what should have been obvious from my own academic work — that reason, however valuable and important in our lives on this planet, has its limits, because it cannot move beyond the evidence and beliefs with which it starts. Reason is a way of drawing conclusions from evidence — it is not a way of deriving evidence in the first place.

Reason, without appropriate values or vision, can even lead to our destruction. As the Australian Nobel Laureate novelist, Patrick White, writes in one of his novels, "Reason finally puts a gun to its head and doesn't always miss." Nuclear weapons, sectarian violence and terrorism are all rational pursuits: it is just that the people who would use them to destroy us, have applied their reason to ideas, beliefs and premises which most of us abhor. The really profound, earth changing and life saving truths have to be discovered using other processes of consciousness.

It is interesting I did not realize this sooner. I had started a career as a sculptor as a parallel activity to my academic research. I would "see" the sculptures in my mind, draw them to remind me of what they looked like and then make them in three dimensions in wood or steel. I was taking an inner vision and making it into something physically visible. I channeled sculptures in the same way that Jane Roberts and Edgar Cayce channeled information. Many artists do this. It took a while to realize that the process of channeling words was similar to what I was doing with art.

I hadn't thought to look in my own consciousness for the lost Gospel!

However, in 1979, after being at Luther College for less than a year, I had to undergo emergency surgery on my back. During the recovery process I used meditation as a way of repairing my back

and other medical issues — with great success. Once I became
aware of how the mind could directly affect the body, how we
human beings are capable of knowing and affecting reality in ways
that are not obvious to the prevailing rational materialism of our
culture, I was ready to start looking within myself. After all, Yeshua
had said that the "Kingdom of God is within you." Perhaps the
information I sought was also there.

I started a program of intense, transformative meditation and,
after a few months of entering regularly into a variety of meditative
states, I was surprised to find Yeshua appear again, almost like seeing one of my sculptures with my inner vision. But he was obviously alive and I could communicate with him.

He smiled and asked me why it had taken so long to get back to
his level again. It was wonderful to see him. Almost fifteen years of
searching had elapsed since I last saw him during the Death Experience. I realized that by doing meditation regularly I had raised my
level of consciousness to where it had been when I died. I realized
that what we called death was merely a shift of consciousness which
could be achieved through meditation instead of dying.

At this point I entered a whole new area of exploration. In my
regular time in the Silence, Yeshua would point out things I needed
to learn or conflicts I should settle and I would proceed to put his
words into effect in my daily life of teaching, marking essays,
research, committee work and all the activities of being a university
professor. I was beginning to get a sense of how I could answer at
least one of the riddles I had been given to solve in 1966. I was
exploring the nature of consciousness.

But what was wrong with the Gospel stories? As I meditated,
Yeshua continued to give me instructions which I would write in
my journal. Gradually, his instructions became longer. As this progressed, I realized that I not only had a large body of teachings
which were helpful in guiding me, personally, but that many of
them were obviously not intended just for me. In addition to this,
I realized that many of Yeshua's words went beyond guidance for
the inner path. They offered a vision of our spiritual nature, and of

the nature of life and of God, which were obviously heretical in terms of accepted Christian doctrines, but which provided much more spiritual and psychological meaning than most of the other Christian writings I had read.

So, I discovered, part of the problem was that the teachings had been distorted over the centuries.

I must admit, I was getting a bit nervous about having this large collection of "Jesus sayings," with their obviously heretical content, almost like *The Gospel of Thomas* from *The Nag Hammadi Library*. I was actually writing a "Gnostic Gospel."

What would my colleagues at Luther College say? What would people in the church say? What would my inner critic say, which still clung to many of the traditional beliefs with which it had been raised?

Perhaps most disturbing for me at the time was wondering what my family would say. My father, Rev. Peter S. MacDonald, was a United Church of Canada minister who had served many congregations in Nova Scotia, India and Bermuda. He had been the President of the Maritime Conference of the church. My uncle, Rt. Rev. W. Clarke MacDonald, was the Moderator of the church. My sister was a United Church minister and my brother was a priest in the Anglican Church. My brother-in-law was a Presbyterian minister in the church in Trinidad. I was active in the church as Chairman of the Central Board of our local congregation and taught at Luther College. I was surrounded with church connections and here I was producing Jesus sayings and listening to Yeshua himself every day as I did my meditation!

Once I had collected enough of these teachings to make a small book of Jesus sayings, I wondered what I should do with them. Yeshua just said to be patient. I was anything but patient. This was exciting, but also in a strange way, quite terrifying. I did not want to be among those who did channeling of this sort. It was, quite frankly, weird. It also seemed to put a lot of responsibility on me. I thought that, somehow, I should be sharing them but I had no idea what to do with the teachings.

And, strangely, I hadn't found the new Gospel: I had written it. It was a "sayings Gospel," like the "Q" [Source] Gospel the scholars spoke of that Matthew, Mark and Luke must have drawn from, or like *The Gospel of Thomas*, which kept cropping up in my research and thinking. That in itself would have been striking enough, if that had been all I received, but there was more to come.

I needed to find some explanation which would help my rational mind deal with all this non-rational material. It was of some comfort to know that others had gone through the same self doubt I was going through as I entered deeper into the mystical realms, the Kingdom of God within. There were people like St. John of the Cross who was severely persecuted by his fellow monks, almost to the point of death, for his mystical discoveries — only after he died in exile and obscurity was he recognized for the great visionary he was.

Thomas Aquinas had been a religious rationalist in his early life but later gave that up, claiming his great rational analyses of the faith were all straw and chaff. He opted for meditative prayer, for "Infused Contemplation," instead. Even Emanuel Swedenborg, who had been a mining engineer, inventor and scientist, later entered through mystical experience into the realms of the spirit and wrote several books about his visions. The list goes on. I was by no means alone in being torn between the life of reason and the growing inner perception of the spiritual potential of human consciousness. But even with this realization, it felt lonely at the time.

There is a concept in Tibetan Buddhism which is helpful in understanding what came next. The Tibetan Buddhists speak of a kind of text called a "*terma*." A *terma* is a text which is hidden in one lifetime in order to be found in another. Sometimes it is hidden in a physical place, so that the person hiding it can find it in another lifetime more conducive to its reception. It might be hidden in a jar in the desert to be found by an archaeologist who does not realize he is the one who actually hid it in the first place.

But a *terma* can also be hidden in consciousness. Since it is the consciousness that survives, not the body, the text can be encoded in the deep levels of the psyche, to be retrieved later, when it is safe and appropriate to make it known. A *terma* is a product of consciousness extended through time.

Time seemed to be important to everything that was happening. As a child I had stood outside of time to wonder about the purpose of being born in 1944. In 1966 I had met Yeshua, Elijah and Moses in a time landscape, discussing the project which had to be achieved in time. Now, in writing the text of *The Thomas Book* I seemed to be communicating through time, as if the past had somehow touched the present.

In meditation I had been able to move to a level of consciousness, either where I could communicate through time with Yeshua or, more likely, where time was no longer a barrier and we were communicating beyond the limits of time. That was surprising enough, but not as surprising to me as what followed.

The Gospel I was receiving was not to be just a sayings Gospel, although the teachings were to be central in the final product. After I had a large body of Yeshua's sayings, there was a switch. This one is difficult to explain. I might say that a narrative "started to write itself" in my journal, but that does not account for the complex process which was involved.

When I entered meditation and moved my consciousness to the level where I usually encountered Yeshua, I sensed a different "voice" speaking in the inner being. Again, it was a bit like the sculptures appearing in my mind, except that scenes and actions and words all came together at once. I would "see" a scene or an event, feel the emotions, sense the ideas and at the same time the words were available to describe what I saw. I merely had to write the words down, with the inner vision as an aid to getting them just right. It seemed like my consciousness had entered into the senses of someone else, seeing and feeling what he saw and felt.

I also sensed that the inner voice was drawing on my extensive language and literary education, so that readers will often find echoes of poems or novels which give just the extra meaning which is required at a particular point in the narrative. All of my consciousness was being used to write the narrative, whereas Yeshua's teachings were almost straight dictation.

As more of the narrative was written, I began to get a sense of how the teachings I had already written fitted into the story. People have told me that the book flows beautifully, each part fitting naturally into the next. But putting the Gospel together was like a giant jig-saw puzzle. I would describe an event, fit in the teachings which I knew were appropriate at that point, then write some more events and perhaps even have Yeshua give me more teachings, then find some of the teachings I already had that were supposed to go in at another point. It was a complex process, not at all like the kind of continuous transmission which was involved in the Seth Books or *A Course in Miracles*.

I sensed almost immediately that the voice writing the story part of the Gospel was not Yeshua. It had a different quality to it and was intensely visual, with a lot of emotional overlay, as if coming from someone who had been searching for meaning for many years, someone who had been deeply hurt and needed to communicate his story. It was not long before I realized that the narrator was Thomas, one of Yeshua's disciples, the one they called "The Doubter."

As you will see later, I discovered through a series of strangely synchronistic events in 2007 that there were two disciples named Thomas in the Bible. This Doubting Thomas was actually Judas Thomas. I guess the doubting part carried into the present because, although my Inner Guide told me about this Thomas while I was writing the book in the early 1980's, I refused to accept who I was until 2007 when the identity came strikingly into focus and could not be ignored.

While writing the Gospel, I was actually reliving the life of Judas Thomas.

You may wonder how anything could shock me at this point, but this discovery that I was seeing through the eyes of Judas Thomas, did. All my preconceived ideas were being stretched to their limits. How could my senses look from the twentieth century into the world of the first century?

I did not really believe that consciousness could bridge the years in that way or that I could see through the eyes of someone I knew was dead. I did not really think that our awareness could reach that far. In spite of all that had happened, I still tended to believe, deep within me, that consciousness was a function of the brain only and that, when the brain died, any communication stopped.

I also considered myself a respectable university professor, doing international research, collaborating with people in the West Indies, England and India. I was publishing articles all over the world and was presenting research papers in places like Los Angeles, Malta, New Delhi and universities in Canada. At the time of writing *The Thomas Book*, in the early 1980's, I was the coordinator of a research team examining the social impact of computerization on universities in Canada and India. The team included the Dean of Science and the Head of the Computer Science Department, among others. We met with government and educational bodies in many parts of both countries. Yet this emerging Gospel, this intensely personal, creative and spiritual part of my life, had to be kept secret.

Universities are very rational places, and the kinds of things I was now doing are not very good for your reputation as a scholar. It was especially difficult having all these biblical characters showing up in my consciousness. I had gotten used to the idea of Yeshua being around. I mostly ignored Elijah and Moses. But to have Thomas, the disciple, show up in such a central role, was a bit of a strain.

I knew, however, that I had to keep going. In spite of my doubts about my intellectual reputation, I realized that this activity was central to the reason for my return to life in 1966. I knew there was something wrong with the Gospel stories: here was an unexpected but profoundly moving solution to that mystery.

The Gospel grew. But there were to be other surprises. As you will find in the text which follows, the book is divided into four sections: "The Life," "The Death," "The Interim" and "The Journey." Most of the teachings found their way into the first, third and fourth sections of the book. There were still gaps in the fourth section and the second section presented me with special difficulty. I was not sure what was going to be there, and I resisted writing that part.

Finally, however, I realized that I had to write the section called "The Death." The pressure to write was just too great. So I got out a separate loose-leaf notebook and started writing. I numbered the pages A, B, C, D and so on, something I had never done before. It was spring and we were coming up to Easter. I was well into the alphabet by the time Good Friday came. On that day, my wife and kids were going to church but I said I would stay home — I knew I had to get back to the book.

As soon as they left the house, I began to write, not knowing what was to come. I wrote that section in a kind of blind fury, and when I got to page "Z," half way down the page, Yeshua died. As you read those pages you may have a sense of why I resisted. I relived the experience as I wrote it and I often wrote through tears, the experience was so intense.

At the moment I wrote that Yeshua was dead, the clock behind me struck twelve. Yeshua had died in my time on Good Friday on page "Z" of the manuscript at exactly noon. I put my pen down and felt sobs emerge from somewhere deep in my body, as if I had been delivered of a great weight.

I didn't write for a couple of days and then took up my pen again. For some reason I began to number the pages AA, BB, CC. When I reached the bottom of page ZZ that section ended. There isn't even room for one more word. Yeshua had died exactly half way through that manuscript and each section, numbered with the alphabet, had taken exactly twenty-six alphabet pages. It was as if this part of the book, written with great intensity, was seared into the pages and into my brain by these amazing coincidences.

You must realize that I was raised in the church with a fairly orthodox understanding of the Christian faith and the place of the Gospels in that faith. I had planned to be a minister. The school I went to in north India had daily Bible study classes and weekly services in which we were told, among other things, that we would go to hell if we disagreed with their doctrines. Although my parents did not have that kind of fundamentalist bias, the fear and world-view engendered by that education has been hard to overcome.

The Death Experience had created a tremendous amount of dissonance at the most basic of levels in my understanding of how the universe works, and writing a new Gospel added even more. There was a great struggle within me as I wrote the story and as the new insights arose. There were many questionings, many doubts about the new material. I was not just channeling. I was changing the very nature of my being as I wrote.

The "coincidences" which were involved in writing this section helped me to deal with many of those doubts and made me realize that this did not just come from an overactive imagination. There is no way I could have planned that section. I knew without a doubt that someone was working in the spiritual background to arrange many of the events around this text. The involvement of "those in spirit" continued through 2009 in some quite dramatic ways.

As you read the account of Yeshua's death, you will realize why I had so much trouble writing it. The traditional story, recorded in the four canonical Gospels, has become so central to the fabric of western civilization that to suggest something different is quite shocking. So I did research into this part of the story as well and realized that I was not the only one who has had problems with the story of the crucifixion.

The Knights Templar, of *Da Vinci Code* fame, were declared heretics in part because they did not place the cross or the crucifixion central to their devotions. The Cathars of southern France were exterminated by the Church of Rome in a crusade around 1244, because the Cathars' teachings and holy way of life were drawing so many people away from the corrupt church and Rome felt threatened. The Cathars also did not place the cross central to their practice. In fact, the cross did not become the central symbol of Christianity until a few centuries after Yeshua's death — after

Christianity had become the official religion of the Roman Empire — the fish was the central symbol before that. Interestingly, composed as late as the 600's CE, the Koran carries the same tradition this Gospel does — that someone else died on the cross in place of Jesus.

There are a great many implications which come from the way Yeshua dies in *The Thomas Book*. I suspect that, if the church were freed from the brutality of the cross and its many images in crucifix, doctrine or film, the Christian world would be a much more loving, peaceful place. The new crucifixion story in this Gospel will require a lot of re-thinking of the doctrines of atonement, the divinity of Jesus and original sin — doctrines which have caused great suffering in their present forms.

Even the emerging computer technology had a role in the writing. By the time I finished writing about the death of Yeshua, Luther College had gotten a new word processor. It was a large machine on its own dedicated trolley with screen, processor and eight inch floppy discs. The final assembly of the privately printed version of *The Thomas Book* took place on that machine.

I would wheel it from the Academic Office into my office and type the material into it. It gradually took shape on those large discs. The new technology made it possible to assemble my jig-saw puzzle manuscript much more easily than by hand. Also, I could sit in meditation and type directly from that state, so that parts of the fourth section, "The Journey," were composed directly there.

Some sections of "The Journey" are obviously visionary experiences which Thomas undergoes, but as with the other narrative, I had to experience those visions myself, as Thomas, before typing them into the word processor.

Through this time, my spiritual connection with Thomas grew more intense and intimate, since it was almost as if we became one person while we were writing. The technology made it much easier to compose that part of the story, because I could enter into the visions and then immediately record them on the disc without returning to ordinary consciousness. It was a bit like Ernest

Hemingway's novels or e e cummings' poetry being partly a product of the typewriter.

I was able to format the document on that machine and print off a copy which was published in a limited private edition in 1985. That was before the fall of the Berlin Wall and during a time when the world feared being wiped out by a nuclear war. The introduction I wrote to that edition reflects those collective anxieties. But now, with this edition to a much larger audience, we are faced with new problems — global warming, the rising of the oceans, over-population, international terrorism, world-wide economic depression, threatened pandemics along with growing violence in society and emptiness in the lives of billions of people. It is not that different now. There is still desperate need for a message of hope such as *The Thomas Book* provides.

The reception the book received, even with very limited circulation, amazed me. I had sold some copies through local bookstores. While presenting a research paper in Los Angeles I had taken a copy to the Bodhi Tree Bookstore and they sold quite a few copies. I received letters and phone calls from Washington, Hawaii, England, Italy, many parts of Canada, India and other places. They were all positive. A number of clergy told me that the book allowed them to finally make sense of the Jesus story. Alison MacNeil, an artist from Nova Scotia, sent me a letter, which I quote because it reflects the views of many people who wrote or phoned:

>...here words fail me, or sound inadequate. I cannot 'put your book down' and no doubt, will read it over and over many times — It is incredible and wonderful, and ... you feel you want to burst with joy and excitement — though I'm fully aware that reading it is only a first step. Thank you, thank you for sharing that huge step of understanding.

In 1966 I knew I had to discover what was wrong with the canonical Gospel stories. I had thought it was only my problem. I did not realize that so many people were waiting for the message of this Gospel. I did not realize that there was such a sense of emptiness in so many people which needed to be filled by exactly this story.

But why, you might ask, didn't I have it published by a publisher earlier? I have found that there is an appropriate time for everything to emerge. In 1991, just six years after the private edition, I had a severe case of viral encephalitis which wiped out large parts of my memory and brought my career as a university professor to a screeching halt.

This seemed like a tragedy and an end to everything I had accomplished. But it turned out to be part of my spiritual education, because in the same way as I had to put my body back together after 1966, I also had to learn to put my brain back together. I was guided again in my recovery from that devastating illness. I was taught new things about consciousness and healing and spiritual growth.

All of this spiritual education was then funneled into *The Prayer of Silence*, the companion book to this one. It was as if I had to complete both of them before either could be published.

But Thomas would not let me go until I included one last comment in the text of *The Thomas Book*. As you will read later in the text of the Gospel, on October 24, 2006 I drove some friends to the airport. On my way home I felt a growing anger within me which I knew did not come from myself. I realized Thomas still had something else to say before the text would be complete, so I wrote his angry outburst and surprising insight in my journal. Then I typed the passage into the following text at the appropriate place. It was as if, through the landscape of time, he wanted to set right something which had bothered him terribly about the way Jesus had been de-sexed by the early church. The outburst had to do with the relationship between Yeshua and Mary Magdalene.

This short passage of invective reveals how he carried his anger for a long time and how his anger transcended time to come to me in twenty-first century North America. He was angry at the way the initial story had been distorted. He was angry how that distortion prevents us, all of us ordinary human beings, from being aware of the potential we have to discover the Kingdom of God, the Presence of God, not in some far away place, but actually within ourselves.

His anger also found expression in surprising ways in events which started in 2007.

CHAPTER TWO

~

IDENTITY MYSTERY

He asked his disciples saying,
"Who do men say that I, the Son of Man, am?"
So they said, "Some say John the Baptist, some Elijah
and others Jeremiah or one of the prophets."
(Matthew 16:13–14)

I HAD THOUGHT THAT WHAT IS NOW CHAPTER ONE WOULD HAVE been the "Introduction" to *The Thomas Book* and that it would have stopped right here. However, a whole string of mysterious things began to happen in early 2007. I realized these things had to form part of the book, even though the most important part had been written more than twenty years earlier.

The events of 2007 opened a great many rifts in the fabric of time, so that Thomas again became a tremendously important part of my life. This was not just channeling. I was going through the process by which I discovered who I was in the past and who I am in the present. It was a painful process, because the pain of Thomas' life came directly into my own. No longer were there two thousand years separating us: we had become one. I include dates in some of what follows so you can see how things progressed in our time. After my long years of preparation, things suddenly speeded up.

As I repaired my burned-out brain from 1991 to 2007, I discovered many levels of spiritual functioning which helped me to heal. I had lost massive amounts of memory, which I naturally wanted to recover. None of the medical people I consulted knew how to do that, so I turned to meditation, which I had been practicing and teaching for years by now. Through experiment, I discovered I could enter into an elevated meditative state where I could re-experience the events of my life.

People have known for a long time that every event records itself, its energy imprint, in the universe. Some people refer to this recording as the Akashic Records. Edgar Cayce, the American "Sleeping Prophet," used to access these records in a sleeping-trance state.

By entering into a particular meditative state, I could re-live experiences by bringing them into focus in my mind (which I discovered to be quite independent of the brain) and then I could will the experience into undamaged parts of the brain to create memories for instant recall. The process of willing memory into the brain was similar to the process I went through to activate the body after my death, in which I willed memories into the cells and life force into the body.

Stored with the experiences, I also found emotional trauma, like the loneliness and fear of going to a residential school in India. I had to re-experience both emotion and action to bring it all into consciousness. This process healed the trauma and, in addition, allowed me to find a deeper peace and wholeness each time I did it. I spent many years rebuilding my memory banks and healing deep levels of the psyche in this way.

I also found that, from some elevated meditative states, it was as easy to access the Akashic Records of past lives as it was to re-experience the events of this life. That had its difficulties, which were different from dealing with present life memories. The series of lives I had lived, starting with Judas Thomas, had been very painful, specifically so that we could enter into the darker aspects of human functioning and find a way of healing even the worst situations. Experiencing in this way brought up pain and torment which had not been consciously carried over into the present life. It was a bit like resolving the pain of present life memory, except that the past life trauma was not familiar, so I had to do a lot of detective work to find out how the experience from the past manifested in the present. Once I had been able to identify it, I could then bring it into the Light of God in the inner being and it was healed. I discovered that many of the issues which I faced in this life were carried over from the past.

So, for instance, I found I had been a Jewish shoemaker in Eastern Europe at the time when pogroms were common. I saw my wife and children die because of the actions of a "Christian mob" in the horror of those times. My present wife and children shared that lifetime with me. During the process of recovering that life, I could not read of the Holocaust or watch television programs about the suffering of the Jews, without intense pain in myself. I remember one night asking my wife to turn to a different channel on the television because I could not bear to hear the program she was watching about Auschwitz.

I also remembered in this life that, when my children were little, I had an intense and irrational fear that they and my wife would be killed in some horrible way. When the children grew older, the fear vanished. It was as if their youth activated the emotion and, once they became older, my deep self knew it no longer had to worry.

The positive side of the process was that I found immense healing in deep levels of my being. I also realized that others could find this same healing and so have included exercises in *The Prayer of Silence* to deal with present and past-life trauma.

It took years of work, but I was finally able to rebuild my memory and also to integrate the lives I had lived, into my present life. In the process the "I" of my consciousness began to transcend the limited ego of "Bruce," and I gradually became the spiritual centre from which my lives had emanated, instead of just the small self of the present incarnation.

All of this spiritual exploration happened in my private consciousness, away from the public eye. Then in 2007 I entered into a past life drama which spilled over into the present in dramatic ways.

In February of 2007, I read *Return of the Revolutionaries* (Hampton Roads) by Walter Semkiw, MD. In that book, Semkiw presents the results of extensive research about the present incarnations of people who had been actively involved in the American Revolution, including his own past life identity as John Adams, second President of the United States. In order to confirm many of his cases, he had consulted Kevin Ryerson, one of the foremost trance channels in the United States and the psychic source which has helped Shirley MacLaine in her spiritual search. Semkiw had gotten very accurate information from Ryerson about the previous lives of many people and had great faith in his abilities.

Since he had done so much work tracking down former incarnations, and since he obviously took this subject seriously, I thought it would be interesting to get his take on the matter of where my material might have come from. At least he would not laugh. I therefore sent him manuscript copies of both *The Thomas Book* and *The Prayer of Silence* on February 25, 2007. I had been told, while writing the Gospel in the 1980's, that I was Didymos Judas Thomas, twin brother of Christ, in a past life, but I could not claim that identity since it would have seemed like empty boasting without independent confirmation.

Of course, in sending my book to Semkiw, I was opening myself to the possibility that he might find that all I had written was nonsense. But I also felt that a serious researcher like Semkiw, with the number of contacts in the intellectual and political life of the United States that he has, would be interested in finding any reincarnation links involved. I was not disappointed.

Walter replied almost immediately to my email after reading the introduction (the present Chapter One) to *The Thomas Book*. He said he had a session with Kevin Ryerson coming up and would bring up my case. One of the "spirit entities" who speaks through Kevin, the one who gives most of the reincarnation information, is Ahtun Re, a former priest from the temples of ancient Egypt.

I was interested to note on Walter Semkiw's website (http://www.johnadams.net) that Ahtun Re had already identified two writers and spiritual teachers, Gary Renard and Michael Tamura, as split incarnations of the soul that had been the apostle Thomas. Ahtun Re asserted that it is possible for a soul to have up to seven incarnations at the same time. I knew that a number of people claimed to be reincarnations of Thomas, so I wasn't keen to try to join the crowd. In light of what Ahtun Re said, I wondered if I was a third (or fourth or fifth) incarnation of Thomas.

There was another connection to Michael Tamura, I discovered. I had vivid memories of a past life as a young woman who died in the Hiroshima atomic explosion: so did he. Were we somehow the same soul wending its way through time? Also, interestingly, that would have meant that I, as Bruce, born in December, 1944, was alive when this Japanese woman died in August of 1945 — another case of a split incarnation.

I include here the description which I sent to Walter Semkiw, of my death as a young Japanese woman, because it illustrates a number of things which come up in regard to Thomas:

I am not sure of the exact age of the Japanese young woman. She would have been in her early twenties, I think, or even her late teens. She was working at a time when the Japanese war machine was badly damaged and I had the sense that they were bringing in any manpower or woman power they could find, which is why I was involved in such a non-traditional role as a factory worker. The whole experience was extremely experiential, as many of my past life memories are. I do not get a lot of semantic information, but the emotional, tactile experience is often intense.

In this particular case I "had a dream," which was not a dream, but a reliving of being a young Japanese woman working in a railway works. I could see the giant overhead cranes like a large steel framework. I knew my brother was off fighting in the war and that my mother was working in the office (which was in a railway car). I don't recall thinking of where my father was — perhaps he had died much earlier, since we seemed to have to make a living without a male provider.

As I watched the sky, I saw a lone, shining aircraft flying high in the air toward the city centre. I thought it might have been an American bomber, but it seemed too high — and also, I thought, one plane couldn't do much damage. Then I saw the plane drop a single bomb and speed away. I thought I would watch the explosion in the city, but then, suddenly, the whole universe seemed to open up, somehow, and I felt myself, my soul, being forced physically out of my body, with a tremendous force I could not have imagined. I have been through a NDE and it was a gradual, peaceful process. This was a violent tearing of the bond between the soul and the body which is difficult to explain but was tremendously intense. It was as if the atomic bomb was creating forces which affected, not just the body, but also the very soul-stuff of the person.

The day after this experience, I went to the library and checked for pictures of Hiroshima and there in the book before me was the overhead steel framework of the railway works I had seen in the vision. I sat for quite a while, staring at it with tears in my eyes. It brings tears to my eyes just writing this — with me it tends to be the emotion and the scene which carry over.

I would have been about eight months old in the Bruce MacDonald lifetime at the time this was happening in Japan. We were living then in Nova Scotia — my father was a chaplain with the Canadian Army, stationed with the Coast Regiment in Halifax. Interestingly, my parents relate that, when I was a baby, they found me in my crib, all blue and not breathing. They brought me down to the kitchen stove (a wood stove always burning) and rubbed me to get my circulation going and worked with me for a while before I started breathing again. They couldn't remember what time of year that was. I am not sure if it was at the same time as the bomb, so cannot make a karmic connection between the two lives in that event. However, I do seem to have been on the edge of life and death many times in this life.

All my life, from the time I was a child in India (we went there when I was 3), I had a deep horror of the atomic bomb and what it could do — until this vision. Following that experience, I knew that even after an atomic explosion, there is life — that death of any sort is still a transition into another stage of life. However, this particular kind of death is a violent rending of the soul and the body and must have its ripple effects through time and lifetimes.

Michael Tamura, who Ahtun Re identified as a reincarnation of Thomas, also remembered dying in the Hiroshima blast, but his memory was of being a young girl at the time, not a young woman. There seemed to be a match of sorts, but not exactly.

March 13, 2007: Walter consulted with Kevin Ryerson and Ahtun Re and reported back, "Ahtun Re said that you were not a split of Thomas, rather, that you were the scribe that wrote down *The Gospel of Thomas*." Ahtun Re is referring here to *The Gospel of Thomas* in *The Nag Hammadi Library*, the book that had kept popping up all through the writing of my Gospel of Thomas.

This was a fascinating development, even a bit bewildering at first. It answered my initial question: I was not Thomas, as some psychics had suggested. I was "the scribe that wrote down *The Gospel of Thomas*." In my present lifetime I am also a scribe who wrote down a Gospel of Thomas. But then, as you can imagine, a lot of questions arose in my mind.

Why would I write a Gospel of Thomas if I was not Thomas, especially if two incarnations of the soul which was Thomas are presently in life? Why not get Gary or Michael to log back into their memory banks and write the book? Why would I go through the long period of training, and all the experiences I have described earlier, in order to write the story of someone not connected directly with me? From a cosmic perspective, you would think there would be a more economical way to do this.

It was certainly a puzzle. But I also knew instinctively that Ahtun Re's brief statement, "you were not a split of Thomas, rather, you were the scribe that wrote down *The Gospel of Thomas*," was a clue to a much larger mystery. He used terms and references which I immediately recognized. Only someone intimately in touch with my knowledge base would know enough to give me those clues. I knew that this statement was not an answer to my question but rather the entrance to a much greater mystery.

I did not realize, at the time, that Ahtun Re's message, which was sent through Ryerson and Semkiw, was one they would not have wanted me to receive if they knew what it really meant. If I thought that Ahtun Re was just an aspect of the consciousness of Kevin Ryerson, I soon discovered otherwise. This ancient Nubian priest could act quite independently of the person who channeled him, and quite decisively in his attempts to set right a great spiritual wrong which he felt was being committed, in part, through the use of his name.

As with much that was to come in the following years, this clue to my past life identity provided an opportunity for me to resolve, for my own sake, and to present to the reader of *The Thomas Book*, some essential background and context for the book. The story of Thomas would not have been complete without the historic background I will now explore, and the need to provide this background was the direct result of the clue from Ahtun Re.

The first part of the puzzle is related to the word "scribe." It meant a great deal to me because I knew I had been a scribe in ancient Egypt. To the modern reader, a "scribe" is usually thought of as a secretary of sorts, typing from the boss's dictation or laboriously copying texts from scroll to scroll. In the ancient world, a scribe was something quite different, as archaeologists have discovered.

In the ancient Egyptian tradition, from which the first writing arose, scribes were almost the only literate people in the country.

They were carefully educated because it was their job to preserve the history, religion and tradition of society.

Some scribes dealt with everyday matters of trade, commerce or administration, but even there they had great influence because they were in charge of the mysterious marks which made it possible for the Pharaoh to administer the realm. In fact, it was writing and the scribes who wielded it, which enabled the Egyptian civilization to survive for more than three thousand years. So important were scribes that some Pharaohs even had themselves portrayed as scribes in their tomb paintings.

But it was in matters of religion and the spirit that scribes had the most power. On a simple level, they could write spells on papyrus, stones or clay tablets which were believed to have great influence over the spirit world. But on a higher level, they were the keepers of the Mysteries of the Temples. They were the ones who learned, wrote and copied the sacred texts. It was their words, written on stone or papyrus, which maintained the Pharaoh's power as a divine being.

The first scribe, and patron deity of all scribes, was the man-god Thoth, son of Ra, who was said to have brought writing to human beings. Thoth was sometimes described as the tongue of Ra and was depicted with an ibis head because the ibis was a bird of the marshes, the realm between water, land and sky. Thoth could live in all of the "three worlds" and so could bring the mysteries of the divine realm, Duat (the Far World), to the world of the human beings living in the land of mortals.

Words, the power of Thoth, could guide the dead, as can be seen in the tomb and coffin texts which instructed the dead on what to do in the Far World of Duat. Scribes, then, were entirely immersed in the word and power of the gods.

It was here, with the words of Thoth, the tongue of Ra, that the belief in sacred writings as the "Word of God" first arose. Thoth was the Egyptian Word, Logos, and Light of God.

This tradition was carried over into Jewish practice through Moses, who had been adopted by Pharaoh's daughter and educated in the Egyptian Mysteries. Jewish tradition holds that Moses was the Scribe who wrote the Torah. He was able to talk to God in "the Tent of Meeting" and bring the words of God to the people (almost like Thoth).

The Jewish scribes who copied the Torah were given a rigorous education, like their Egyptian counterparts, so that they could accurately and with devotion and prayer, copy the words of God onto new scrolls. It was a great responsibility and was exercised by a special class of people so that, as Jesus says in reverence of the Torah, "For assuredly, I say to you, till heaven and earth pass away, one jot or one title will by no means pass from the law till all is fulfilled" (Matt 5:18).

There was a special class of people, called the Scribes, at the time of Jesus. As the Jewish Encyclopedia puts it, "The original meaning of the Hebrew word 'soferim' was 'people who know how to write'; and therefore the royal officials who were occupied in recording in the archives the proceedings of each day were called scribes (comp. II Sam. viii. 17; II Kings xix. 2, passim); but as the art of writing was known only to the intelligent, the term 'scribe' became synonymous with 'wise man'."

The Scribes became the teachers, especially of the young, and it was their task to maintain schools and interpret and explain the spiritual meanings of the text of the Torah.

Jesus was angry with the Scribes of his day, not because of any animosity against authority, but because he felt the Scribes were missing the spiritual meaning of the scriptures and were only teaching the "doctrines of men." Scribes, in his understanding, should have been wise men, involved in the things of the spirit, not just copyists interested in the "letter of the law."

With this background, we can begin to appreciate some of the implications of Ahtun Re's reference to "the scribe who wrote down *The Gospel of Thomas*." Who was this scribe? We know that he would have been highly educated, would have been literate and was someone interested in the things of the spirit. In fact, I understand from a couple of spiritual sources that Judas Thomas, the person who claims to have written the Gospel, was actually raised and educated as a Scribe.

The opening lines from *The Gospel of Thomas* in *The Nag Hammadi Library* state: "These are the secret sayings which the living Jesus spoke and which Didymos Judas Thomas wrote down. And he said, 'Whoever finds the interpretation of these sayings will not experience death.'" (Marvin Meyer, Translator, *The Gospel of Thomas*. HarperSanFrancisco, New York, 1992.)

Interestingly, the words of the divine speaker, "the living Jesus," are first conveyed to the scribe, Didymos Judas Thomas. The "living Jesus" was the resurrected Jesus, so this Gospel was channeled, much like the Torah and the Gospel for which I was the scribe. Judas Thomas had listened in his spirit to the living Jesus speak and then had recorded the sayings in his Gospel.

Salvation does not come, in *The Nag Hammadi* Gospel, from believing doctrines or from the intervention of any person, including Jesus, or from some mystical effect of the cross or crucifixion. It comes when the seekers of truth find the interpretation of the words which Jesus speaks — from inner searching and a change in the nature of the inner being. The same is true of the Gospel which was written through me, as well as of *The Prayer of Silence*. My role in writing a new Gospel was, thus, very similar to that of Didymos Judas Thomas in writing his, and the process of finding enlightenment is also similar.

Ahtun Re is quite specific when he says that I am the scribe "who wrote down" the Gospel. Didymos Judas Thomas claims to be the person who "wrote down" the words of Jesus. This repetition of phrase is the simplest level of the code identifying Didymos Judas Thomas, the scribe, with me, the modern scribe.

But this is only the beginning of a much more complex puzzle. In fact, with his simple phrase, Ahtun Re, through Walter Semkiw, has opened up a very large mystery indeed, one which takes us deep into the nature of Christianity.

The next stage of resolving the mystery hinges on the question: who is the scribe who claims to have spoken to the living Jesus and who records the words of life? Who is this Didymos Judas Thomas? Although he seems to have three names, we will find that, in a sense, he is almost nameless, especially when we try to track his identity in the New Testament.

Didymos is the Greek word for twin. Thomas is the Aramaic word for twin. Here is a man with the odd name of Twin Judas Twin. A Jew of Jesus' day, living in Judea or Galilee, might carry the Aramaic nickname, Thomas, "the twin." A Jew who had traveled and studied in Greece or Egypt (where Greek was the language of education at the time) might be called Didymos. In this scribe we seem to have a man named Judas (perhaps named after the great Jewish hero, Judas Maccabeus) who was from Galilee or Judea but who had studied in Egypt and Greece.

What else do we know about this Judas? Quite a bit, actually.

In some traditions, including among many Syrian and Coptic [Egyptian] Christians, Judas Thomas was considered to be the twin brother of Jesus. There is ancient record of such a belief. In *The Nag Hammadi Library*, in a book called "The Book of Thomas the Contender," Jesus is quoted as saying to Judas Thomas,

> "Brother Thomas, while you have time in the world, listen to me and I will reveal to you the things you have pondered in your mind.
>
> "Now since it has been said that you are my twin and true companion, examine yourself that you may understand who you are, in what way you exist, and how you will come to be. Since you are called my brother, it is not fitting that you be ignorant of yourself."

There is another highly moralistic, and wildly fantastic third century book, filled with magic appearances and disappearances and talking animals, called *The Acts of Thomas*, which also carries this tradition of Jesus having a twin (in *The Other Bible: Ancient Alternative Scriptures*, Harper Collins, 1984). In this book, Thomas talks to a man and woman just after their marriage. Then Thomas miraculously disappears and Jesus appears in his stead. The groom mistakes Jesus for Thomas, but Jesus says, "I am not Judas who is also Thomas: I am his brother." The miraculous switch serves no other purpose in the text except to show that Jesus had an identical twin. Later in the book, a magical serpent speaks to Judas Thomas and says, "For I know that you are the twin brother of Christ."

The twin brother of Christ? For most people, this claim that Jesus had a twin brother would be almost inconceivable. The church has been indoctrinated with the idea that Mary was a virgin, even after she conceived, and that Jesus was the only son of Mary, without an earthly father and without sex. In this atmosphere, the idea that a twin could have shared Mary's womb with Jesus, is not acceptable. There can be only one Son of God in this kind of tradition. There is not even room for the assertion that Mary had other children besides Jesus.

Whether we agree with these texts or not, we can at least conclude that some early Christian groups believed that Jesus had a twin.

Now, more importantly for our purposes, we must ask if there is any evidence beyond the apocryphal writings of the early church to support even the suggestion of Jesus having other brothers and sisters, let alone a twin brother. Actually there is, but decoding the matter requires some more complex searching and a brief tour through some biblical scholarship.

The oldest books (first to be written) in the New Testament are the letters of Paul and Mark's Gospel. These do not mention a virgin birth.

Unlike Matthew and Luke, who start with stories of virgin births, Mark's Gospel starts with John the Baptist proclaiming his message of repentance in the wilderness. For Mark, writing the earliest canonical Gospel, Jesus is declared Son of God at his baptism, not at his birth.

Paul seems to know nothing of a virgin birth tradition, either. He even writes in his letter to the Romans, "Concerning His Son Jesus Christ our Lord, who was born of the seed of David according to the flesh, and declared to be the Son of God with power according to the Spirit of holiness, by the resurrection from the dead" (Romans 1:3–4). Paul says here that physically, "according to the flesh," Jesus is descended from the line of King David (through Joseph as we will see in a minute) but was declared to be Son of God, not because he was born of a virgin, but because he was filled with the spirit of holiness and rose from the dead.

Even John's Gospel, which was likely the last to be written, has the following statement, "Philip found Nathaniel and said to him, 'We have found Him of whom Moses in the law, and also the prophets, wrote — Jesus of Nazareth, the son of Joseph'" (John 1:45). John has no information about Joseph not being Jesus' father, even though he is writing almost sixty years after the resurrection. That is a long time without a virgin birth tradition.

In the earliest traditions of the church, reflected in Paul's letters and Mark's Gospel, there was no belief in a virgin birth. In that atmosphere it would not be difficult for members of the Syrian and other early churches to believe that Jesus had brothers and sisters or even a twin brother. That would even be the norm, and any suggestion of a virgin birth would be the aberration. In fact, the Jewish followers of Jesus continued to believe that Jesus was the son of Joseph and Mary up to at least the third or fourth centuries.

In his Gospel, Mark actually lists the names of Jesus' brothers. The citizens of Nazareth refuse to believe anything special was in Jesus because, they object, "Is this not the carpenter, the Son of Mary, and brother of James, Joses, Judas, and Simon? And are not His sisters here with us? So they were offended at Him" (Mark 6:3). Interestingly, Matthew's Gospel (13:55–56), from which one of the virgin birth stories comes, has an almost identical list of Mary's children. As we shall see, Matthew seems to be arguing both sides of the case.

Some people, especially in the Church of Rome, suggest that these brothers and sisters are not Mary's children but children of Joseph from a previous marriage or "nephews and nieces of Joseph and Mary" (the term also used for the children of the "celibate" medieval Popes). But Mark seems to be aware of a growing movement, even at his early date, where some people were asking questions about Mary and her children. At the end of his Gospel, after the resurrection, he has three passages in quick succession in which he repeatedly emphasizes that these are Mary's children, not someone else's.

In Chapter 15:40 Mark writes, "There were also women looking on afar off: among whom was Mary Magdalene, and Mary the mother of James the less and of Joses and Salome." Then just seven verses later, in Chapter 15:47, he writes again, "And Mary Magdalene and Mary the mother of Joses beheld where he was laid." In the very next verse he re-emphasizes, "And when the Sabbath was past, Mary Magdalene, and Mary the mother of James and Salome had bought sweet spices, that they might come and anoint him." The names are interchanged in such a way that there is overlap and it is obvious Mary is the mother of all of these children.

Matthew seems to reflect an even more striking tradition. He describes a number of women standing far off from the crucifixion, "Among whom were Mary Magdalene, Mary the mother of James and Joses, and the mother of Zebedee's sons" (Matt. 27:56). Here we have the same overlapping of names as in Mark, but some scholars have even suggested that the passage carries a tradition that, after Joseph's death, Mary married Zebedee who fathered some of her children, so that at least some of the "sons of Zebedee," who were Jesus' disciples, were also sons of Mary but not of Joseph. They would have been Jesus' half-brothers.

Luke also has a similar passage following the resurrection, "It was Mary Magdalene, Joanna, Mary the mother of James, and the other women with them, who told these things to the apostles" (Luke 24:10). "Mary the mother of James" would also be Mary mother of Jesus, since, as we shall see, James was almost always referred to as "the brother of our Lord."

It should be noted that, in all these passages, Mary Magdalene is always mentioned first, as the wife of the deceased would be named.

In the Gospel which follows here, it is asserted that Mary Magdalene was, in fact, Jesus' wife, only with an interesting twist which illustrates something more about learning of sex and unconditional love.

We might wonder where Mark gets his information. Scholars have determined, through intensive study of the first three Gospels, that Matthew, Mark and Luke drew on a common source which they call "Q," from the German "*Quelle*," which means Source. But there is an additional bit of information which is helpful here.

A few years ago, a scholar by the name of Morton Smith wrote in his book, *The Secret Gospel of Mark*, of his discovery of a fragment of a letter of the early church father, Clement of Alexandria. Clement claims in his letter that Mark was living in Rome with the disciple Peter. Peter had written a number of notes he used for preaching about the life and teaching of Jesus. Mark brought those notes to Jerusalem and composed his Gospel from them.

As a word of caution, some scholars now believe that the document which Morton Smith claims to have found in the monastery of Mar Saba in the West Bank, may be a forgery, a scholarly joke played by Morton Smith on his fellow academics. But even if this is the case, the tradition that Mark wrote his Gospel, either from Peter's notes, or from his own notes of Peter's teachings, is expressed in the early church historian, Eusebius, and by the Church Fathers, Iraneaeus and Justin Martyr.

According to these ancient sources, Peter was the main source for Mark's Gospel. Peter's notes might even have been "Q." But for our purposes, we can conclude that, because Mark has no virgin birth stories, Peter also must not have believed in a virgin birth or it would have found its way into Mark's Gospel.

It is interesting that Paul met with Peter in Jerusalem for two weeks not too many years after the resurrection. In his letter to the Celtic church in Galatia, Paul writes, "Then after three years I went up to Jerusalem to see Peter, and remained with him fifteen days. But I saw none of the other apostles except James, the Lord's brother" (Gal 1:18–19).

There are two important points in this passage. First, the mention of James, the Lord's brother, confirms that the James in Mark's list of Mary's children is Jesus' brother. But also, if Paul spent fifteen days with Peter and James, and if they knew of a tradition of a virgin birth, then Paul would have learned it from them. James would certainly have known who his mother was.

It would appear, from both Mark's Gospel and Paul's writings, that the tradition of a virgin birth, even if it existed in some parts of the early church, was not accepted by the major apostles.

The virgin birth is reported in Matthew's Gospel and in Luke's Gospel. However, there are some strange things going on even there. Both Gospels begin with a genealogy of Jesus, tracing his lineage back through King David to Adam, in order to show that Jesus is the rightful heir to David's throne and thus a candidate for the role of kingly Messiah (anointed one). The problem arises when we look at the genealogies. Both of them trace his descent through Joseph. If Jesus is not the son of Joseph then he has no title to the throne of David, and there is no sense in putting these genealogies in the Gospels.

So we have two alternatives. If Jesus was born of a virgin, and Joseph is not his father, then these genealogies are wrong and Jesus has no claim to the throne of David. On the other hand, if Jesus is David's heir, then he must be Joseph's son and the stories of virgin births must be later, non-Jewish interpolations.

From the Jewish perspective, a non-virgin birth announcement by angels would make sense. Other important births in the Bible are announced by angels, either directly or through dreams. One thinks immediately of the angels who met with Abraham and Sarah, to tell them they would have a child, Isaac, in their old age. John the Baptist's father had a vision in the temple, telling him of the birth of his son. A birth as important as that of Jesus would also be announced by angels.

However, we can begin to see how the Jewish tradition of angel announcements could have been corrupted by the gentile belief in virgin births. It would take only a couple of changes to the text to include the idea of a virgin birth in an otherwise traditional Jewish angel announcement.

Somehow, it would seem, the story was transformed from a Jewish story, told by the predominantly Jewish followers of Jesus, into a gentile story, designed to appeal to the gentile world after the destruction of Jerusalem in 70 AD. And, once all the machinery of the church had developed beliefs, doctrines and institutions around the "virgin" part of the story, they had to defend their interpretation even when it was not supported by the Bible itself.

We might wonder where the virgin birth story originated. Part of the cause may actually have been Jewish. The orthodox, monastic Essenes, an important sect in first century Judaism, and the group among whom Jesus was born (according to the text which follows here and according to Edgar Cayce), were very suspicious of sex and nakedness.

Among these ultra-conservative Essenes, sex was forbidden, and for those who were permitted to reproduce, sex was for procreation only, not for pleasure. Couples often lived apart and husband and wife usually "came together" at a particular time of year only, when a child was planned. Within this sect of Judaism, which was trying to be absolutely pure, in order to bring in the "Acceptable year of the Lord" and the end of the world of corruption and foreign domination, it was felt that physical, especially sexual, pleasure, was something which might tie the Seeker to the flesh and the world of the flesh. Since they sought to escape the flesh and all of its entanglements, they had to overcome the desire for sex and all other "impurities."

By the time *The Acts of Thomas* (from which we quoted earlier) was written in the third century, this anti-sex, anti-children tradition had already grown so strong that the writers of that book even have Jesus preaching to a newly wed couple that, "if you abandon this filthy intercourse you become holy temples, pure and free from afflictions and pains both manifest and hidden, and you will not be girt about with cares of life and for children, the end of which is destruction." Here, sex becomes the root of all evil, all illness and all pain. Children become a curse. Salvation consists of giving up sex.

One can hardly imagine anything less like the teachings of Jesus than this passage, but it gives us a sense of the great fear of sex which would have developed into the virgin birth stories. The frightened writer, who believed sex was the original curse, and who would put these words in Jesus' mouth, must have said, "Mary, mother of Jesus (and later 'Mother of God') would surely not have had this 'filthy intercourse' with a mere man!" Another way to have Mary give birth would have been necessary, and the gentile world had many examples of virgin births to follow.

In *The Thomas Book* which follows here, it is suggested that James, an Essene and the brother of Jesus, may actually have been involved in part of the downplaying of the sexuality of his mother Mary (who seems to have had many children and may have remarried after Joseph's death). He would also, most certainly, have downplayed the sexuality of Jesus. Thomas is quite angry about the whole process of de-sexualizing Mary and Jesus.

But Jesus, all his life, refused to be enclosed in the confines of any of the orthodox views of his time and invited tax collectors, prostitutes and sinners into his fold. According to a number of texts, he also used to kiss Mary Magdalene often on her mouth. And in John's Gospel, we have a tremendously sensuous scene where Mary Magdalene pours a costly jar of pure nard perfume on Jesus' feet and wipes them with her hair (12:3). One can hardly think of a more sensual, or even sexual, scene than that.

A comparison of Jesus' description of marriage and Paul's attitude provides a stark contrast between the two positions, even at the very beginning of the growth of the church. At the end of a long passage of "marriage counseling" Paul concludes:

But I say this as a concession, not as a commandment. For I wish that all men were even as I myself [celibate]. But each one has his own gift from God, one in this manner and

another in that. But I say to the unmarried and to the widows:
It is good for them if they remain even as I am, but if they
cannot exercise self-control, let them marry. For it is better to
marry than to burn with passion. (I Cor. 7:1–9)

For Paul, marriage and sexual relations are to be avoided if possible. At best, they are a necessary evil because of the weakness of
the flesh.

Jesus, in contrast, as a knowledgeable Rabbi teaching the spiritual meaning of Scripture, draws his definition of marriage from
Genesis 2:24–25:

"Therefore a man shall leave his father and mother, and be
joined to his wife, and they shall become one flesh. And they
were both naked, the man and his wife, and were not ashamed."
(Genesis 2:24–25)

The attitude he quotes from Genesis (in Mat 19:5 and Mark
10:7) is obviously very different from Paul's approach and that of
the Essenes. Here couples not only hug, but cleave to each other,
emotionally, sexually and spiritually. Husband and wife come
together, not only to procreate, but to become one flesh — almost
a mystical idea of sexual union. There is no fear of nakedness or the
body here, because in the Garden of Eden, in the primal state of
innocence represented in marriage, nakedness is without shame.
Paul and Jesus could hardly be more different.

I spend this much time on the anti-sex bias of the churches
because these doctrines have distorted sex to such an extent that it
has caused great harm. The sexual scandals among clergy and often-
reported abuse in conservative religious families are a direct result
of this distortion.

The anti-sex, anti-intimacy bias of the virgin birth stories is
closely related to the beliefs of Paul and the conservative branch of
the Essenes and runs counter to the kind of love and intimacy
which are so central to the message of Jesus. They also set up a

standard of such strict morality that it is impossible to meet and therefore excludes all those obviously "immoral" people whom Jesus included in his group of followers, including the oft mentioned prostitutes.

Jesus spent a lot of time with the "sex trade workers" of his day because he knew the importance of sex in the lives of people. The holy people of his day were offended by their inclusion, and the holy people who promote perpetual virginity and celibacy, and who denigrate sexuality as an aspect of the "original sin" of humanity in our day, run counter to the whole tenor of Jesus' teachings.

The other source of the virgin birth stories is no doubt gentile. Many of the Greek and Roman religious heroes were born of virgins. The religion of Sol Invictus, for which the Sun was the central deity (he was even born on December 25th), had celibate priests and nuns. Emperor Constantine, who legalized Christianity, was considered an incarnation of Sol Invictus, and more than one theologian has suggested that, when Christianity became the religion of the empire, the priests, nuns and the Pope (*Pontifex Maximus*) of the religion of Sol Invictus, merely renamed themselves "Christians" and kept their organization going as they always had. Hundreds of years after that, Roman Christians were still accused of worshipping the Sun instead of the Son.

Any religious figure who wished to compete in that Roman arena would also have to have divine, virgin parentage. For the gentile Christians, Jesus had to have more credentials than the Emperor, and so were developed the stories to give him just those credentials.

The Mother Goddess was also very popular in the Roman world, especially the goddess, Isis, of Egypt. Isis was portrayed exactly like Mary — holding the babe, Horus, in her arms. She stood on the crescent moon, wore a blue mantle and was referred to as Queen of Heaven and Mother of God, just like Mary under the later church. It would seem that, in order to deal with the great popularity of Isis, the church merely adopted her, as they did so many pagan customs, renamed her Mary, mother of Jesus, and even kept her title, Queen of Heaven. She thus became the new/old female deity of the new Christianity.

Problems arose in the text of Matthew's and Luke's Gospels, when they tried to meet the criteria of two very different religious traditions. Jesus as a gentile religious hero born of a virgin impregnated by God cannot be made to mesh with the Jewish genealogical credentials as the heir to David's throne. The genealogies and the virgin stories clash so badly that they cannot both be true.

In spite, then, of the importance of the virgin birth to many Christian churches, especially the Roman Catholic Church, it would seem that there is really very little evidence for that doctrine in the earliest documents of the faith.

We can put it quite bluntly, based on the Bible witness — the Apostles and members of the early church did not believe that Jesus was born of a virgin.

Our discussion can take a great leap forward at this point. Without the impediment of trying to maintain the insupportable position that Mary was a perpetual virgin, it is not difficult to imagine that she had a number of children, as the Gospel writers say, and that Jesus had brothers and sisters. It may not even be so difficult to imagine that he could have had a twin brother.

This brings us to a very important question. We know a number of texts outside the Bible speak of Didymos Judas Thomas, twin of Christ. Are there any indications in the Bible that Didymos Judas Thomas was a brother of Jesus, or even existed at all? Actually, although Judas Thomas is not mentioned by exactly that name anywhere in the Bible, it is fairly easy to find him, and once found, we will discover that there is quite a bit of information about him.

To start our search we need to look at the lists of the twelve disciples in the Gospels of Matthew, Mark and Luke and The Book of Acts.

At first glance, it seems easy to find our scribe. Look at the seventh person in all the lists and there you will find Thomas. However, this is not our man. Strange as it may seem, we are not looking for a Thomas at all. We are looking for Judas, for an important

Matthew 10: 2–4	Mark 3: 16–19	Luke 6: 14–16	Acts 1:13
Simon called Peter	Simon he surnamed Peter	Simon named Peter	Peter
Andrew his brother	Andrew	Andrew his brother	Andrew
James son of Zebedee	James son of Zebedee	James	James
John his brother	John brother of James	John	John
Philip	Philip	Philip	Philip
Bartholomew	Bartholomew	Bartholomew	Bartholomew
Thomas	Thomas	Thomas	Thomas
Matthew the tax collector	Matthew (Levi son of Alphaeus)	Matthew	Matthew
James son of Alphaeus	James son of Alphaeus	James son of Alphaeus	James son of Alphaeus
Simon the Canaanite	Simon the Canaanite	Simon the Zealot	Simon the Zealot
Labbaeus Thaddaeus	Thaddaeus	Judas brother of James [some texts: "son of James"]	Judas brother of James
Judas Iscariot	Judas Iscariot	Judas Iscariot	[Judas Iscariot is dead]

reason.

If you look at the names above, you will discover that there are some men known by only one name: Philip, Bartholomew and Thomas. The rest of the disciples have a name along with a qualifier: Simon the Canaanite, John brother of James and the like. There was no way of tracking people by family name in the first century, so if you wanted to be more accurate, you added a qualifier:

son of, daughter of, brother of, etc.

This system was not terribly efficient, and after the generation which actually knew these people died, there was no way to track their identity farther.

The reason we know we are not looking for a Thomas is that Didymos Judas Thomas is actually a man called Judas, along with two qualifiers — Didymos and Thomas. These qualifiers can be moved around without changing the identity of the person we are looking for. As we have seen, both these qualifiers mean "twin." So it doesn't matter if we say Judas Thomas, or Didymos Thomas or Judas Didymos or Thomas called Didymos — they are the same person.

That makes it easier. We are looking for a "Judas" with a qualifier, not a Thomas. We know, then, that the Thomas in the disciple lists is not the Didymos Judas Thomas who wrote *The Gospel of Thomas* (so named by the translators) because the "Thomas" named in the lists is a proper name, not a qualifier of another name. The scribe who wrote the *Gospel of Thomas* was actually a Judas who was a very important Thomas (twin).

In the disciple lists, we have two people named Judas. There is Judas Iscariot, the one who betrayed Jesus, and then there is the eleventh disciple, "Judas brother of James." This one is the only Judas in the disciple lists who would qualify.

What else do we know about this Judas?

As you look at the columns, you will see that all of the names agree until we come to the eleventh disciple. Matthew and Mark list Lebbaeus Thaddaeus or just Thaddaeus while in the same position Luke and Acts (the same author wrote both) list Judas, brother of James.

First we need to ask, "Why would two Gospels give the name as Thaddaeus or Labbaeus Thaddaeus, whereas in Luke and Acts it is "Judas brother of James"? Most sources assume that this is the same person, only with different names, and that seems a logical conclusion. But why change the name?

Since Mark's Gospel is the older of the two who include the

name, Thaddaeus, he is likely the originator of that name. But since he seems to have composed his Gospel from notes written by Peter, we would assume that Peter is the ultimate source of this name.

It may be that the name was unclear in the notes and Mark copied as well as he could. Perhaps it was a garbled version of Didymos which was copied as Thaddaeus. Matthew then copied what Mark had written, but wrote another similar name just to make sure he was getting close to right.

Luke's choice of "Judas brother of James" is odd because, in so many other things, Luke follows Mark, but not here. Luke was Paul's traveling companion and seems to have gotten his information from Paul or Peter or even from James himself, when he visited them in Jerusalem, and so "Judas brother of James" is likely more accurate than "Thaddaeus" because James would have known who his brother was.

There is another possibility — that both names are accurate but come from different traditions. Matthew and Mark may be drawing on the name by which the other disciples knew Judas Thomas while Jesus was alive. Luke did not know Jesus before the resurrection, since he seems to have been introduced to Christianity by Paul. Is it possible that while Jesus was alive, the eleventh disciple had a code name to hide his identity, whereas, after the resurrection, that name was no longer necessary for some reason?

Let's speculate for a moment. If Jesus was indeed heir to the throne of David, his life would be in constant danger, as we can see in the "slaughter of the innocents" by King Herod as well as in the sentence which is posted over the cross. He was accused, by the Romans, of being the "King of the Jews."

If Judas Thomas was the twin brother of Jesus, he would have been considered heir to the throne if Jesus died and he would be in danger as well. So it would be necessary to hide his identity and he would need a code name by which he was known among the inner group of Essenes who expected the Messiah, the heir of David's throne, to deliver them from bondage.

Let us suppose, further, that Judas Thomas, twin of Jesus, was named after Judas Maccabeus, the great Jewish revolutionary leader. Jesus (Yeshua) seems to have been named after Joshua (Yeshua) who led the Hebrews out of the wilderness into the Promised Land after Moses died. These twin brothers had revolutionary names, to say the least, and carried tremendous expectations on their shoulders.

A code name aligning Judas with Maccabaeus would be a logical choice. If you sound out the name "Didymos" along with the others, you discover that they all sound the same: Thaddaeus, Labbaeus, Didymos, Maccabaeus. "Didymos" then becomes as much a code name as Thaddaeus.

After Jesus' death, and especially after his resurrection, a major shift took place in the hopes people had concerning his role in the reformed Judaism he had founded. No longer was he seen as a king: now he was thought of as a spiritual guide. Once people began to think of him as more than a kingly Messiah, the whole idea of support for a Davidic king began to fade and new expectations grew.

In that changed atmosphere in the Jesus movement, it was no longer necessary to promote Judas as the heir to the throne, and consequently his life would no longer be at risk. With the new expectations, which would have developed around the time Luke began his career as a companion of Paul, the need for a code name would also disappear, and he could be known openly as "Judas brother of James" instead of as Thaddaeus.

The Gospel for which I was the scribe says that, after the resurrection, Judas Thomas spent some time in Jerusalem and was then called by the Christ to go to the East. Tradition holds that he went to Syria (where he was known as the twin) and to India.

Although some of this is speculation, the whole argument is built on good evidence. Judas Thomas was certainly known outside of the Bible. As we have seen, in the Syrian church Judas Thomas (not Thomas) was known as the twin brother of Jesus. It is claimed that he wrote *The Gospel of Thomas*, as we have already seen. He is the central character in *The Book of Thomas the Contender* and *The Acts of Thomas*. There are two hymns —"The Hymn of Judas Thomas the Apostle" and "The Song of the Pearl" — both of them said to have been written by Judas Thomas. In all of these cases he is called Judas Thomas, with Judas as his given name and Thomas or Didymos as a qualifier.

John's Gospel also mentions Didymos Judas Thomas, but with some differences. John does not list all the disciples and, as you read his account of the disciples he does name, you get the sense that he was not really sure who they all were. He was likely as bewildered by the lists as we are, if he saw these lists at all.

We know for a number of reasons that his account was written later than the other Gospels — perhaps around 90 CE. Actually, by the time Matthew's and John's Gospels were written, Jerusalem had been destroyed by the Romans (70 CE), much of the population of Judea and Galilee had been either killed or sent into exile, many towns and cities had been wiped off the map and the Judaism of the Temple which Jesus knew had come to a violent end.

When John wrote his Gospel, any hope of having a Jewish king had been destroyed by the Romans. Now people wanted to know who Jesus was in theological, not political terms. The speculation around who Jesus was had developed to such an extent that much of John's Gospel is involved in defining exactly that: who Jesus was in theological terms. In John, then, we have all the "I am" sayings: "I am the bread of life," "I am the gate" and the like.

John also seems to have been more involved with the former disciples of John the Baptist than the other Gospel writers, and it is possible that he wrote out of the theology which they had developed, as distinct from the branches of the church which followed Peter or Paul or James.

It is not much wonder that John is a little more hesitant in referring to the names of the disciples, because the group for which he was writing seems to have lost touch with the Christians for whom Matthew, Mark and Luke wrote. They were dangerous times and John could not just walk down the street and ask Mark what the names of the disciples were.

John has two Judases, like the disciple lists, but, unlike them, he also has two disciples named Thomas. For instance, John records a Thomas without a qualifier: "Thomas said to Him, 'Lord, we do not know where You are going, and how can we know the way?'" (John 14:5).

However, John is also aware of another Thomas, one identified as different because of a very important qualifier. We hear that "Thomas, who is called the Twin [Didymos], said to his fellow disciples, 'Let us also go, that we may die with Him'" (John 11:16). This Thomas Didymos shows up later. He is recorded, for instance, in the famous "Doubting Thomas" scene: "Now Thomas, called the Twin [Didymos], one of the twelve, was not with them when Jesus came. The other Disciples said to him, 'We have seen the Lord.' So he said to them, 'Unless I see in His hands the print of the nails, and put my finger into the print of the nails, and put my hand into His side, I will not believe'" (John 20:24–25).

From this last passage we know that the Thomas of the earlier disciple lists, the one without a qualifier, is not the Doubting Thomas. We also know that "Thomas called Didymos" is "one of the twelve" disciples. That means that he must have appeared with another name in the earlier disciple lists. The eleventh disciple, the one whose name changes constantly, seems to be the only candidate. This Doubting Thomas passage becomes very important in the text of the Gospel for which I was the scribe, by the way.

Like the other Gospel writers, John also knows of a second Judas: "Judas (not Iscariot) said to Him, 'Lord, how is it that You will manifest Yourself to us, and not to the world?'" (John 14:22). John does not seem to know that in the disciple lists, this second Judas (not Iscariot) is called "Judas the brother of James." Perhaps in the small area of the Empire where he lived in exile, inheriting the teachings passed on among the former followers of John the Baptist, this piece of information had not been preserved.

John seems to have inherited some details which in themselves make little sense and which he does not seem to understand: that there was another disciple named Judas, not Iscariot, and that there were somehow two disciples named Thomas, the one named just plain "Thomas" and the other called "Thomas Didymos." If we did not have any texts outside the Bible, these fragments from the New Testament would make little sense. But with the evidence we have given, the passages from John's Gospel take on a new significance.

We can conclude that John's "Thomas called Didymos" and "Judas not Iscariot" are actually two names for one person — Didymos Judas Thomas.

We have thus found Didymos Judas Thomas in all four Gospels, although, because of the system of names with qualifiers, it has been difficult to track him down.

I had initially thought that I had found another reference to Judas Thomas in the Jude (short for Judas) who is recorded in the list of Mary's children and the Jude who wrote the Epistle of Jude — the one known as St. Jude, saint of lost causes, whose name shows up in the daily newspaper classifieds.

However, through a series of discoveries over the last two years I have realized that Mary actually had two sons named Judas.

It is here that matters become even more complicated.

I have found, through the many years of seeing the life of first century Judea through the eyes of Judas Thomas, that it is possible to converse with the other lives in which our Spirit is involved because, outside of time, they still exist as centers of consciousness, linked firmly to our own consciousness.

I had felt the presence of Judas Thomas in meditation when I was writing the Gospel in the early 1980s but, in the last two years (since 2007), he has made himself increasingly felt in my life at other times as well. This is because I have been integrating all of my "lives" into the present life and it is no longer necessary to enter a meditative state to make contact. Judas Thomas especially makes his presence known when something causes him pain or anger.

The life of Didymos Judas Thomas was full of suffering. The reason there was so much pain in his life is the same reason there were twins and not just one son of Mary. They had two missions but were "twin souls," I have been told.

Yeshua came to teach the message of the all-inclusive Love of God and, after the resurrection, serve as a helper to those who followed him and sought his help. Judas Thomas, on the other hand, came to start a whole series of lives in which he could learn at first hand the deep experience of pain in the world, the anger, hatred, fear and other negative emotions which keep people from seeking and asserting their divine nature.

Over the centuries, many attempts have been made to lead people out of the trap of the world of negative beliefs and actions. I had met Yeshua, Elijah and Moses during the NDE in 1966 for an important reason — because they put me in touch with a project which had been going on for many centuries.

Moses had wanted to teach the people to talk to God as he had — "as a man talks to his friend" — but they were afraid and wanted to keep God at a distance, so he gave them a law to live by instead. Elijah had started the "schools of the prophets," in which he taught those who wanted to find God, how to be in touch with the inner, "still small voice" of God. Yeshua came to teach the same thing: how to speak to God as one would to one's loving father, Abba — with a prayer beginning "Our Father who art in heaven" and a daily "Prayer of Silence" which would gradually break the bondage of the negative aspects of the world and bring them into union with God.

None of these worked completely, although they have made a difference to those who could find inner peace using their methods. But most people still continued on their destructive way, even perverting the messages these prophets had brought, teaching cruelty and violence instead of love and forgiveness.

The mission of the soul, which Judas Thomas and I share, was to find why people keep returning to violence and pain even though many prophets have brought messages of God's love. By entering in a profound and sustained way into the pain and darkness of life, it was hoped that, through the lives we lived, we could learn of the condition of humanity and then teach people how to move beyond its self-imposed limits.

The lives of Judas Thomas extended to my life, which I understand is the last in a series. In my life the aim has been to write a new Gospel and books on a new kind of meditation which will help people take the next step in their spiritual evolution — before it is too late and we destroy the earth itself as a place where we can incarnate. I have built on the insights of many traditions, but have introduced new elements as well. The Gospel presents a new "mythic" story, a new pattern of meaning, designed to correct some of the errors in the other Gospels.

The soul which was in Judas Thomas has lived many painful lives, including my own. The physical pain of a broken back, encephalitis and other ailments has reminded me vividly of the other lives we have lived together. It has also provided a challenge for me to learn and teach, how we can heal our lives and our bodies and our relationships. I have had to enter all those lives, re-experience them and integrate them into a vision of how we can move beyond the darkness, to become the transcendent Self which is no longer trapped in the narrow confines of our fears and hatreds.

Interestingly, it was the pain I shared with Judas Thomas which made me realize that Jude was not Judas Thomas. And it was the readings of Edgar Cayce which brought my feelings into focus.

Cayce's readings are like the New Testament in that they do not directly mention Didymos Judas Thomas, but they do hint at his existence. In the collected Cayce readings, the "Report of Reading 294–161" discusses the dissatisfaction of most of the disciples at the time before Jesus' death "because of Jesus not taking advantage of the desire of the crowd the day before ... of making him the leader of their group." Then the report says, "Judas, not Iscariot but the other Judas, being among those most outspoken at the time." Here is the Judas Thomas we have been tracking in the Bible. His reaction is consistent with what is recorded in the Gospel I wrote.

In reading 5257–1 F 12 is another hidden reference to Judas

Thomas. Section 17 in the online database reads, "The entity (5257) was well acquainted with Judas, Thomas and with John the Beloved." Note the comma between Judas and Thomas, as if this is a series of three people. The editors of the oral readings would quite naturally have put in the comma, since there is no Judas Thomas in the Bible. But knowing what we know now, it makes more sense, grammatically, to leave out the comma, because the repetition of "with" indicates that we have two phrases rather than a series of three names. Thus, the person getting the reading was, during the time of Jesus, "well acquainted with Judas Thomas and with John the Beloved."

There are a number of readings for a "Stockbroker, Hebrew" under number 137. He was a reincarnation of Jude, youngest brother of Jesus (not the second born twin). Judas Thomas and Jude are different people in the Cayce readings. But this raised the question, "Why would Mary have named two of her children Judas?"

We often repeat patterns from life to life, and this repetition helped me to understand the emotion I felt coming from Judas Thomas.

As I explored the life of Judas Thomas in meditation, I discovered that he felt completely isolated from his family. He often felt bitter and lonely, because his family didn't seem to be aware of his existence. He had been separated from them early in life and had been raised by the equivalent of a foster home in Egypt. The educational methods of the time were often brutally cruel and he hated what was being done to him. He finally ran away from the school in Egypt.

The pattern repeated in my life. I went to a boarding school in north India, far from my father and mother who lived in central India. There I was beaten by the matron and some of the teachers. I disliked school and learning and didn't learn to read until Grade Three in this life. As an adult, I always lived far from my family, just like Judas Thomas — in England or western Canada.

For a long time, I sensed in meditation that Judas Thomas had been educated in Egypt among the Therapeutae, a group of Jews associated with the Essenes. They had combined a number of features of mystical Egyptian religion with Greek philosophy and Judaism. I also sensed that he had finally run away from them (as I did from boarding school at one point) and had gone to Greece.

In his loneliness and bitterness at being separated from his family, and being merely a "spare" to the heir to the throne of David, he had also rejected Judaism. It made no sense to him, this belief of a minor sect of Judaism that they were going to have the Messiah born in their ranks. He knew that they could not possibly defeat the Romans. He was bitter at being forced to live as a minor player in their deluded drama, forced to be separated from his family and forced to follow what he considered to be their delusional spiritual training.

His education was mostly in the Greek language, and the trauma of that time also carried over into my life in my first years at university. I wanted to study Greek philosophy as a basis for entering the ministry of the United Church of Canada. To that end, I had studied classical Greek and had gotten 97% in my first year exams, since I found it very easy to learn. But about half way through the second year of Greek, my mind suddenly refused to learn any more. I had the strangest sense that in some way my mind just decided of its own accord to shut down.

I was translating Thucydides' *History of the Peloponnesian Wars* in the Library at Mount Allison University one afternoon in the fall of 1964. I had gotten to the bottom of one page but, when I looked at the next, I discovered that I could not understand any of what I was reading. My mind blocked any further learning of Greek. I had not been able to figure out what happened there, especially since it did not affect any of my other learning and, therefore, was not a neurological problem. Now I realize that the trauma of Judas Thomas' experience with Greek education had carried over the centuries into my Greek classes.

I have also sensed great conflict related to Judas Thomas' search for meaning. He had rejected Judaism and the religion of the

Egyptians, into whose mysteries he had been initiated. In Greece he hoped to find some direction for his life, but it did not come. When the Gospel which follows here opens, Judas Thomas has returned to Galilee. He is on his way to Persia and India, where he hopes to find meaning among the Zoroastrians or Buddhists.

Thomas has been separated from his brother for many years. He does not even recognize him on their first encounter, and he is not identified as his brother in the text itself (likely because, when I was writing it, I did not want to acknowledge that connection with Yeshua). However, Yeshua becomes more than a brother to Thomas. To his great surprise, Thomas finds that his brother's teachings, especially the Prayer of Silence, offer him an alternative to the empty life he has been leading.

It appears that when Judas Thomas fled Egypt, he completely severed contact with his family and with those who were educating him. He was away so long that they thought he was dead. That is why, when a young son was born to Mary, she named him Judas (shortened to Jude) in memory of her other son who was lost.

Yeshua says that the story of the Prodigal Son was modeled after his twin, Joseph's son, who had run away. The sorrow was especially deep after Judas Thomas rejected his Jewish heritage and went "to feed the pigs" among the gentiles. His exile from the family and from his Jewish traditions became a metaphor for the exile of the soul from God. Joseph had stood on the road daily, waiting for his return, until Joseph died. I finally discovered why the story of the Prodigal Son always moves me almost to tears, even to this day.

Judas Thomas was very sensitive, even in the present, I found, to any suggestion that he didn't belong or to any story which related to his isolation from his family. When he returned to life in me and found that someone had stolen his name in the present, he was livid. I could feel his anger burning through me as the conflict, which I will discuss in Chapter Four, evolved. I have had to do much work on resolving his anger because it was affecting my life and my writing. But it is interesting that he was able to provide me with essential background knowledge which I needed to solve the mystery of his stolen name.

It is intriguing that alone among all the disciples this eleventh disciple almost seems to disappear in a flurry of names: Didymos Judas Thomas, Judas brother of James, Thaddaeus, Lebbaeus, Thomas also called Didymos, Thomas the Contender, The Doubter, Judas not Iscariot. To have so many names is to be almost nameless. It was even thought he was dead, so another brother was given his name.

Perhaps that is also why I was called "Bruce Fraser MacDonald." To have that name in Nova Scotia, where I was born, is to be indistinguishable from many hundreds of people with the same name. We were both anonymous in many ways.

Perhaps, also, that is why the scribe who wrote *The Gospel of Thomas* in *The Nag Hammadi Library*, a Gospel which has survived almost miraculously for two thousand years, asserts defiantly, "These are the secret sayings which the living Jesus spoke and which Didymos Judas Thomas wrote down." It is as if he is claiming that he does exist with a full name, Didymos Judas Thomas, in spite of being hidden from view for so long. The brother and disciple who cannot be named, who is always subordinate to someone else, finally has a name.

That brings us back to the question with which we began. Am I, Bruce Fraser MacDonald, a reincarnation of Didymos Judas Thomas, the scribe, as my Inner Guide says and as the clue given by Ahtun Re, speaking through Kevin Ryerson, passed on by Walter Semkiw, also suggests? Since there is obviously no physical evidence to confirm or deny any of this, we need to look at some "spiritual sources" to answer that question.

Chapter Three:

～

Drawing on Spiritual Sources for Clarification

He said to them, "But who do you say that I am?"
(Matthew 16:15)

I WENT THROUGH THE ABOVE DISCUSSION CONCERNING BIBLICAL evidence for Didymos Judas Thomas for several reasons. First, the whole structure of the argument and the nature of the evidence presented above seemed to form in my mind almost as soon as I read the hint from Ahtun Re that I was the "Scribe who wrote down *The Gospel of Thomas.*" It was a bit like when I was channeling the Gospel itself.

I felt compelled to write that chapter, even though I was attending my mother's funeral in Nova Scotia on March 17, 2007, with all the difficulties of a death in the family. I continued with my research and with a profound spiritual learning process through the death of my sister-in-law in June and the death of my father in August of the same year. It was a time of much emotional upheaval but was also a time when I had to deal with pressing issues involved in this Gospel.

I know there are contradictions and difficulties with the Bible, as with all religious texts, but I also have a great deal of respect for the Bible as the repository of the major documents which record the development of the Judeo-Christian tradition, even if you do have to approach them with a knowledge of the historic context to understand what is really being said. If there had been no evidence in the Bible for the existence of the twin brother of Jesus, I would have been hard pressed to accept the claim. In the 1980's, I refused to accept that identification, even though it came from my Inner Guide. I did not think it was important to claim any such thing.

I have been trained as a literary historian. I needed some kind of historical evidence. So I suspect the discussion above was as much to persuade me as to persuade you — this does, after all, directly impact the rest of my life in a very profound and unexpected way, and I do not want to build any of my life on sand. To be a university professor, who also happens to be the channel for a Gospel, is one thing: to be the reincarnation of the twin of Jesus is quite another, as you might imagine!

However, as you can see from our exploration of the evidence, even the New Testament has a lot of fragmentary, but collectively very convincing, evidence for the existence of this twin brother of Jesus. The fact that it is fragmentary and hidden even makes it more convincing, because it is obviously not the result of someone manipulating evidence to prove a particular party line. Editors may even have been trying to obscure who he was and, if this twin was also someone whose identity was being hidden for his own safety, it is amazing that there still is any evidence at all!

It is important, as well, to evaluate everything on the spiritual path to keep from falling into the many pits along the inner road. We should not merely accept things because they come from "spirit."

Many so-called prophets have led people astray into violence, hatred and even suicide in the name of God. One has only to think of Jim Jones and Jonestown, Guyana, or even Joseph Smith, whose original message involved a violent overthrow of the government and polygamy, to realize that not all messages which claim to come from God actually have a divine source.

Many messages, especially the violent ones, come directly from a distorted ego, the attempt of the "prophet" to gain personal wealth or power or sexual favors. Test the words of anyone who brings you a message from "spirit" — including me. Do not believe me or anyone without doing your own work on the subject. If the message proclaims love, joy and peace, then follow it: otherwise beware.

On the other hand, just because some messages which claim to come from God are false, does not mean all are. Cynicism often throws the good out with the bad. In the process of my own spiritual growth I have had "messages" which pandered to my ego — for wealth, power, influence or popularity. These are the same voices Jesus had to deal with in his "forty days in the wilderness being tempted by Satan." Anyone who wishes to follow the spiritual path will find themselves tempted by ego gratification in the same way.

This is why I am concerned about programs like "The Secret" which start people on the road to spiritual enlightenment by telling them they can get anything they want. It seems to me that these kinds of "make as much wealth as you want" processes are starting and stopping with ego gratification without going through the hard learning which is involved in coming to appreciate, at a deep level, the love, joy, compassion, humility and peace which can be higher aims of the spiritual path.

The Bible has been an important resource for me, as it is for many other people, but I know some people will feel I have weakened my case by including so much information from Ahtun Re, Edgar Cayce or other similar sources. However, if I am to be honest with my own experience I must include all of it.

You hold in your hand a book which has come almost entirely from spiritual sources. Over more than forty years, since the NDE of 1966, I have been immersed in spiritual realms and have never accepted any of it without testing and re-testing what I received. That is why I did a PhD in a conventional subject like literature, so that I would have the critical background to test what I found.

Almost the whole of Chapter Two has been an attempt to put Ahtun Re (and my Inner Guide) to the test. I have examined his comment in the light of biblical evidence, early non-biblical Christian literary sources, historic evidence and my own experience. His hint was very fruitful and seems to have stood up rather well.

I have already spoken of how someone stole Judas Thomas's name. It is at this point that I need to introduce that person who has carried a first century theological debate and conflict into the twenty-first century. I discuss this matter fully in Chapter Four.

There is a best-selling writer and teacher of the principles of *A Course in Miracles* named Gary Renard. Other very capable people have suspected him of fraud and have tried to expose him, but have failed. I think I have succeeded and must give credit to Judas Thomas and to Ahtun Re — spiritual sources — for the evidence which has succeeded where other, more conventional methods have not.

What I am doing in this chapter, in looking at "spiritual" sources of information, is very important. It seems to me that we human beings are moving into a time when we will be increasingly able to access information from "spiritual," "psychic," intuitive" sources. Even many scientists report seeing "visions" which solve their scientific problems — experiences like seeing atoms dancing before their eyes to demonstrate the principles of the theories they are working on, for instance. We are opening "the doors of perception," as William Blake calls them, so that we can function more as spiritual beings who have bodies rather than bodies which cannot see beyond themselves.

It is important that I affirm these kinds of experiences so that others coming after me may realize these are appropriate sources of information.

But I must also emphasize, as strongly as I possibly can, that we need to use our reason, our analytic and evaluative faculties, in order to determine what is valid and what isn't. In the case of Gary Renard, for instance, I will look at some of the credulity which has gone into accepting his claims without even basic analysis of the implications of what he says.

If we are not vigilant, we will end up being consumed by super-stition, instead of moving to greater understanding of the psycho-spiritual phenomena which have the potential to liberate us from the prisons of the self.

The other extreme, of course, is the materialist claim that none of these phenomena are valid "because they could not be because the world is made up only of material phenomena." That is merely a tautology which claims that "A is not A because A cannot be A." That is not helpful either.

The period of over two years since hearing from Walter Semkiw about being "the scribe" who wrote *The Gospel of Thomas*, has been a period of intense spiritual learning accompanied by profound physical and psychic changes. On April 17, 2007, exactly one month after my mother's funeral, it seemed like I was almost liter-ally "hit in the head" with powerful spiritual energy. On that day, I suddenly developed heat, pain, burning and a feeling of immense energy flowing in my neck and head — pain so severe that I could hardly walk. I consulted a neurologist at the Emergency Depart-ment of the hospital. After tests, he diagnosed it as post-encepha-litic headaches and treated it accordingly. I knew he was partly right but suspected there was more to it than that.

The discomfort persisted, and I sensed a resumption of the pow-erful Kundalini experiences (the powerful flow of creative, trans-forming energy in my body) I have had since 1991 — much like the experiences which Gopi Krishna describes in his books. On June 26, 2007, I went to see Melody Jones, a skilled spiritual healer in town, who has clients from as far away as South Africa. All I told her was that I was having recurrent headaches.

After focusing on the problem areas, Melody said, "It's amaz-ing. I have never experienced this much energy in anyone. It is as if your brain is rebuilding itself, getting rid of damaged parts and constructing whole new areas." This was a confirmation of what I already knew from my own meditation, but it was good to get her reaction. The powerful flow of energy (and discomfort) has continued till now.

I knew that this was connected with the unfolding of the story of Judas Thomas, and I knew that deep changes were taking place in me, physically and spiritually, in order to be ready to deal with whatever was coming. But it was not only in me that things were happening.

Something was going on at different levels of consciousness, in different countries, through different spiritual channels and even over stretches of two thousand years, and it was related to this book you hold in your hands. Thomas was always present in my consciousness. Yeshua obviously had an interest in the results and now Ahtun Re came dramatically into the picture.

Walter Semkiw had been encouraging me to have a reading with Kevin Ryerson so, on July 12, 2007, I finally spoke directly to Ahtun Re. I had another reading in September.

A couple of months after the readings, I read Gary Renard's first book, *The Disappearance of the Universe*. Putting the readings and Gary's claims together, I found evidence that strongly suggested this popular, best-selling author was perpetrating a fraud in his works. I communicated this to the Ryersons and Walter Semkiw, as well as to Renard's publishers, Hay House, since I thought they would want to act on this information with my help. After all, fraud in the area of our interest affects us all negatively.

Walter Semkiw told me that he cannot help me because Renard is his friend. He continues to promote him extensively on his website, even though he has a recording of the reading from Ahtun Re on whose testimony he says he bases much of his research. At least in this case he is not paying any attention to Ahtun Re.

The Hay House editors said that what I told them was interesting but they seem to have done nothing about it. Of course, as long as Gary's word is not seriously questioned, they have a best seller on their list.

And the Ryersons, without any explanation, will not give me permission to quote from the July and September readings which show fraud, even though Walter Semkiw quotes freely from Ahtun

Re in his books. I assume Gary is a friend of the Ryersons as well, and perhaps that is the reason for their blocking me from quoting from the readings. I feel that Kevin Ryerson is doing a valuable service in helping people see the potential of spiritual perception in very convincing ways, so I am disappointed they are blocking this attempt to set right a spiritual fraud.

As you can see, I have run into yet another mystery. I am very disappointed that none of them is willing to investigate this further, even though they have evidence which they usually accept implicitly. Something else is obviously obstructing the search for truth in this matter, even though they all say that truth is what they seek. Perhaps, because I am currently unknown, Gary seems like a better bet.

To an extent, I can understand their problem with me. Gary Renard has established his reputation and has made friends, at least partly on the basis of his claim to be a reincarnation of Didymos Judas Thomas. Then I come along with a Gospel and the report from Ahtun Re that I am a reincarnation of Didymos Judas Thomas. There is obviously a conflict there, but is it enough of a conflict to accuse their friend and best selling author of fraud? Obviously, it is not enough in their eyes. That means the burden of proof rests on my shoulders, and in Chapter Four I give that proof in detail.

Since I cannot quote from the readings, all I can say is that the readings confirmed my inner guidance.

My own inner sources had already told me, before the readings, (Chapter Two is based on their guidance) that Jesus had a twin, Didymos Judas Thomas, who was the author of *The Gospel of Thomas* in *The Nag Hammadi Library*. I am a reincarnation of the twin. The twins were raised for a while together in Egypt where the Holy Family fled to get away from the threat to their lives. The twins were then entrusted to two different groups: Yeshua to the Essenes in Palestine, and later in Persia and India, and Judas to a Jewish family in Egypt and then to be educated by Jewish Therapeutae near Alexandria.

Jesus was to be raised as the heir to the throne of David as well as a spiritual Messiah: Judas was groomed to be the scribe who eventually would keep a record of Jesus' words and actions, in the traditional way of Jewish kings. The education of such a scribe in those days was as demanding as the education with PhD which I have gone through in this life. Judas' identity was kept a secret in order to protect him, so that he could take over in case anything happened to Jesus, the first heir to the throne. I had picked up spiritually almost all of what Ahtun Re told me.

Actually, I had been told in the 1980's, while writing the Gospel which follows here, that I was the twin of Christ. But at the time I was taking in so much new information, much of it quite shocking to my traditional ideas, and certainly a threat to my reputation as a Professor at Luther College at the University of Regina, that I had shuffled the information deep into my subconscious.

It has taken me a lot of meditation and prayer, over more than two years, to come to terms with the implications of all of this. This is not just intellectual knowledge. This "information" is causing a profound change in my physical, emotional, intellectual and spiritual being. Much of the change is very uncomfortable, even painful, but I have been learning much faith, humility and patience in the process. Although I am not fully adjusted to this new identity, the adventure has certainly begun and the publication of this book will start things moving in earnest.

I also realized from my own questions, and from more information coming from Spirit, that I had to clarify a few things before publishing the Gospel. I may not be able to quote from the Ryerson readings but something interesting followed from them.

As you know, I have been talking to Yeshua and Judas Thomas, in spirit, for many years and can, like Moses, talk to God "as a man talks to his friend." Not long after the Ryerson readings, Ahtun Re spoke to me in my time of meditation and showed me a scene of him leading a procession between the massive pillars of a temple in Karnak in ancient Egypt. I had been his teacher, he said, in that lifetime. That is why he arranged to have the coded message sent to me through Walter Semkiw. He hoped I could expose a fraud in which he was being implicated.

I asked directly about the virgin birth and Ahtun Re insisted that, although the twins may not have been born of a virgin, they were a "divine birth," as he calls it. He would not elaborate, but it felt almost like he was speaking on behalf of a group of people in Spirit saying, "explain this part of the story more fully." He says that John the Baptist's birth was also a similar "divine birth."

Something special happened with the birth of the twins. It was announced by angels, as with all important Jewish births, and obviously the world was changed by the birth of Yeshua and John the Baptist if not directly by that of Judas Thomas.

There were a number of important questions which arose from this comment about "divine births." If I am the reincarnation of Judas Thomas, and it was necessary that Judas Thomas and Yeshua be divinely conceived, why would I, the same soul, be conceived in the usual sexual way by Peter and Edna MacDonald this time around? Wouldn't it be necessary to have the same kind of divine conception each time this soul came into human existence? Or was Judas Thomas not as special as the others? In another sense, the question boiled down to, "Is sinlessness or divine birth the same as sexlessness?"

I realized that we were dealing with something quite different from the usual ideas of a virgin birth. Divine conception, whatever that was, did not seem to require a virgin mother. Could it have involved a human father and still be considered a divine conception? What does it mean to be "divinely conceived"? Ahtun Re seemed to be giving me the opportunity to clarify that difference, thus providing you, the reader, with another level of understanding in relation to the Gospel which follows here.

On June 19, 2007, almost a month before talking to Kevin Ryerson, and anticipating some of what I might be told, I had put those questions to my Inner Guide and this is the reply I received:

"Yeshua was not born of a virgin in a physical sense, since he was the child, according to the flesh, of Joseph and Mary. But, in a spiritual sense, you could use the terms, 'virgin birth' or 'immaculate conception,' if you like, except that in aligning itself with sexuality or non-sexuality it muddies the waters."

"In order to understand what happened with his birth, you need to be aware that all people are incarnations of the Divine. However, after many incarnations, every Spirit (Atman) becomes a soul, or a karmic spiritual body. This soul carries the karma, the experience, the learning, the positive and negative of all lives. When this soul incarnates, it brings with it all the weight of the past and all the causes of the future. At its centre is always Atman, the pure Divine Essence, but this Divinity is masked by all the experience and consequent consciousness which follows karma."

"Every once in a while it is necessary for the pure Divine Essence, the Atman, the Christ, the Logos, to incarnate directly, to remind souls, lost in their darkness, of who they really are and what they can become."

"The Soul-Spirit which incarnated as Yeshua also incarnated as Judas Thomas. Atman/Logos/Spirit incarnated directly, without the karmic soul cloud, in the person of Yeshua. On the other hand, Judas Thomas was the incarnation of the same Spirit/Atman but carried also the remaining karma of the entity-teacher which was born as the twins."

"In this sense one can speak of Yeshua as being born of a virgin, not because of the physical state of his mother, Mary, but because of the spiritual state of the incarnating Spirit.

"You, Bruce, are an incarnation of the soul which was in Judas Thomas and which still had to work out the remaining karma it had taken on and find its union with the Divine Atman. That you have done. You are, as Eugenia Argue [a very spiritual and much admired friend of mine who leads a regular meditation group] told you, one with the God Force. There are just a few karmic residues you must deal with before you will be consciously aware of your Oneness and its implications for the rest of your life."

In order to understand what this means, it would be helpful to have a brief explanation of the model of consciousness which underlies this statement.

Think of the human being, not as a physical body, but as a kind of complex magnetic field. Within this field are a number of frequency levels: what appears to be a physical body (the most dense part of the field); the emotional field; the field of ideas in the mind; the soul field; and the spirit field, which is the centre of the whole thing — "the True Light that lights everyone coming into the world," as John's Gospel puts it (John 1:9). At the centre of every person is this Divine Light. The darkness of life experience gradually dims the light of the soul in the world and so it is necessary to go through processes of cleansing in order to see the inner Divine Light again.

When you think of reincarnation, think of this total field (minus the body which is replaced in each lifetime) being reincarnated. The emotions, ideas, beliefs and accumulated spiritual perception all adhere to this "entity." Like a magnet, when it is born into the human world, it attracts to itself all the results of its actions and ideas and feelings in the past. Violence in a past life attracts violence in the present life. Love in a past life attracts love in the present life. Each person draws on skills and knowledge acquired in former lives.

Technically, it is not the soul alone which reincarnates. The feelings, beliefs, ideas, attitudes and the results of action also accompany the magnetic field which moves from life to life. Although the body changes, the psycho-spiritual field attached to the soul provides continuity from life to life.

The different fields can be developed to different degrees — the athlete develops the body field, most people have a strong emotional field, some people work on developing the mental field, fewer people are interested in the soul field and at the present, only a very few are aware of the Spirit/Divine field at the centre of their being.

All of these fields can be developed in positive or negative ways.

Our beliefs, ideas, attitudes, prejudices and actions all affect the field we are and also affect what we attract to ourselves.

When we become aware of the Divine centre of our own personal field, and of our oneness with that centre, we can say with Jesus, "I and the Father are one." This is what is referred to as the Christ Consciousness. As people move into the awareness of the Divine centre within them, they literally "become Christ." Everyone can become Christ: it is not something which applies only to one person at one time in history.

With this background, it might be easier to understand the clarification I received from my Guide on July 17, 2007, after talking to Ahtun Re:

> "When someone has reached the level of the Christ Consciousness, the Logos Consciousness, then they can choose to be born in any way they see fit. That is a divine act because it comes from the divine centre of their being. In terms of the flesh, they choose their parents and their siblings based on their suitability. The process of impregnation is by a man and a woman who, in most cases, have not reached the same level of spiritual consciousness as the incoming entity."

> "The "Christ soul" as you might now call it, is responsible for building its body and life circumstances to match what it wishes to achieve. I say 'It' because at this level there is neither male nor female, and the Christ in the flesh can be either male or female."

> "Mary was not a virgin physically, since the father of the twins was Joseph. She had not reached the Christ level when she conceived, although that experience and the intense spiritual preparation for the birth propelled her to that level in her lifetime. It must be emphasized that this is the level of being that all people are to achieve sometime in their many lives. Those who have achieved this level now are merely forerunners of what is expected of all people. Jesus was not the "only son of God," since all people are manifestations of the Divine.

He was the "elder brother" of what will become the full family of God, but there were also others who had achieved this level before he was born."

"God consciousness is an aspect of yourselves and so you cannot avoid what is most deeply you. You will all achieve this, although it may seem to take thousands of years to achieve. If you cultivate love, kindness, joy and peace, you advance the date on which you achieve this condition of consciousness."

"If you practice hatred, violence and murder, especially in the name of God, you have put a great chasm between yourselves and the Christ Consciousness level of being. And if you teach others to commit murder in the name of God, you have endangered your very spiritual existence. This is not merely what you call sin. It is what is known as blasphemy, a betrayal of your central divine nature in a profound and persistent way. It is very difficult to find your way out of this kind of spiritual maze. It is important to point this out at the present time, when many abominable things are being practiced in the name of God. They are not acceptable."

"Once you have achieved the state of the Christ, you too can decide to incarnate to serve others. You do not need to find a virgin to do that. The Christ can be incarnate through the womb of a well experienced prostitute if that is appropriate — she too is inherently divine. That is why Yeshua knew that he could accept prostitutes and sinners into his group of followers, even when the righteous people objected."

"In other words, sex has nothing to do with this. It is the condition of the inner awareness which dictates at what level you are."

Over the centuries, the humanity of Jesus, Mary and Joseph has been lost in the doctrines of the churches. Many Christians have been so focused on sexual virginity that they could not see the importance of the spiritual processes involved in the birth of the twins. They have even undercut the importance of the love between man and woman in making of Joseph an old man and Mary a teenager uninterested in sex. They have implied, or even stated directly, that you must avoid sex if you are to be "saved," whatever that means. However, Yeshua says that we can all strive for the experience of the Christ Consciousness and even our sexuality can be part of our spiritual development.

In the same way that I have talked to Yeshua and Thomas, I have also been able to talk to Mary and Joseph in the spirit for many years. One time, when I was at a conference in Quebec City, I drove to the Basilica at St. Anne de Beaupre not far away, where I had a very intimate afternoon of conversation and communion with Mary. (St. Anne was the mother of Mary.) She emphasized that she and Joseph were very much in love and their marriage was not merely a convenience to hide her pregnancy. Their story is a bit sad, actually.

Mary had been raised among the Essenes to be one of the "hand-maidens of God," women so pure that the Essenes thought they could be the vessel for the coming Messiah. She was an heir to the priestly caste within Judaism. Joseph was also an Essene, about thirty-six years old, a direct heir to the throne of David. Their marriage was planned to produce an heir who would be potentially both a royal and a priestly Messiah. The Essenes had many such handmaidens and hoped that at least one of them would prove worthy of the Anointed One finding a home among them. It was thought this child, although not a priest technically, would be a priest after the order of Melchizedek: a priest of the Most High God and a King of Israel at the same time.

They were betrothed by the elders, having no say in the matter. It was their lineage that was of concern, not their personal feelings. For the Essene elders, it was almost like breeding a race horse. But during the period after their marriage when, according to the strict sexual laws of the Essenes, they were supposed to abstain from conjugal relations, they could not prevent their love from blossoming into both spiritual and sexual love, producing Mary's pregnancy as well as an appreciation for the importance of human love in the divine scheme of things. It was partly from observing their love in later life that Yeshua knew that marriage could make two people into "one flesh," which he counseled as the aim of the union of man and woman.

This was the scandal which so much bothered the Essenes, because of their overly strict sexual morality, even though most people would not have been shocked. They could not reject Mary or her children, since they were heirs to David's throne and to the priestly caste. However, because of what the Essenes considered their sexual indiscretion, Mary and Joseph were no longer allowed to remain among the ritually pure Essenes and lived as exiles among the lay Essenes who lived like others in the villages. Joseph had to make his own living instead of sharing the communal life. The attempts to cover up the rumors of what happened produced many mixed accounts from the first century and in later years the story was distorted farther with the accounts of the virgin birth.

Both Mary and Joseph, however, knew that their love had brought two very special children into the world. The story of angels, seen by those who were sensitive to these things, was correct. And as the boys grew, the parents knew they had conceived something out of the ordinary, two souls they felt were somehow directly from God. Having to give up the children, in order that they could be trained by the Essenes in two separate, unknown locations, nearly broke their hearts. (As I pointed out earlier, the story of the Prodigal Son is also the story of the loving father, Joseph, who waited anxiously for the return of his son.)

Joseph, over the years, has often told me with a great deal of hurt, of how he was written out of the story for the sake of expediency and doctrine, and how the love of a father had thus been denigrated through the last two thousand years. Mother's love had a scriptural model in Mary (even if a distorted, sexless model), but the loving father of the twins had been denied his role as a model for fathers. Thus fathers have always felt less than pure in the Christian tradition, since sex was also denigrated and sexlessness was held up as the ideal. I have promised Joseph that I would correct that here by telling his story.

So you see, there was indeed a "divine conception" on a number of different levels, not least the sexual love of Mary and Joseph, which brought them together as "one flesh" in spite of the strict religious condemnation of anything to do with sex among the Essenes. Contrary to the belief of many branches of Christianity and other religions, sexual love is not evil. It is not the cause of "the Fall of Man" or of original sin. Jesus even saw nakedness and the union of man and woman as an aspect of the primal innocence of the Garden of Eden. Sexuality can be yet another expression of the divine, creative force in our lives.

(As I revised this account on the evening of November 4, 2008, suddenly the whole room was filled with the powerful, almost overwhelming scent of roses, as if in approval of what I was writing. As I write I am often aware of a "great cloud of witnesses" watching what is being said.)

In clarifying this matter, I see that I have provided a "nativity story" for my Gospel of Thomas. I think it is much better than the virgin birth stories, because it highlights the tremendously important human love, which is an expression of divine love, in the birth and early lives of the twins. It can be the model for all human and divine love in the birth of every child coming into this world.

The other area in which I feel someone in spirit wants clarification is in regard to certain aspects of the death and resurrection of Jesus. I have already described in the first chapter how the account of the death of Jesus wrote itself with the numbering system A, B, C and then AA, BB, CC and so forth. But as I thought back over this event, I realized that I was not "channeling" in the usual sense of having words automatically write themselves. I was not even writing from memory. I "experienced" the events in my inner being and then recorded what I saw as if I was actually there.

I can still see the room in which Yeshua died, for instance. I can visualize the layout of that part of Joseph of Arimathea's house to which I was admitted, but not any other part of the house. I can visualize looking out of the wooden window shutters, onto the darkened streets of Jerusalem, and can still hear the frightened calls of the people. I can see where the couch and the chair were that Yeshua and I used, and the rough stone walls of the storeroom where Yeshua died. And I can often feel the pain and pressure of the "Stigmata," the wounds which Judas Thomas made in the flesh of his twin brother. What I was not aware of when I wrote the account was the relationship between Yeshua and Judas Thomas.

The fact that they were brothers makes so much more sense of what happened. When I go back over the event now, I know that Thomas, the twin, wanted to be the substitute in the plot to save Yeshua's life, but because he was "the spare," the potential heir to the throne, he was not allowed to do that, and Saul volunteered. Judas Thomas felt some resentment against Saul, because Saul was allowed to do what Judas Thomas was not. Not being allowed to act as he thought right in this important matter, re-emphasized the feeling that Judas Thomas had all his life — that he could not actually live his own life, because others were always directing him. In my present life this has manifested in a strong resistance to being controlled by anyone.

The violence of the death scene still haunts me at times, and to know that it was two brothers involved in that tragic event, and then in the absolute forgiveness which came later, is still deeply moving to me. I have come to realize that there really is no such thing as death, and there is no final condemnation, because we can always work with God to overcome the effects of even the worst of our actions. We have many lives to do that.

A very important additional conclusion from this is that there is no hell. God is love and could not put people into eternal torment without contradicting that love. Hell is merely a projection of our worst fears. It was invented by religious authorities (originally by the Zoroastrians, long before the time of Christ) in an attempt to control us through fear.

There is one last thing which I feel needs clarification in this chapter. This involves the humanity of Jesus. Over the centuries, he has been dehumanized in a variety of ways. He has been denied feelings or pain. He has been emptied of anything to do with sexuality. He has been portrayed as the consummate victim. He has become a sacrificial lamb to appease the "just wrath" of God. Some groups have even denied that his body was real at all. He has been drained of anything which would make him "one of us." In the most extreme case of dehumanization, he has been turned into God.

Now, it is time to see him as a human being again, but a human being who has become "fully human," even bringing into his "magnetic field of awareness" the knowledge of his own Christ Consciousness, his oneness with God. He is an example of what all of us can become. He was human as we are human. The only difference is that Yeshua knew, as the very basis of his life and action, that he was one with God. Most of us do not know that yet. Once we do, we have also "become Christ."

Remember how the people who knew Yeshua's family, the citizens of Nazareth, did not want to see anything special in him "because we know his mother and father, his brothers and sisters"? They could not accept their own holiness, so denied that anyone they knew could be holy.

Jesus always emphasized that he was human, like everyone else, except that he expanded the meaning of what it is to be human. The fact that he was a man and was still capable of being one with God meant that there is hope for the rest of humanity. To be human is to be capable of the same oneness with God which Jesus experienced.

The writer of John's Gospel realized this when he said that Jesus is not the only Light of God, but that this Light is in everyone who comes into the world (John 1:7–9).

If we continue to assert that Jesus was merely a product of a virgin birth, like the emperor and countless other godlings of the Roman world, then we destroy the whole substance of his message. There is obviously no hope for humanity if we have to be born of virgins to be acceptable to God.

And we are not forgiven by God because of the crucifixion. We do not have to depend on a human sacrifice on the cross to appease God's anger or "just wrath." Jesus did not say to the cripple, "Wait for a couple of years until I die on the cross to appease God's anger so you can be forgiven." He said, long before his death, "Your sins are forgiven." The cross had nothing to do with it. We are divine in our very core. The Kingdom of God is always within us. We have only to look within, diligently, often, to find it.

I know that I will be criticized for making the claims I do in this book. Some people will say scornfully, "Who is this retired university professor to think he is the reincarnation of the twin of Christ? How can he be holy? He has a wife and kids. He sometimes gets angry and sick. He is sexual and physical and all too human."

But I hope I can turn that around and persuade people that I am special as they are special: we are all inherently divine. It is in our human love — in our joy, peace, honesty, kindness, friendliness, sincerity — that we actually show our divinity. We can all do that.

Yes, there is great suffering and pain and darkness in human life. I have experienced a good bit of it myself. Yeshua told Judas Thomas that he would have to find the heart of this human darkness before he could overcome it and move fully into the light. But we can start here, now. We can experience love and kindness by giving love and kindness and then build from there.

In order to explore the darkness of humanity, the Spirit which was in Judas Thomas and is presently in me, has incarnated many times in many lives. Through many lives it (collectively "we") has experienced some of the greatest horrors of human existence, including the Holocaust in Europe and death by atom bomb in Hiroshima. "We" have been a Jewish merchant, persecuted by the Spanish Inquisition and a Zoroastrian merchant in Persia, killed by the advancing Muslim armies. We have been an aboriginal prostitute artist in western North America who, out of desperation at having lost her family and her love, committed suicide, as well as an abbot of a small monastery in 12th century England, who hated women and sex and was burned at the stake. We have been many negative things. But we have also experienced the potential of human love to transform the world. We have followed the road back to the Light of God, which is to be found within each one of us.

This Spirit was also in the twin brother of Yeshua, separated from his family for the sake of security, who wandered into a far country, looking for spiritual meaning among the educated and sophisticated of his time. He forgot, or more likely never even knew, his relatives and the land familiar to his ancestors. The story in the Gospel which follows here picks up where this stranger returns to the place of his birth, still unsatisfied after all his searching, where he finds, in the most unlikely place, what he had been looking for all along.

And now, after two millennia, Judas Thomas has returned, as I have returned, to make the two one. It really isn't either Judas Thomas or me who has returned: the Spirit which has entered human experience through us, has returned to teach people to seek within themselves for the Kingdom of God — in the place where spiritual sources can instruct them to move beyond the limits of hatred and fear.

Like Didymos Judas Thomas, I have heard the living Jesus speak for many years, conveying his divine message of love, forgiveness, joy, peace and transformation. I, too, have written a Gospel which contains the keys of the Kingdom of God which is within each of us. In a spiritual sense, it can be said of the teachings and stories of this Gospel, as Didymos Judas Thomas claimed for the sayings in his:

"Whoever finds the interpretation of these sayings will not experience death."

CHAPTER FOUR

~

RECLAIMING A NAME
THE EXTREMELY
UNFORTUNATE CASE
OF GARY RENARD

THIS IS THE SADDEST PART OF THE BOOK. IT HAS TO DO WITH
something which bothered Judas Thomas all his life — his name —
or lack of name. This chapter also gives a sense of how consciousness can bridge the centuries and how information from Spirit can
even be used to solve a case of suspected reincarnation identity
theft, fraud and plagiarism.

Imagine returning home from another life to find someone has
stolen your name and has moved into your house. All the neighbors think the impostor is you. When you claim that you are you,
they all say you are lying. Those who think you have evidence to
prove the impostor is perpetrating a fraud try to prevent you from
speaking the truth. They put blocks in your way and forbid you to
use any of their words which might have inadvertently revealed the
truth of the matter. They have become friends with the impostor
and don't want you back because you have become an embarrassment.
They want you just to go away and forget about trying to get your

identity back. You discover, to your dismay, that you have been the victim of reincarnation identity theft.

It seems almost impossible to prove your case. It is hard enough to reclaim your identity if it is stolen in this life. How can you, after two thousand years, get together enough evidence to persuade others that the impostor is not who he claims to be? And worse, you have returned after many centuries, ready to publish the fruits of your labor, but almost no publisher will touch your story because the person who stole your name is Gary Renard, the self professed "Bad Boy" of spirituality, who has developed a large following around the world through his lectures and books.

This is what happened to the Didymos Judas Thomas we have come to know in the pages of this book. However, although his case is certainly difficult, it is not hopeless, as we will see.

Many people have suspected that Gary Renard, international teacher of the principles of *A Course in Miracles*, has perpetrated a fraud in his best-selling books, *The Disappearance of the Universe* and *Your Immortal Reality* (Hay House). But we will go farther here in asserting that, not only does he seem to have perpetrated a scheme to defraud the public, he has also plagiarized an important part of his second book from a published source, thus providing the most damning proof of his errors.

Miracles Magazine, a *Course In Miracles* journal, recognized, in 2006, the serious nature of what they felt to be Gary's lack of truthfulness, so they devoted a special issue to "The Extremely Dubious Tale of Gary Renard." Jon Mundy, PhD, Greg Mackie and Robert Perry examined what they felt were extremely doubtful aspects of Gary's claims (Sept/Oct, 2006). Even more striking has been the action of Beverly Hutchinson (of the Miracles Distribution Center in California which deals with *Course in Miracles* materials) who, following her inner guidance, refused to stock Gary's best selling books.

(Just for clarification for those who may not know: *A Course in Miracles* is a series of three books which were written in the 1970s by psychologist Helen Schucman. She heard a "voice in her head" and "scribed" the books from a source which she, and many Course readers, consider to be Jesus Christ.)

The negative reaction to Gary is countered by prominent writers, clergy, psychologists and film makers who speak highly of his work. He has spoken in many countries, to many groups of admiring fans and, according to his website, is booked to speak almost every week for many months to come.

Gary claims that his ideas are drawn from two "Ascended Masters," Pursah (a woman) and Arten (a man), future incarnations of St. Thomas (Pursah) and St. Thaddaeus (Arten). Gary claims he is the intermediate, present incarnation of St. Thomas, so that Pursah is Gary in the future. These Masters traveled back through time to appear in Gary's living room and instruct him on the subtler meanings of *A Course In Miracles*. He recorded the conversations, he asserts, then copied them into book form and destroyed the tapes.

A number of problems have been pointed out in regard to Gary's account of the Ascended Masters. First, this kind of time travel (Pursah and Arten even take Gary physically into the future) is fine in movies, but hardly believable as actual experience. If this had actually happened, it would be the most amazing event in human history and would make all of Jesus' miracles, his resurrection and his ascension pale in comparison.

Having so-called Ascended Masters, who are future incarnations of oneself, return to teach, also counters all we know about the freedom of choice which we enjoy. Pursah is supposed to be Gary's future self. How does Gary know that he is on the path of becoming an Ascended Master? Is it inevitable that he become Pursah? Is there some kind of determinism involved here? What if he commits fraud in this life and that prevents him from becoming an Ascended Master in his next life? Will Pursah have to disappear in that case, since she could no longer exist if Gary failed to meet the criteria for "Mastership"? Will the books which she dictated also disappear, because they no longer have a source to write them? And will all those people who published and read the books, suddenly be changed once the books have disappeared, because they could not have read them?

It is a measure of how much we have been influenced by science fiction that this account has been so readily accepted merely on Gary's word. The unquestioning acceptance of this "dubious tale" undercuts those who are seriously trying to explore spiritual subjects and who are all too often accused of credulity. One wonders why people of the caliber of Wayne Dyer and Louise Hay, to name only two "big name" supporters of his work, accept this kind of tall tale without thinking about its implications.

In order to understand the importance of establishing the truthfulness or falsity of what Gary says, we can examine one of the issues which has been raised by others. Even Gary admits that his ideas (or Pursah's and Arten's ideas) are very similar to those of Kenneth Wapnick, a prominent teacher of *A Course in Miracles*. It is argued by his critics that Gary's writing adds nothing new and that he seems to be merely copying from Wapnick.

Those writing in support of Gary say that, even if the teachings do not actually come from Pursah, but from Kenneth Wapnick, it would seem that the only damage that is done is that, by a kind of logical magic, Wapnick's ideas have become Pursah's ideas which have then been presented as Jesus' ideas. Many people have benefited from Gary's teachings, they argue, so the question really only comes down to whether we are to believe that these are Gary's ideas, whatever the source, or whether they come from Jesus.

But, when you think of it, that may be very important. If these are actually the ideas of Jesus, then we should all pay attention, because something profound has happened in bringing actual teachings of Jesus to a modern audience. If they originate with Gary, and not with Jesus, that is very important to know, because in that case all the machinery of Ascended Masters is merely an elaborate way of lying to the public.

Gary claims he recorded what the "Ascended Masters" told him and then transcribed the tapes before destroying them. We are told that what we are reading is transcribed conversation, yet there are no distinguishing features in any of their dialogue, except the features which characterize Gary's speech. As other writers have again pointed out, they all use the same catch phrases, the same grammatical errors, the same crude, adolescent sexual jokes and innuendos, the same vocabulary and ideas. One could substitute any of the names, move them around or remove them entirely and it would be impossible to tell who was talking without the tags. This does not happen in real dialogue with real people. Looked at from a stylistic perspective, it would appear that these "conversations" all come from one consciousness — Gary Renard's — and that the claim to have recorded the conversation of so-called Ascended Masters, is itself a fraud. Even a half-rate novelist could have created more convincing dialogue.

Pursah and Arten also make a basic error, which is common in parts of the Course community, when they say that "J" (Jesus) wrote *A Course in Miracles*. This cannot be the case, as the Course itself reveals. The Course has many inspiring ideas and the consciousness from which it arose is very subtle. But it is not Jesus writing, as can be seen in *Manual for Teachers*, the third book in the series, when the text reads:

> Jesus has led the way. Why would you not be grateful to him? He has asked for love, but only that he might give it to you. You do not love yourself. But in his eyes your loveliness is so complete and flawless that he sees in it an image of his Father. You become the symbol of his Father here on earth. (p. 55–6)

Jesus is spoken of here in the third person and is not the speaker, as is obvious in other parts of the Course, so Jesus cannot be the person who wrote the books. Pursah and Arten are thus blatantly wrong in this most important of matters.

These are just a few of the serious objections other writers have raised. Gary has failed to answer any of them, yet he is still supported by a large part of the Course community and continues to be invited to travel the world giving talks. One wonders why people do not object more strongly to what appears so obvious to many and why he has such strong supporters. People on both sides of the debate feel so strongly about him that he seems to have split the Course community. Those who continue to object — and there are many — are now reduced to making caustic comments in internet chat rooms, because there seems no way to prove that Gary is a fraud.

Part of the reason for the support may arise from the fact that Gary's claim to be a reincarnation of St. Thomas is confirmed by Walter Semkiw on his website. But it is precisely because Semkiw quotes Ahtun Re to this effect that Ahtun Re tells me that his name is being used to support fraud.

Ahtun Re has great authority in the present day spiritual community because of his role in helping Shirley MacLaine in her spiritual adventures. Gary has become an almost unassailable writer and speaker in consequence. On the one hand we have a writer whose writings, without Ahtun Re's support, would likely have been questioned long ago. On the other is a person who many people think could not possibly be a fraud because he is a reincarnation of one of Jesus' disciples.

Another reason for the remaining support seems to be that many people think "Gary is such a lovely person so he wouldn't lie." Of course, con artists are always persuasive and friendly, and from all accounts, Gary is very persuasive.

However, after reading much of the debate engendered by the three critical articles and Gary's rebuttal (http://www.circleofa.org/articles/GarysResponse.php) I realized that there is another, more important reason, which is not at all obvious to the outsider.

Members of the *Course in Miracles* community "think differently," and are actually quite open in claiming that they use a different logic than the rest of the world, as I will summarize briefly in what follows here.

The starting point of the philosophy behind *A Course in Miracles* is the assertion that the world as we know it is not real and the usual logic which we use is one of the sources of our suffering.

The only reality is the Divine Trinity of Father, Son and Holy Spirit. Humanity, collectively, is the "Son of God." The world is an illusion, like a movie which the Son of God (humanity) has projected out of ignorance. It may appear that the Son of God (humanity) suffers in this self-created world, but suffering, and our whole physical existence, is really only a dream.

The way out of the dream is forgiveness. Once we are able to forgive others and the world, to "overlook," or forgive, the error which brought the world into being, and continues to maintain the illusion, we will literally no longer see the world and its suffering. The title of Gary's first book, *The Disappearance of the Universe*, reflects these beliefs: once we "forgive" the universe, it will disappear.

One of the weaknesses of the philosophy is that it is not made clear what "forgiveness" or "overlooking" are. Much of the difference of opinion (and outright animosity) within the Community, revolves around these terms. It is not clear either how "forgiveness," whatever that is, can cause the world to disappear.

In the Course view, Jesus did not suffer, because he knew the truth that there is no suffering and consequently did not manifest it for himself. We only manifest suffering when we "make it real" for ourselves by doing something like get angry or sad or frustrated or jealous. If we can "forgive" every event, we can make it not real. Gary apparently says in his lectures that Jesus never got angry because anger would only make the reason for the anger, which is illusory, into something real.

When we think Jesus suffered (as in the "Passion of Christ" movie), the Course says that what we are really doing is projecting our own fears of suffering onto Jesus. We do this also every time we think there is error in anyone else — the error is actually in us and we project it into the illusion which seems to be around us, by the mere fact of recognizing that it is there. If we choose not to recognize the error, to "choose a better way," then the error is supposed to disappear.

Jesus' ability to "overlook" or "forgive" all error leads, in this view, to the possibility of the disappearance of the universe — and hence the end of our suffering. When enough people can overlook error, can stop projecting error into the illusion, then the Course claims the universe will cease to exist.

It is not clear why the universe still exists, since Jesus is supposed to have been perfect and is supposed to have given the complete forgiveness of God to the universe. One would think that the universe would already have disappeared if the philosophy is at all correct.

Although the Course does not go this far, Gary (or his Ascended Masters) even says that God cannot be aware of our suffering and does not care about our suffering, because God cannot know any illusion. God does not know about our pain and so does not make it real. We are thus free to make it unreal by overlooking or forgiving it. God is completely separate from the illusion which we live and cannot help us with our problems. If He did help us, He would be acknowledging that our suffering is real, which is impossible for God to do. In order to help us, God created the Holy Spirit to help us change our way of seeing the world.

It is not clear from Gary's writing or from the Course how God was aware enough of our suffering (without actually being aware of our suffering — thus making it real) to decide to create the Holy Spirit. It is not clear either how the Holy Spirit can be aware of our suffering without God (who is inseparable from the Holy Spirit) being aware also, but these are some of the contradictions within the system.

If this seems like circular logic, it is. It is only with a lot of work that people are able to adopt this logic. In fact, there is a *Workbook* with daily exercises which, when practiced regularly, make it possible for the reader to enter more fully into this circular logic. My conclusion, after trying the exercises, is that it is a form of brain washing where any sense of the reality of the world and our place in it is replaced with the views outlined above. I notice on the internet that there are a number of people helping former Course members overcome the effects of this logic on their lives. They speak of the ideas as a trap, a cult, a distortion which poisons relations with family and friends.

There is an interesting similarity here with an early Christian sect called the Docetists, from the Greek *dokeo*, "to seem." This similarity will be important later in our discussion of reincarnation identity theft. The Docetists also argued that Jesus did not suffer — he only "seemed" to suffer, because God cannot suffer. For the Docetists, as for the Course Community, the world and our suffering likewise only seemed to be real.

Like Gary, the Docetists felt that, as soon as we see the unreality of suffering and the world, and replace it with the realization that the only reality is God, we will be free, because our suffering only exists as long as we believe in the pain. (This also has similarities with Christian Science which is essentially a docetic movement.) The only differences between the Course and the Docetists is that the Docetists felt it was necessary to perceive the world differently and the Course says we must "forgive" the world, "overlook" the error — which may actually be the same thing.

The effects of this philosophy on human relations are quite striking. The Course teachers often use the metaphor of the theatre. You need to think of yourself as a projector, they say, projecting a movie, which is the world. Since whatever is outside us is illusion which we have projected there, if we see error in someone else (outside), we are really only confirming that it is in ourselves (the actual source of the projection). When we "forgive" the other person, we are actually forgiving ourselves, from whom the error came in the first place.

Applying this logic strictly in the case of murder, for instance, if the police accuse someone of being a murderer, which is by definition an illusion, then the police must be the murderers for having seen an error which does not exist. The police, or even the victims of murder, are projecting this image into the world and are thus making it real. Instead of accusing, they should forgive and the murder will cease to exist — if only it were that easy.

The logic of this position becomes especially difficult for anyone who wants to question the morality of any action and correct it. If Gary's critics see dishonesty in Gary, the Course view is that they are actually only seeing it in themselves and projecting it onto Gary. Thus, in the view of many members of the Course community, it is the critics who accuse Gary of fraud, not Gary who is accused of fraud, who are guilty as soon as they have seen the fraud and named it.

To an outsider, this logic seems hopelessly contradictory and in practice it leads to an inability to deal with conflict within the community, as a number of members have discovered as they try to deal with the problem of Gary and his critics.

If the fault which we see is in the fault-finder, not in the one who seems to have committed the offense, people will be at pains not to see error in Gary's writings (or in anything else) for fear they will be convicted of the fault they point out. Instead, they are encouraged to "overlook" and "forgive" the fault, instead of pointing it out and asking for an explanation. Demanding that others be accountable for their actions is seen as "attack" instead of "love." Thus, although forgiveness is the aim of the community, members are forced to accept anything that anyone else does as valid, for fear of being seen as the perpetrator of any error they point out.

We can see this played out in Gary's case. Gary's critics merely asked for clarification of certain apparent contradictions in his work. In response, Gary wrote a vicious, personal attack against them, without addressing any of the contradictions. After Gary's reply to his critics, in which he said that he pitied Jon and accused him of "Professional jealousy and mindless attack on a fellow Course teacher," as well as dishonesty and acting from vested interest instead of integrity, Jon withdrew in seeming hurt and bewilderment and published an "Apology" in which he said that he still did not believe Pursah and Arten were real, but that he acknowledged that Gary did. "Let's sit down in San Francisco and talk about more pleasant things," Jon Mundy says, and that seemed to be enough. Jon cannot call Gary to account for dishonesty because by doing that, Jon is acknowledging that he is the source of conflict, not Gary. Many other members sided with Gary and attacked Jon in language which was so offensive the journal said they could not print it. There was obviously no room to address the whole question of honesty or truthfulness in this case because the only value held up by the community is a vague "forgiveness." Strangely, this "forgiveness" did not seem to apply to forgiving Gary's critics. Members even felt free to use extremely offensive language in condemning them.

To an outsider, the whole exchange seems a bit ludicrous. Either Pursah and Arten are real or they are fabrications. It would seem that one should be able to bring up questions about honesty without feeling guilty for doing so, but the logic of the community makes this impossible.

The problem becomes more serious in regard to the blatant intimidation which Gary uses against his opponents. He teaches forgiveness, yet his reaction to his former colleagues and friends is not forgiveness but vicious attack. He even admits he emailed Beverly Hutchins with the following, when she refused to sell his books: "If you care about your image and your place in Course history then you'll give very strong consideration to changing the nature of our relationship." In another email to Beverly he says: "The way things stand now, you will not be happy with my next book." This is direct blackmail. Gary does not feel he has to change anything — it is Beverly who must change. He threatens to portray her in a negative light if she continues to refuse to sell his books, but if she will sell his books, he will change how he portrays her.

Similarly, Gary quotes an email he wrote to Jon Mundy: "If you continue to try to attack me, I predict that only one of us is going to be hurt, and it's not going to be me." In whatever context, this is a threat, and his whole reply was obviously letting any future critics, including me, know that the critic was the one who would be hurt.

If the only value in relationships is forgiveness, then questions of honesty, blackmail, intimidation and betrayal of trust are swept under the carpet — and very few people in the Course community seem to be willing or able to question this kind of conduct on Gary's part. As we have seen, in the logic of the Course, these issues cannot be raised.

This does not seem like "such a nice guy who would not tell a lie." Gary will obviously change what he says about Beverly if she sells his books, which suggests that he is perfectly willing to twist truth for self interest.

It will be interesting to see what happens in my case, when the critic is not a member of the Course community and does not accept the illusoriness of the world in which we live or the defense that, "if you see fault in me, it must be in you." This is not a sufficient defense outside of the Course community and especially does not apply in the courts in the case of theft of the property of another writer. In the world most people live in, theft, intimidation and lies are still theft, intimidation and lies and, although they may be forgiven after appropriate changes are made, they are not condoned and they do have consequences.

Spiritual teaching about forgiveness, cloaked in threat, refusing to address questions of honesty, yet claiming to be the word of Jesus, becomes increasingly objectionable. In examining Gary's writing I assert that there are substantive issues which can be addressed, important questions of truthfulness which must be examined. Too many people are being hurt by the lies.

But we still have that assertion by Ahtun Re on Walter Semkiw's website that Gary is the reincarnation of St. Thomas. Ahtun Re has a history of being very accurate in his readings, so we have to take that seriously.

We have been dealing with contradictions in Gary's writing and in his behavior, things which can readily be identified. In going farther, we must realize that we will be dealing with evidence which comes from "spiritual" sources, and trying to prove anything from this material is a bit more difficult than proving observable facts.

Kevin Ryerson is a trance channel and Ahtun Re is a personality who exists in "spirit," not in the flesh. *A Course in Miracles* is a channeled work from a spiritual source. Gary's "Ascended Masters," Pursah and Arten, are supposed to be future incarnations of St. Thomas and St. Thaddeus, who materialize from the future to talk with Gary in his living room. Any evidence of their existence has, we are told by Gary, been destroyed. In all of this material there is very little "concrete" evidence we can deal with, so we will have to proceed in unconventional ways if we are to get at the truth of the matter.

However, we do have a basis to begin our discussion since Ahtun Re told Walter Semkiw that Gary is the reincarnation of St. Thomas. Even if you do not believe in channeled information that is a premise from which we can begin to work.

Gary begins to get into trouble because he goes farther than Ahtun Re's reading would justify. Not only does Gary accept Ahtun Re's assertion that he is St. Thomas, he also claims, in addition, that he is a reincarnation of Didymos Judas Thomas, Doubting Thomas and the author of *The Gospel of Thomas* in *The Nag Hammadi Library*.

We don't need a quote from Ahtun Re to tell us there is a problem here. In our detailed examination of early Christian documents in Chapters Two and Three, we discovered that St. Thomas and Didymos Judas Thomas were two completely different people. Gary cannot possibly be both, as he claims. And we discovered that St. Thomas did not write *The Gospel of Thomas*, even though it would seem natural to make that assumption. If Gary was St. Thomas in a past life, as Ahtun Re says, then Gary could not have been the writer of the Gospel, as he claims, and he could not have been "Doubting Thomas" either. These are only the first of a number of problems which arise from Gary's ignorance about the followers of Jesus. It is this ignorance which makes it obvious that Pursah and Arten are fabrications, not real "Ascended Masters."

Gary's claim that he was Didymos Judas Thomas in a past life is what I call reincarnation identity theft, and the proof of that charge can be seen only in the context of a number of things which happened to me over a period of years. Therefore, in order to clarify this aspect of our discussion, and given the strange nature of the evidence we are working with, I ask your forbearance at this point as I give you a short account of my experience. This is of tremendous importance, since this may be the first provable case of reincarnation identity theft in history.

I refer to myself in the third person in the account which follows, as Bruce MacDonald, because the logic of the contradictions will be much clearer that way. I know you have heard this story earlier in the book, but for the sake of those who have forgotten the details or who have not read that part, I repeat some of what I have already said.

In 1966, Bruce MacDonald had a Near Death Experience, after a fall down a 37 foot shaft on a construction site in western Canada. During the NDE, he met with Jesus and discussed a "project" which was then taking shape, a project which involved many thousands of people. He was given the choice of whether to remain on "the other side" or to return to his broken body. He decided to return.

After coming back to life, he was convinced that there was something terribly wrong with the Gospel stories in the Bible so, instead of becoming a minister in the United Church of Canada, as he had planned, he completed a PhD from the University of Leeds in England and became a University Professor, with the underlying aim of finding what was wrong with the Gospels.

In the early 1980s he channeled a Gospel of Thomas which he published privately as *According to Thomas*. He did not claim any particular past life identity, but assumed that he was merely a university professor who happened to write a Gospel. He has been going through a very intense spiritual training program, guided from within, from 1966 to the present.

In 2007, Bruce felt the time was ready for the Gospel to be published to a wider audience, so he sent a copy, now called *The Thomas Book*, to a publisher, along with a book about meditation (*The Prayer of Silence*) which incorporated many of the lessons from his Near Death Experience and a life of meditation and spiritual search.

He also sent a copy of the books to Walter Semkiw, author of *Return of the Revolutionaries*, (a book on reincarnation), thinking Walter would be interested in any reincarnation connections involved. This is where Ahtun Re entered Bruce's life.

Walter consulted Kevin Ryerson and Ahtun Re and sent Bruce an email in which he said that Bruce was not a reincarnation of St. Thomas but "was a reincarnation of the scribe who wrote down *The Gospel of Thomas*" in *The Nag Hammadi Library*. Bruce's research and his inner guidance led him to realize that the scribe who wrote the Gospel was actually Didymos Judas Thomas and Bruce's spiritual Guide told him that he, Bruce, was a reincarnation of this Judas Thomas.

Walter encouraged Bruce to consult Kevin as well. Bruce had two readings, one in July and the other in September, 2007. On both those occasions Ahtun Re confirmed what Bruce's Guide had told him.

(It is important for this discussion to state that, although Bruce was told by his Inner Guide that he was the reincarnation of Didymos Judas Thomas, he did not make this claim. It was confirmed by Ahtun Re, through Kevin Ryerson, the same person who said that Gary was the reincarnation of St. Thomas. It has the same weight, logically, then, as the statement about Gary being the reincarnation of St. Thomas.)

Ahtun Re reiterated that Gary Renard was a reincarnation of "St. Thomas," but not of Didymos Judas Thomas, and that "Thomas" (of whom Gary is said to be the incarnation) did not write *The Gospel of Thomas* in *The Nag Hammadi Library*. As you can readily see, this information from Ahtun Re immediately conflicts with Gary's and Pursah's claims.

There is a very troubling implication in this: either Ahtun Re is contradicting himself or the person who has been identified as the reincarnation of St. Thomas, one of the disciples of Jesus, is perpetrating fraud.

Concern about this fraud was not confined to people in the flesh. As you are aware, Bruce has his own spiritual sources (he did, after all, channel a Gospel through his communion with Jesus and Judas Thomas).

Bruce has been told by his spiritual Guides that those in Spirit were concerned that in the 1990's Gary had claimed identity as the reincarnation of St.Thomas in a new book he had published privately and was distributing on the internet. They were also concerned that he was leading many people astray by teaching in the name of Jesus, things which are very different from what Jesus would have taught. It was therefore decided to follow a course of action that would take a few years to unfold.

They knew that it was almost impossible to prove Gary wrong in any conventional way because his claims were related to events long gone and only someone with "inside information" would be able to expose him. Three people within the Course community tried, without success.

It was therefore decided that Ahtun Re, because of his connections with Bruce in a life in ancient Egypt, would orchestrate the plan. He would first tell Walter Semkiw that Gary was St. Thomas in order to confirm Gary's claims and to make him feel so over confident that he would lower his guard and make critical mistakes through which he could be exposed. This was a "white lie" passed on to Gary to pander to his pride.

Bruce was on the scene but was not yet ready to act because he was going through an intense period of training before publishing his Gospel and other works.

When Bruce was ready, however, he was first led to read Walter Semkiw's book and to read on Semkiw's website that Ahtun Re said Gary was a reincarnation of St. Thomas. This was the base from which all the rest would follow. Walter Semkiw and Kevin Ryerson were friends of Gary, so information could not be presented openly through them to Bruce. Only hints and code phrases could be passed on to Bruce.

(The evidence of Gary's fraud was most persuasive, however, because it had to be conveyed through channels who would have resisted it if they had known what was happening!)

As we have seen earlier in this book, Bruce was then told he was "the scribe who wrote down *The Gospel of Thomas*." Only Bruce would know the implications of this phrase, and Walter would pass it on without being aware that he was actually passing on information which would lead to the exposure of his friend, Gary. If Ahtun Re had said, "Bruce is the reincarnation of Didymos Judas Thomas," Walter and Kevin Ryerson would immediately have seen the conflict and might have been reluctant to pass it on (as they were reluctant to help later).

Once Walter had passed on the information, all the players were in action. It was hoped that, with his training as a literary historian and writer, accustomed to looking for obscure hints and patterns in the documents of the past, Bruce would be able to find a way to put all the clues together in a way that would succeed in exposing the fraud.

Bruce, the actual reincarnation of Didymos Judas Thomas, had enough inside information about the life and teaching of Judas Thomas to be able to find the errors in Gary's writing. To Bruce, the fraud was blatantly obvious, even though to others, unfamiliar with the life of the early church, it was hidden.

Bruce tried first to persuade Walter Semkiw, Kevin Ryerson and Gary's editors of the fraud, but they would not act and in some ways even tried to block his attempts to expose what Gary was doing. So he had to act more directly, himself coming up with the present chapter as the way of revealing the truth.

Bruce's sources even say that, in spite of what Ahtun Re had said about St. Thomas earlier (to put Gary off the scent) Gary is really a reincarnation, not of St. Thomas, but of Simon Magus (Acts 8:9–24). He was a magician and healer who claimed to be the Messiah. In the Christian tradition he is known as someone who perverted spiritual truth for money, hence the term "simony." He was a Docetic philosopher, just like Gary. In fact, Bruce's Guides say, it was not Jesus who was the source of *A Course in Miracles*, but Simon Magus, who then incarnated as Gary in order to promote his ideas more directly. This is the reason Gary is so successful in his teaching of a philosophy which was his own in the past.

Most people know very little about the early church, and even scholars are vague about what actually happened. Gary thought it was safe to draw on that area of history for his fiction because few people could expose him. However, Bruce had special knowledge of that period in history and realized that it was in the murky area of the early Christian church that Gary made his greatest mistakes in creating his Ascended Masters. Gary's errors could actually be exposed quite simply.

First, Gary made the mistake of thinking that, because Ahtun Re said he was the reincarnation of St. Thomas, he could also claim that he was the incarnation of Didymos Judas Thomas. Not so. Gary did not realize that they were two separate people and that he could not be a reincarnation of both at the same time.

Second, Gary thought it would be easy to get away with talking about St. Thaddaeus, because almost no one knew who that was. There was a Thaddaeus who was one of the "Seventy" who Jesus sent out and there was the disciple Thaddaeus. But most people have never heard of him. Gary did not realize that in the disciple lists in the New Testament, Thaddaeus was another name for Didymos Judas Thomas. In making Pursah into the later incarnation of Didymos Judas Thomas and Arten into the incarnation of St. Thaddeus, he had actually made them incarnations, not of two people, but of one person with two names.

Gary also thought that, since Ahtun Re said he was a reincarnation of St. Thomas, it was safe to claim he was the author of *The Gospel of Thomas*. He did not realize this was a title given by scholars and that *The Gospel of Thomas* was actually the Gospel of Judas Thomas and was not written by Thomas at all.

Finally, Gary tells us that Arten and Pursah are married to each other, but also that Pursah was the reincarnation of Didymos Judas Thomas and Arten was the reincarnation of St. Thaddaeus. Because, historically, "Didymos Judas Thomas" and "St. Thaddaeus" were merely two names for the same person, Gary had inadvertently constructed a story in which Judas Thomas is married to himself.

This is impossible, of course, even in Gary's illusory world.

Gary's ignorance of early church history betrayed him into all of these fatal mistakes, as Spirit knew would happen if they allowed his pride to get the better of him. His carefully crafted illusion has finally fallen apart.

For most people this will be enough evidence of fraud. But if what we have presented here is still not enough, then we can look in his second book for the most convincing evidence — plagiarism.

Pursah is said to have recited a new version of *The Gospel of Thomas* under the title of "Pursah's Gospel of Thomas" in Gary's second book, *Your Immortal Reality*. Gary claims that he recorded it for accuracy and then transcribed it directly from the tape. It was supposed to be a new, authentic, original translation by the person who wrote it in the first place. In *Your Immortal Reality* Pursah says the following:

> "I consider it an act of completion to have J's words in *The Gospel of Thomas* recorded accurately by a later incarnation of myself. I recorded J's words 2,000 years ago, and now you will record them again. Thus will the Gospel be corrected and passed along in its original form." NOTE: I [Gary] inserted the title below. Pursah spoke all 70 of the sayings. They were recorded for accuracy.

We now know, without any doubt, that all of this is fabrication because real "Ascended Masters" would not have to quote everything they say from a modern translator, especially when they claim to be making the translation themselves. Pursah's "Gospel" is actually plagiarized directly from Marvin Meyer's translation of *The Gospel of Thomas* from *The Nag Hammadi Library* (Meyer is Griset Professor of Bible and Christian Studies at Chapman University in Orange, California).

If you compare Gary's version with Marvin Meyer's translation of the work (originally in *The Gospel of Thomas: The Hidden Sayings of Jesus: New Translation, with Introduction and Notes* by Marvin Meyer. HarperSanFrancisco, copyright 1992, well before Gary's book was published) you will see that Gary's rendition is an almost verbatim copy of Meyer. I include just a brief sample here, taken from an online version of the Gospel so that you can compare easily with Pursah's Gospel, to see the extent of the plagiarism — except for minor changes early in the work, the whole thing comes directly from Meyer. The web address is http://www.gnosis.org/naghamm/gosthom.html .

Note the similarities:

(Meyer/Patterson) 90. Jesus said, "Come to me, for my yoke is comfortable and my lordship is gentle, and you will find rest for yourselves."

(Gary/Pursah) 90. J said, "Come to me, for my yoke is comfortable and my lordship is gentle, and you will find rest for yourselves."

(Meyer/Patterson) 91. They said to him, "Tell us who you are so that we may believe in you." He said to them, "You examine the face of heaven and earth, but you have not come to know the one who is in your presence, and you do not know how to examine the present moment."

(Gary/Pursah) 91. They said to him, "Tell us who you are so that we may believe in you." He said to them, "You examine the face of heaven and earth, but you have not come to know the one who is in your presence, and you do not know how to examine the present moment."

[Even in the following rather convoluted passage Gary plagiarizes word for word from Meyer.]

(Meyer/Patterson) 92. Jesus said, "Seek and you will find. In the past, however, I did not tell you the things about which you asked me then. Now I am willing to tell them, but you are not seeking them."

(Gary/Pursah) 92. J said, "Seek and you will find. In the past, however, I did not tell you the things about which you asked me then. Now I am willing to tell them, but you are not seeking them."

[Compare this passage to Thomas O. Lambdin's translation of verse 92 to see that the Meyer/Patterson translation is not somehow inevitable but their own careful choice which Gary has copied word for word. A translation is actually an act, not just of mechanical transposition, but of creativity in trying to match meaning to meaning.]

(Lambdin) 92. Jesus said, "Seek and you will find. Yet, what you asked me about in former times and which I did not tell you then, now I do desire to tell, but you do not inquire after it."

It is interesting that, in the early part of "Pursah's Gospel of Thomas," Gary changes a word here and there. By the time he gets to these passages, he must have grown tired or careless, because he doesn't even bother to change anything. He must have merely used the cut and paste function of his computer to copy directly from Mayer. It almost seems as if he was getting weary of the game he was playing with the public, and wanted to get caught.

Translators are writers and they make their living from their work. Plagiarism is stealing their livelihood and is worse than stealing their car or wallet.

Marvin Meyer and his publisher will likely want to talk with Gary and his publisher. Rogier Van Vlissingen may want to talk to Gary's publisher as well, since this scholar's book, *Closing the Circle: Pursah's Gospel of Thomas and A Course in Miracles*, is now almost worthless. All his labor has been in vain.

Interestingly, Gary has stolen twice, first from Meyer and secondly from Didymos Judas Thomas, claiming for himself a Gospel which was not his. Although Didymos Judas Thomas cannot sue, he has at least been able to set the record straight, even though there is still a long way to go before all the implications of this fraud work their way through the world spiritual community.

Those in Spirit who came up with their plan and gave me the information I needed to expose Gary, are very pleased at the success of their group action. There will be celebrations in their area of the heavens when this is published.

I have learned from my own experience with reincarnation that it is all too possible to keep punishing ourselves by committing the same offence from lifetime to lifetime. I have spent the last forty years learning of things from many past lives which I have had to change in order to live a full, spiritually mature life. In all of this, forgiveness is essential, as Gary and the Course say. But honesty, kindness and accountability are also important. Life is not an illusion, but an opportunity to learn and to grow spiritually and emotionally and in favor with God and our fellow human beings. In spite of what Gary says, God does care about us, deep within our own being where we can find the Divine Presence. By coming regularly into the Silence, we can discover this Presence. We do not have to wait for the universe to disappear before we can grow out of the suffering we create for ourselves.

Gary has obviously continued his life as Simon Magus, distorting religious truth and misappropriating the work of others for money. I hope he can move beyond yet another case of simony, to use his considerable abilities for something more creative and honest. He has changed the lives of many people for the better with his work, teaching them the value of forgiveness. Perhaps, after a time of reflection, he may be able to continue to help others, if the members of the Course Community are willing to forgive him. It is sad that his lack of self confidence led him to adopt the fiction of the Ascended Masters and to present the work of a well known scholar as if it had come from them. He had the ability to present his ideas on his own — but perhaps he became trapped in his own fiction and didn't know how to get out of it.

As far as I am aware, this is the first case in history of provable reincarnation identity theft. Now that it has been cleared up, it will be possible to look beyond Gary's deceptions and to realize that Didymos Judas Thomas is back as Bruce Fraser MacDonald. What follows here is another Gospel, *The Thomas Book*, actually written as collaboration between Bruce, Judas Thomas and their beloved brother and teacher, Yeshua.

The first *Gospel of Thomas* was written after the death and resurrection of Judas's twin brother, Yeshua, who he encountered in spirit as "the living Jesus." His Gospel survived almost miraculously to be discovered, hidden in a jar, in Nag Hammadi, Egypt in December of 1945, one year after I was born in December of 1944. In December of 1947 I traveled on a ship through the Suez Canal, not far from the site of the find, to land in Bombay on my third birthday, December 8, 1947, thus picking up the life of Judas Thomas which had ended in India. Ironically, December 8 is both Immaculate Conception Day and the day for celebrating the enlightenment of Gautama Buddha. I wonder what that says about the present drama. In 1966 I was reunited with my earlier life when I encountered the living Jesus in a Near Death Experience and was subsequently able to write our Gospel by listening to the words of the resurrected Christ and seeing the world of the first century through the eyes of Judas Thomas.

As the Gospel which follows here opens, Judas Thomas has returned from Greece on his way to India. He had been separated from his twin brother when he was young and had rejected his Jewish heritage, seeking meaning among the Egyptians and Greeks. When he encounters Yeshua and his followers on a Judean hillside, Judas Thomas does not at first recognize him. But the words of this strange teacher spark a fire in his heart and he becomes his disciple. Even when he does realize who this teacher is, he has to keep his identity as the twin of the heir to the throne of David a secret for security purposes, so does not tell anyone how he is related to Yeshua. As the story progresses, he gradually realizes that he has encountered more than merely a brother or the heir to the throne. Yeshua becomes his teacher and then much more than a teacher.

Now, almost two thousand years after that event, and a little more than sixty years after the discovery of the Nag Hammadi text, a fuller Gospel by the same author is in your hands. It has been two thousand years in the making. It can change your life.

PART TWO

~

THOMAS SPEAKS: THE GOSPEL TEXT

CHAPTER ONE

~

THE LIFE

THE OTHERS WRITE AS IF THEY DO NOT KNOW HIM, THIS MAN OF Nazareth. As we sit down following the evening prayers to record and remember the One who is gone, they remember teachings and sayings and argue over how he said them.

For them he is outside, like a street they can follow to somewhere, so they try to get his words down exactly, the events, the things. But there is no fire in their words.

And they start their stories with him, with a birth, with genealogies, as if that is where it began. I am not learned in the scriptures of my forefathers because I was often a rebel and sought after the wisdom of the Greeks or the secrets of the Egyptians in their temples and libraries.

So I see him through different eyes, not the eyes seeking the fulfillment of prophecies, but eyes seeking spiritual unfolding, the wisdom which is greater than Greek or Roman, which comes from within.

It does not start for me, then, with a birth, nor does it end with a death. These things are only incidental to the story.

"Thomas," they say, "You have always been different from us, doubting where we believe. Why do you persist in your error? Why not join us? Is it too much to believe what we believe?"

Even Peter, who knew the true account of that death, chided me because, by siding with them, he could lay the whole guilt on me. Judas had already killed himself and Joseph of Arimathea had moved into a far country, so there was only Peter and me, and now there was only me who admitted the secret to himself.

It would have been so easy to believe in their simple truths, to recall in the peace of an evening, the days of walking as disciples of this Master. But the burden I carried now was heavy, not with guilt, but with the need to find those who would believe.

That was long ago, in another land, and because their account has been spread wide and accepted by most of the Brethren, mine will not be looked upon with favor. So I live now among a different people, going daily to the place of worship early in the morning to meet with the group who have believed my words. We seek in quietness, through the spirit of the Christ, to grow in this life, so that in this and the next we may become the teachers of the Christ, preserving the truth which He has given us.

When I first met him I was hesitant because I did not look like most of his other followers. I had traveled and had the foreign clothes of one who travels. I did not look like a Jew as he and his other followers did.

So when he called me by name and asked me to follow him, I drew back.

"You have been frightened," he said, "and you feel wounded by life. Follow me, and I will show you the roots of your pain."

This is where the story begins — not with a birth, but with that promise — the roots of my pain.

You see, I had sought. From the Greeks I had hoped to gain a deliverance from the pain of my life. But their abstractions finally mocked me in their pillared courtyards. "Jew," they would say, "there is too much darkness in your soul. How will you attain to the Good if you dwell on the darkness of the soul?"

And the ritual of the Egyptians led me only part way out of that pain at the heart. They had power — there is no denying it — and I learned much of life and the powers of life from them. But again that darkness.

He was patient, you see, as I stood hesitating before him and his followers. Some of them looked like they did not want me anyway, and I could have left easily to go into another country, as I had done often before, running away. But he seemed to know my thoughts, too.

"When you go from here you will take your pain and darkness of soul with you," he said again. "I will take you to the heart of this darkness."

And welling before my eyes came all the days of search and loneliness, all the days far from home seeking and seeking. Yet here was a man among the hills of my home who offered some sort of deliverance or understanding.

"What can you give me?" I asked.

"Nothing," he replied, "But I can show you what is within you, for that is where the giving comes."

"But is not truth in the world and in the hands of God?" I tested.

"Yes, but the gateway to life is within and your inner eyes will be able to see the truth."

"But I have sought among the wise of the world for answers. How can you offer me anything, man of Galilee?"

"You have gone to the wrong teachers," he replied patiently, as if he did not care about insults. "Become pupil to yourself and you will have sufficient to provide you for many days."

"But it is the wisdom I do not have that I seek. How then can I learn from myself? Must I sit in front of myself and both teach and learn?"

"You are full of pride," he said. "You think your darkness is too great to have its own solution within it. You think all the world must try to solve the conflicts of your heart. The world cannot solve even its own problems. How will it solve yours?"

And after some silence, as he sat and drew in the sand in that way of his, he looked me in the eye: "Learn from yourself, for there is the true wisdom and there you will meet your God face to face. I am the guide who can show you the Way."

And then, sitting again in quietness with his followers behind him, he seemed to struggle to see what was within himself, to recognize what was growing there, and with great effort he said, "You will carry the secrets of the Kingdom within you for many lifetimes. Come, follow me."

With that he turned and began to stride down the road with hardly a glance over his shoulder. Soon I was alone again as the trail wound through the hills and only the sound of the wind in the tall grass filled my ears.

Where would I go now — to Greece, to Egypt again, perhaps to Persia? I had heard that one of the kings of the East had set up monasteries where one could go.

And then over a rise I saw this Galilean walking again and knew that his words had sparked fire in me such as I had not seen in all my travels, and I ran quickly down the road until I reached his group.

I fell in walking with the man at the end of our procession. Matthew was his name. Some of the others looked suspiciously at me, but Matthew turned and whispered, "You think you look strange in your foreign garb? I was a tax collector. Only the Master accepts me so far, but maybe we can be friends, too."

"We can," I said as we walked under the hot sun with grasshoppers jumping against our legs.

Those first few days I seemed to learn little, but a great peace grew steadily over me. It was the prayer he instructed us in which brought this peace. Every morning and evening we sat silently for a time, letting the cares of the world drain from us and being filled in imagination with the light of the Father.

When we did this meditation on fine mornings, outside, while we faced the rising sun, we began to feel all the light and life of the world rise up within us.

In the evening, we let the day die within us, that we might not be bound by it, but might be born anew each evening and morning.

This was the centre of our life, this prayer, this meditation. And I began to see those inner doors open, which I had closed out of fear or hatred. Gradually, as my eyes turned inward, I began to see as I had never seen.

"You will indeed see and hear and speak things which have been hidden from humanity since the founding of the earth," he told us one morning as we sat on a grassy slope. "You see with your eyes like all people, but you do not see. What can the eyes show you or the ears tell you? They can tell you of the surfaces of things. But I will lead you into a deeper way. You will see into the things themselves."

"And with your hands and eyes you know your body, but I will show you a knowledge of your body and your heart and mind and Spirit. You will see your mind and know your Spirit and understand the longings and desires of the heart."

"Do you not already feel within you the peace which leads to understanding? You will be able to move in that peace to know the Father as I know the Father."

But we were troubled among ourselves because we did not know about this sort of knowledge, and our traditions did not have these practices, except among the prophets of Mount Carmel.

So Peter asked, "Will you make us all prophets, then, that we may be like Elijah and Isaiah? We are but common folk. How can this be?"

To which he answered, "You will be prophets and more than prophets. The prophets warned the people of what was and what was to come. But you will be the very Sons of the Living God. The prophets were servants and did not have it within them to take part in the creating. But you will be called Sons because you will create."

We could not believe his words and sat for a time plucking grass and staring into the distance.

Then he continued, "The time has come when the Father desires not servants but sons and daughters. A servant does not know the will of the Master and so can only fulfill his commands and the laws which he has established. But a son knows the will of his father, and the son has an interest in the affairs of the father."

"So if I tell you that you are Sons of the Father, do not fear. You are no longer servants of the Law, because you have an interest in the affairs of the Father. You share in the possession of the Kingdom."

"But where is this Kingdom?" we asked, because we were wanderers sitting on a common hillside. Our clothes also showed signs of wear, and people on the roads often mistook us at a distance for a band of thieves.

"The Door of the Kingdom is within you and the Way of the Kingdom is within you. I lead you in the Way that you may possess what is rightly yours."

"Again, do not look at your clothes for a sign of the Kingdom. King Herod died consumed of worms, yet he possessed a whole earthly kingdom. Why then do you seek the signs of such a kingdom in yourselves? Do you also wish to be like Herod?"

"No. Seek first the Kingdom of God and what you need in this world will be given to you. Look at the flowers of the field. They do not toil or spin, yet even Solomon in all his glory was not dressed like one of these."

"As yet you are people of little faith because you would still be servants. When you know in yourselves that you are Sons and Daughters and not servants, you will have the power of the Father within you."

"Show us how to have this faith," James asked.

"I cannot show you faith," he replied. "Is it a stone or a stick that I can hold in my hand? Faith will grow within you as you follow my Way. Out of the silence of your prayer will come faith. Out of the peace of your living will come faith."

This was indeed something new which I had not seen in any place I had gone to seek. So I asked, "Master, the Greeks teach that in refining the mind and in the mastery of words is to be found wisdom. The Egyptians seek enlightenment in the complex rituals of their temples. And our fellow Jews seek fulfillment in the Laws of God. What then do you preach?"

Again he pondered for a time, as he often did before replying.

"Thomas," he replied at last, "You seek to justify yourself with your knowledge. Yet if you knew the wisdom of every age and every people you would still not be satisfied. And now you seek by asking this question to show your learning and justify yourself."

"Your search has been hard and, in your attempt to break your bonds, you have sought farther than any of these followers of mine. Great things can come from you. But I tell you that even a small child can learn to see more of the Kingdom than you have seen for all your searching."

"What are words and rituals and Law to the Kingdom of God?" he continued after a pause. "These are things for this present age. But through me is conceived a new age which will grow and ripen through you. When the new age is ripe and ready to be born the birth pangs of the earth will destroy the old and bring forth the new."

"Then there will be no need of words or ritual or Law. But now you all come from the world and are servants. You will become Sons so that you may leave behind the Law and the rituals, and you will no longer be ensnared by words."

"Thomas, you will see far, but in a world where people do not wish to see, you will have much pain. I proclaim not words, law or rituals but simplicity, the true simplicity of the silence within. Follow my Way and it will lead to eternal life."

—

So we would talk and question as the days went by. At first we doubted and even feared that our loyalty to this man was leading us into false ways, and we continued to question him until, gradually, we began to gain the faith and insight he had promised.

As we traveled, I discovered that we twelve were not the only followers. Indeed, we were not the first, because there seemed to be those who had known him from childhood. Also, in many towns, there were devout men and women who learned from him and practiced the Way.

There were those who had helped his mother when Joseph, his father, died, and who had been with him in times of trouble. They proved a kindly and loving fellowship who desired to possess him and all he did.

We never got too close to these people. They were mainly of the Essenes, who, with the Pharisees and Sadducees, divided Judaism into three groups.

As Jesus chose us to be his inner circle, many of the Essenes withdrew from him. They had, they said, educated and provided for him, and felt that they should have some control over his words as well. I felt a sadness as I saw this conflict grow.

Some of these people, Mary and Lazarus and Martha, as well as a group at Capernaum, remained loyal, and from being teachers became followers.

One day, as we were at the home of a man of influence who was a member of this party, he asked Yeshua why he chose twelve men who were not of their group. "Why, even I would be one of your band," he said.

"You Essenes have come far in your spiritual learning, from the schools of the prophets even to the present day," he said. "But a new thing has come into the world from the Father, a thing which cannot be contained by your righteous and disciplined life. For you require your members to face a long period of probation to show that they are perfect. And you exclude those who have fallen. But the Father now seeks not perfection, but life; not strict behavior, but love."

"You follow the Inner Silence, but you do not know where it goes or how to get there. And you think that I am one of you. But you should know from your own prophets that although I have been born into your family, I am not from you. I have come from the Father with the new covenant from the Father, that all people may learn of the Kingdom and turn to the Father. He does not require probation."

We were asked to leave that house and Yeshua was rejected by that household, although some secretly believed. There was great disagreement among the Essenes about Yeshua's mission, some saying that they should control his words, others that what had been born among them was greater than they expected and that they should listen to him.

But we were an odd group among these. Fishermen, laborers, tax-collectors, zealots, wanderers — what must we have seemed to Yeshua's friends? It must have seemed indeed that he had fallen among bad companions, when people of such strict discipline looked at him.

"You bring discredit upon us," they would say, or, "Why did you not draw your followers from us?"

Finally, Yeshua spoke about these murmurs, and his words became well known among them. "I have come to usher in a new age and, although your life was appropriate to the old, it is not the Way which I bring. Leave your old way and become my followers."

Many came with him, so that in many towns there were small groups of those who met regularly in the practice of the Prayer of Silence and sought the Scriptures to learn. He traveled around meeting with them and helping them to grow in knowledge and wisdom and love. These groups welcomed anyone and drew even prostitutes and sinners to their company — anyone who desired to lead a new life.

Our job, the job of the Twelve, it soon appeared, was to learn of the Master, so that we also would be able to travel to these communities to assist their growth.

"I have chosen you," he said, "because you belong to no sect or group, yet you seek for holiness. Often what we believe can keep us from the truth, but you believed very little and were open to the Way. So, too, the sinners are open to the Way because they have not been perverted by the strict morality of the Law in its many forms. You can grow new branches, whereas they cannot even grow new leaves, so stunted are they. The Pharisees and the Sadducees are even more stunted, although they have Seekers among them as well."

"Do not expect to see the full flowering of the Kingdom. I sow in you, that you may sow in others, so that the Seekers may be nourished and grow in many generations. I am the beginning, but the whole world will be our harvest."

"The Essenes are a holy people, and preserve much of the spirit of the Law in their gatherings. But they have also fallen victim to the Law, in that they take it upon themselves to judge by the same Law. So they exclude many who are not as zealous as they, even if they seek the Father. Do not be like those who judge the heart by looking at the body."

"Rather, in your gatherings, admonish gently the errors you see in each other and nourish with vigour those things which lead to the strengthening of love, joy, kindliness, honor, gentleness, simplicity, purity and the pursuit of good."

"The practice of the Prayer of Silence will gradually deliver even the most obstinate from evil. So do not condemn. You have not been excluded. Why would you drive others away?"

"The Essenes and Pharisees and Sadducees condemn, but they pay a price. They draw into their ranks only those who are saved already, but make it impossible for them to progress far beyond where they entered the sect."

"I seek the lost. I have come to deliver those who have no hope, who are not moral or upright and cannot stand before the judgment."

"And I have chosen sinners to be my Disciples so that, knowing your origins, you will not be able to condemn, without condemning yourselves. So have patience with the weak. They will fall many times into their error and will need to be saved again and again, but with your love, constant for them, they will learn also to be constant of spirit."

"Judge not that you be not judged, for whatever measure you give to others, it will be measured back to you."

"Do not seek to take the speck out of your brother's eye when you have a log in your own eye. Take the log out of your own eye, and you will see clearly to take the speck from your brother's eye."

"I have chosen followers with many logs in their eyes. But as your inner eye becomes clear, you will be able to cast out the logs from your eyes."

⁓

So he taught us, and his words sank deep within my soul. Every morning and evening, as part of our meditation, now, we would bring into the silence and the light of our prayer, the words which Yeshua spoke to us.

Did he speak of judgment? Then we would examine judgment within ourselves that we might understand the springs of our judgments.

The Law had taught us to judge, our parents and relatives had taught us the same, and in our meditations we examined how this affected us, and through us, others.

And he guided us, each one, in our own Way, for he said that the Way is one, but each of us has a different path within the Way.

"You do not understand this life," he said on a later occasion, "so you do not understand what you can achieve. You think that you are born and die and have only the time in between to live. The Sadducees do not even believe in the resurrection. And the Pharisees and Essenes believe you are saved or damned on the basis of what you do here in this life."

"So you judge and condemn others and forsake love in order to enter heaven. Yet I tell you that the Father has many heavens and many homes for you. This is not your only life, and these are not the only things you have to learn. You will have lives in other times and places."

"Do you judge the gentiles? You may have been a Gentile. Do you judge the prostitute? You may have been a prostitute. Do you judge the Roman or Greek? You may have been those."

"The Father wishes you to know the life of the world in all its conditions so that you may be able to love those in all conditions. He wishes you to learn poverty and wealth, weakness and strength, sickness and health so that, in all these, you may seek Him and find Him."

"Is He the Father only of the righteous? No, he is Father of all and Mother of all. All may come to God and find the love appropriate to their condition. Are you poor? Learn to love your fellows. Are you rich? Learn to give of your surplus to those who have nothing. Are you in a place of power? Learn to use your power for the good of others. Learn the love appropriate to the condition you are in and all conditions will become blessed."

"So, do not fear what people can do to your body, because you will have many more of those. Rather, avoid those who can kill the soul within you, those who would destroy love and the light of your soul. I tell you, you will have much more to learn then, and at the end of the Age, those who have not learned love will enter the Long Sleep, while those who have learned love will inherit the New Earth which the Father prepares for them."

"In each life, you are affected by what happened in other lives, but you in turn can affect those lives. The Father has not put you in a prison, that you can change nothing. Rather, you can do anything when your inner eyes are opened and you see the Kingdom within."

"Now, even you who follow me see dimly as through a fog. So do not, in that condition, set up laws for others to follow. Rather, teach others to grow in spirit so that their eyes may be opened to the peace and love of the Father."

"The Father wishes good for you, not evil. If then, you bring your fears and errors before the Father in meditation, He will help you to understand and be free. The Father does not condemn: you condemn yourself."

"If you judge, you will be judged. If you condemn, you are already condemned. If you do not love, how will you know love? If you are cruel, cruelty will come to you. What you are within yourself — that you will draw to yourself."

"Do not drunkards drink together and the rich consort together and the righteous pray together? There is a great law of the creation that like is drawn to like, in order that those in any condition may learn, in full force, the nature of their condition. Thus, seeing themselves in their fellows, they will be able to judge themselves through what they see in those around them."

"Your soul is free to grow, then, in this and other lives. You are bound only by what you wish to bind you. If you change your desires and beliefs, you will change your life, because gradually you will draw the new to yourself and become a new creature. You will find yourself attracted to new friends and new deeds."

"But the other lives in which your soul takes part will also change for the better or worse, depending on your decisions. See that you learn peace and love and, in your deepest experience, you will come closer to God."

"The home of your soul is in many mansions of the body that it may learn in all conditions to draw nearer to the Father in peace and love. You are greater and more powerful than you think, if you believe you only live in this time and this place. There is much power and knowledge which can come from the soul, if you turn to your inward eyes to see."

"Your condition in this life reflects what you have failed to do in other lives, and what your soul has learned as well. We have all come short of the glory of God, yet He has put it within us to find His glory, and to set right whatever error or ignorance we have."

"Praise God that He has created us out of His bounty and that He has given us freedom to be like gods, so that, separated from Him, we might yet seek His ways and draw close to Him in peace and love and the bliss of His presence."

"Draw close to the Father, then, and seek Him, that gradually you may become like Him and remain in His presence always."

"You who have followed me, and been faithful to me, have heard the words of life and have learned to come into the presence of the Father in silence and light. You have not yet been perfected, but you have overcome some of the temptation of the world."

"Now I will lead you into knowledge of the powers for good which are within you. Beware lest the power for good, by seeking only personal gain, become evil. The laborer is worth his wages, but the laborer does not seek to have the power which belongs to the king."

—

Yeshua's main interest, during the first year we were together, was to teach us of love and of the Father who does not require sacrifice, but mercy and justice. He taught us much about the mansions of the soul and how we are joined in Spirit with the other lives of our soul.

"This is the way to perfection," he explained. "You must be perfect, as I am perfect. Do you expect in one lifetime to be perfect?"

When Nicodemus asked him how to be perfect and enter eternal life, Yeshua explained that he must be born again — for Nicodemus was an old man.

"Must I enter again into my mother's womb, then?" he asked.

"You must be reborn in the Spirit, and you will have a new body. You have been seeking in this life and you will be able to seek further in the life to come. But are you a ruler of the people and do not know of these things?"

Yeshua asked this because the Pharisees held these beliefs also, although just the inner circle of initiates knew them, for fear that the knowledge would be polluted by common possession.

"I know, Master," Nicodemus replied, "I have been taught these things from my youth, and I have sought the perfection of the Law to become perfect."

"One thing you lack," replied Yeshua. "Seek also the perfection of the Spirit. The Law is nothing, unless the Spirit agrees. Learn love, kindness, patience, humility, devotion, and cast out of yourself hatred, greed, envy, lust, fear, for all these things, even with the Law, will draw your soul far from the Father. Strive for those things which bring peace, rather than division, and the Father, who dwells in peace and light, will draw you to Himself."

"Master, what is it to be perfect?" asked another.

"You are told to love the Lord your God with all your heart, soul, mind and body, and your neighbor as yourself. If you can achieve this, you have gone far."

"But what can take me closer to the Father?" urged the questioner.

"Would you be perfect? Then I give you a further command. If a man strike you on your right cheek, turn the left also, without anger or spite. If a man sues you for your coat, give him your cloak also. Love your enemies and do good to those who despise you. Do not condemn, but seek to win back those who sin. When you can do all these, then you are like the Father who loves all people, even when they turn away from Him."

"I am come because of the love of the Father. If you have been loved in your sin, should you not also love others in their sin? Work, then, not to find reason to condemn, but to find reason to love."

"And if the Father has loved you, should you not also love yourself? Would you hate what the Father loves? The Law teaches you to hate yourself and to despise and fear your weakness. Look at yourself in the Spirit, rather than through the eyes of the Law. You are here to learn, and the Father will guide your learning if you turn to Him."

"My disciples meditate morning and evening that they may come into the presence of the Father and learn to view their error as He views it. The Father has love and understanding, and will guide you gradually out of error, into life."

"But how can we approach the Father?" asked another. "When our forefathers approached too closely to the Presence, they were killed. Do we not need the priest to come between us and the Lord?"

"The priests have themselves been corrupt and have used their position to keep you from the Father. They have taught you fear and guilt, until you felt that the Father hated you. They have made it impossible for others to enter the Kingdom of God because, knowing they could not get in themselves, they have closed the door on others. They have much suffering ahead before they will learn the truth."

"But, all of you! Consecrate your hearts and minds to seek truth, and you may come into the presence of the Father with no intermediary."

"Do you think the Father is evil, that He will give a stone when you ask for bread, or a serpent when you ask for fish? Even an earthly father would not do that."

"So approach the Father in confidence, knowing that He wishes your good. He wishes to draw you to Himself that you may share His bliss. Believe in His love. Do not doubt. Ask, and He will give to you; knock and the door will be opened to you; seek and you will find."

"No priest is necessary, for you are all priests. Yes, and more than priests. You are the Sons and Daughters of the Living God. Does the child need someone else to carry his words to his father? Hardly! And you do not need anyone to carry your words to the Father."

"Come into His presence with thanksgiving, and into His courts with praise. Know that it is He who has made us and not we, ourselves."

"Read what the Scripture says and you need not fear. For fear is an evil as much as guilt and greed and murder. All these keep you from the Father and the glory He has prepared for all of you."

"And do not say to yourself, 'I will not be first in the Kingdom but will let others pass in before me.' Is there a tax collector at the gate of heaven that you must stand in line? No. If the whole world were to come at once, they could all enter into the presence of the Father."

"For I tell you that you do not need to travel to some place, like Thomas, in search of the Kingdom. The Kingdom of God is within you. Turn your eyes inward and there, in the stillness of your heart, you will find the Father who is within each one of us."

"You have sought the Father outside, as if He lived in a great house in the heavens. This is because you thought of the Book of the Law, which is external, as a manifestation of the Father, who must be external as well. So, looking outside of yourself for perfection, you also sought the source of all perfection outside of yourself."

"Even your prayer has been directed outward, as if to some outward deity."

"But the Father seeks no worship in temples, except the temple of yourself. Why do you argue about the right place to worship the Father? The Father seeks not place, but rather those who will worship Him in Spirit and in truth."

"And why do you argue whether the Pharisees or Sadducees or Essenes have the right interpretation of the Scriptures? They are all in error who seek only to interpret the Scriptures. Your life must reflect the divine will which is revealed in the words."

"Do you imagine that the Scriptures are themselves the Word of God? Are they not words in a human language, and do they not tell of human treachery and lust? How is this the Word of the Father?"

"I tell you that the Word of the Father is with the Father, the Father is the Word and the Word is the Father. The Scriptures may guide you to the Father, as my words will guide you to the Father. But if you would know the Word, the Light of the World, the True Scripture and the True Priesthood, you must yourself take it upon you to enter into the presence of the Father and become one with Him."

"Do you think it sin that I should speak of becoming one with the Father? I wish you could all be one with the Father, as I am one with the Father, and that you could all be one. You cannot be one in the flesh, but in the Spirit you can be one."

"We are created in the image of God, male and female; we are in the image of God. So God is not only the Father but the Mother. But as you draw near to God in yourself, God is neither Father nor Mother, male nor female, as we are neither male nor female in the Spirit. How much more are we neither of one sect nor another in Spirit, neither Jew nor gentile, neither slave nor free."

"Enter into the Kingdom of God, which is within you, and you pass beyond the divisions of this world into the unity which is in God, the All."

"Do you imagine limitations — there are no limitations, except those you lay on yourself."

"Can we then do anything we want, even when the Law speaks against it?" someone interrupted.

"What is the Law but the covenant of God with His family, not for slavery, but for freedom? If you commit adultery, are you not a slave to the flesh of the one with whom you are unfaithful? And are you not slave to the intrigue and the pain which you cause?"

"Or, if you steal or murder, are you not a slave to the fear, guilt, anger and hatred you cause?"

"God is no tyrant who keeps you in the right track with the whip of the Law. No. Rather the Law is there to guide you in the Way. People have turned it into a whip, but, in the Spirit, the Law is a gentle guide to freedom."

"But the Law is still outside, and I tell you that in this new age, the Law will become a thing within, so that in the Inner Way and in the Prayer of Silence you may be able to draw near to God without the fears and guilt and hatred that come from breaking this Law."

"Is everything, then, to be inside of us?" asked another, puzzled. "How will we know it is from God and not from the imaginings of our hearts?"

"The tree which bears good fruit is left to grow in the orchard," he replied. "Those who bear good fruit are in the Way. If a man claimed to be holy but bore hatred, lust, fear, contentiousness, would you not know where his 'holiness' came from? It is not from God."

"Yet, if you are doubtful about your worth, but still bear acts of love, kindness, patience, humility and strength, then you can know that you are in the Way."

"You will know others by their fruit."

"Do not fall into the trap of words. You can imagine that what you say is sufficient justification, but no one is ever justified before the Father by the words he uses. No, let the words be silent and let your life speak."

"Then others will know that you are with the Father and will be drawn to Him."

"In the beginning, God created the heavens and the earth out of the plenitude of His love. He created Spirits to oversee all His creation, with their set bounds and duties. Then He created human souls and gave them freedom to be what they would."

"The souls desired to experience all the qualities of the creation, so they took upon themselves bodies to come into the Earth. At first they knew that they were in the image of the Creator, but gradually they lost that knowledge and thought that they were themselves the Creator. In the pride and envy of their hearts, they drew away from the Father, until they thought that the bodies they had taken were their whole self, and that they had all power in that realm."

"So, because of their error, God destroyed all flesh, that the souls, freed from the flesh, might look upon Him again and recognize from where they came."

"He gave them the Law to guide them, and chose a people from among them to carry His truth to the world. But they broke the Law and refused to draw near to Him."

"I am the New Covenant which He is sending into the world. My Law is different from the old law which you practiced. My Law is the Law of Freedom."

"If you would draw near to God, draw near to yourself, for you are created in His image and you are reflections of His glory. But most people have sullied the reflection and have bound themselves to this earth. You imagine that your body is yourself, so you also think of the Father as having a body."

"God does not have a body or the limits of a body, and you are not a body, although you adopt a body to experience the world."

"In the Prayer of Silence, as you draw near in yourself to the Silence of the Father, you will find yourself moving away from or beyond the body which you have adopted. Do not be alarmed. The body is necessary for your experience in this world, but the Spirit also must find itself in closeness to the Father."

"Now, you imagine a great gulf set between the body and the soul, but there is no such division. Now, in order to meditate, you have to turn from the body deliberately, to the perception of the soul but, with practice in the Prayer of Silence, you will be able to perceive both the body and the soul as a unity. You will see that the body exists that your soul may learn to draw away from the attachment to the things of the earth, to draw near to God."

"You must remember that you have free will; you can will to follow many courses in your lives. But be aware, also, that the soul has learned through many lifetimes what is profitable and what is not. Do not think only of your ease in this life, for that may cause suffering in your inner self, in your soul. Rather, seek those things which free you from bondage to the flesh and attachment to the things of the earth. Seek love and peace and kindness and fellowship and patience — these things are of the Spirit and bring you closer to the Father."

"Do not seek to follow the Law, because that is merely to become slave to the Law. Rather, use the Law as a measure of your spiritual progress. As you meditate, the actions which are against the Law will slowly melt away. Ask not in your meditations that you may stop the actions: rather ask that you may understand the springs of error within yourself, and thus cleanse the inner motive, so that the action will be completely foreign to your changed nature."

"Thus, if you are an adulterer, do not merely stop the act of adultery — I tell you, the desire will still be there and you will commit the deed in your heart over and over. Rather, if you are tempted that way, bring this temptation, and the act, into the light of your meditation. Seek to know why you desire union with one who is not your husband or wife. Seek to know why in your own marriage you do not find fulfillment of your desire or need. Seek to know how you can learn love in your own marriage, and patience and kindness and forgiveness."

"I tell you, there is much more than the physical act of adultery here. There is much that your soul can learn of love and faithfulness and patience and forbearance here that reach far beyond the Law."

"And when you have found the springs of your adultery, you can find that love and unity, in your own marriage, which can bring you closer to the union which is in the All."

"Do you steal or murder or serve false gods? All these things can bring you closer to the Father if you are faithful in exploring them."

"The Father does not condemn you. Even the flood of Noah was not a punishment, but rather a means of freeing the souls from the prisons they had created for themselves."

"Death gives you another opportunity to learn, if you have so befouled one life, or it can be a gateway into rest for those who have learned and advanced toward the All. Death also can be an expression of love."

"Do not think of life as a place where you are rewarded or punished by a great judge. You reward or punish yourself. Do you live by the sword? Sometime you will die by the sword to learn the plight of your victims. Are you victorious in battle? You will be defeated. Are you great in the eyes of others? You must also learn how to live in humility. For, in these things, you seek to follow the laws of the world, and you become imprisoned in the world."

"But seek first the Kingdom of God and His righteousness and He will give you what you need for the body. If you serve the body that is all you have, but if you truly seek the things of the Spirit, then you have all things, as the Father has all things."

"So again, do not fear those who can destroy the body, but avoid those who can destroy the soul and bring all into darkness and sorrow. The Father seeks to bring you to Himself, but the laws of the body tend toward bondage. Seek then to control the body, so that the soul may come to a knowledge of God. As you draw nearer to the All, the earth will appear to you in a new light. The earth also is the child of God and is full of the angels of God. Plants and animals and rocks and wind are of the Spirit as well."

"You see the earth with imprisoned senses, so you see a thing dead or like an engine of war. Open your spiritual eyes and you will see a kingdom of spirits serving God and bringing their creations as an offering to God."

"You, living in the Spirit, will be able to do all things, for the spirits of earth have a command to work with the souls of those who have drawn close to the Father."

"You marvel at the things which I do. You wonder how a man can heal the sick or cast out the spirit of evil from a person, or command the storm to be still."

"Why do you wonder? You, too, can do these things, and greater things than these will you do when I leave you to go to the Father. For I will continue the work which I have begun here and will draw you to myself, that where I am you may be also."

"When you are in the Father and the Father in you, you can do all things. You are from the Father and you can return to Him. You are the child of the Father, yet you are the Father. You are in His image, yet you are His image."

"Do you understand what I am telling you? You are afraid to accept that you are in the image of God. How can you then accept that you are His image? You are all the body of the Father in the earth."

"Do you still not understand? I tell you that whatever the Father can do in the world, you can do, when you have freed yourself from the bondage which you have brought upon yourself."

"Can the Father still the storm? You can too. Can the Father bring increase in the crops? You can too. Can the Father bring drought to teach His people? You can too. Can the Father heal the body and mind and soul? So can you."

"But the Father wishes greater things than this: that you love mercy, do justly and walk humbly with Him. If you would be great, be the servant of all. If you would be a child of God, make peace among others. If you would be like the Father, learn love and patience and peace and humility."

"For, out of His love, the Father has given you love; out of His patience, He has waited for you. The Father does not seek to be great among you: He has become the servant of all."

"Learn to be like the Father, showing love and patience, sharing joy and sorrow, and yourselves becoming servants of all, that you may show forth His glory in the earth."

⌐

With many of these teachings he taught us, stirring our hearts within us and drawing us to the Father, so that Matthew and I, who had been outcastes, became part of the group of those faithful to Yeshua. Love grew among us.

What manner of man this was, we knew not, for he seemed to have entered his heart and soul and he had found the Way to God.

We had all sought in our ways, and we had all been dissatisfied with the traditions which had been handed down to us.

So I had gone off to Greece and Egypt and Matthew had sought company with money and the Romans. Peter and James and John had been with the Essenes and Simon was a Zealot, trying to bring in the kingdom by force. We had all rebelled, yet had found no lasting answers.

Here was a man who promised much and showed many powers. And it worked. As we meditated each morning and evening, we did draw into a greater peace and love, we did begin to glimpse the will of the Father.

And his words were like manna in the desert. His words drew from us recognition of ourselves and our deepest longings.

The traditions as taught by the priests and rabbis meant little to us. We felt guilt because we could not find meaning in them, and our countrymen condemned us as not fit to be Children of Israel, but our hearts did not speak and our minds found no lasting food, and we were all more desolate than rebellious.

This man, Yeshua, spoke to our hearts. His words pierced to the centre of our emptiness and brought hope.

"Why is it that we don't find fulfillment in the Law and teachings of the Pharisees?" we would ask.

"Because the Law brings death, but the soul seeks life," he replied. "Are you commanded not to commit adultery, not to steal, not to take the Lord's name in vain? But there are more and more prohibitions as well."

"These are fine. You should not steal or murder or worship false gods. But the Law only goes as far as telling you what not to do. Where do you read how to love your wife or husband and be faithful instead of committing adultery, or how to love your enemy instead of murdering, or how to give gifts to those in need instead of stealing?"

"The Law can only condemn, it cannot save. And the teachers of the Law can only condemn, they have no power to save. Obey the Law, but go far beyond the Law if you would be saved."

"The Sadducees do not believe even in the prophets, but follow the Law only, so they believe only what they can see with their eyes and judge with the intellect. Of all the Jewish sects, they are the most empty."

"The Pharisees listen to the prophets and study what is to come and accept the resurrection, but they have forgotten that the prophets also said to love mercy, do justly and walk humbly with your God. They will only accept what will fit in their limited system."

"So, when I heal a lame man, they cannot accept that and think it is trickery or else that it is from the devils. They think that they know all there is to know about God, and anything they cannot understand, they condemn."

"They do not understand me, so they condemn me, and they will condemn you for the same reasons. I offer the spiritual food they cannot, and instead of accepting the food themselves they warn others not to taste."

"This is a perverse generation that will hear the words of life, and because they are attracted to them, because the words offer freedom from the bondage of the Law, because the words would bring them closer to the God they claim to serve, they fear and condemn."

"If you are starving, and I offer food, do you kick it in the dust?

Yet this generation starves for the Spirit, and still rejects the words of the Spirit."

"How long will the Father bear with this generation? Flee from their perversity and seek life that you may escape the destruction that will come upon them. The earth will be turned upside down, and they will be no more. But those who hear my words and do them will enter whole into the New Earth which is planned for those who find life."

"All can find life. There is not one who needs live in darkness and death. Turn inward to find the Way and the Kingdom of the Father. Find in my words and in the Prayer of Silence the path to eternal life."

"You are not merely a body subject to Law, but you are a soul inhabiting a body in order that you might learn of the love of the Father. Accept His love and you will live."

"Turn to Him and you will find life and food and drink for the soul."

―

Who can express how it was with us in those days? Meditating together on the hillsides or in rooms, watching together the sun rise above the earth and in ourselves, we saw the light of the Anointed One rise up to give peace and love.

There was no trouble, in those days, from the authorities, and we had not yet broken into factions. Together with Yeshua, we grew.

The Prayer of Silence! That prayer drew us closer to the Christ-consciousness. It was often hard to do as well, because the material mind wanted often to pull us back to a concern with the things of the world. But Yeshua would bring us back with his often repeated maxim, "Seek first the Kingdom of God and His righteousness and all these things will be added to you."

And from time to time a voice within would tell us that this was all nonsense — we should be working, making a future, raising a family.

Sometimes people laughed in the early days of our gathering, at all these grown men, wandering around with this unorthodox teacher. We were surely lost, they thought. Some dropped away. They expected to be instantly blessed with some form of power, and when they were not, they went their way. This, in spite of Yeshua telling us that we would not be given anything; rather we would discover it in ourselves.

So, gradually, for those of us who stayed, the inner doors began to open, and we began to see the world as the Master told us it was. It was not a matter of saying, "Yes, I believe," but rather was a seeing, a perceiving of the world as he said.

And as we grew in Spirit, he could tell us more of Spirit and the Way. Sometimes he told us generally, and sometimes he led us into our individual Way.

For he told us, "There is one Way, and the Christ is that Way, but you each have an inner path to follow to walk in the Way."

"The Kingdom of Heaven is like a Master who went into a far country and left his servants to look after his possessions. To one servant he gave the responsibility for five sums of money, to another, two sums, and to another, one sum."

"When the Master returned after many years, he called the servants together. The first brought the five sums and in addition five more. The second servant brought two sums, and in addition two more."

"These servants the Master praised and said, 'In this life you have been faithful with a few things. In the life to come you will have the responsibility and rewards of many more. Go into the Kingdom, blessed of my Father.'"

"Then he called the third servant, the one who had only one sum to look after. But when that servant came to the Master, he brought only the one sum he had been given. He had buried it in the ground, fearful lest he lose even that one sum, because, as he said, 'I knew you to be a hard Master, reaping where you have not sown, and I was afraid.'"

"The Master was angry at this servant and, taking the one sum, gave it to the man with five, saying to him, 'You have been faithful with much; you can be trusted with more.' But to the unfaithful servant he said, 'Your fear has destroyed you. In this life you have been unfaithful; in the next you must bear the fruits of your unfaithfulness.'"

And then, speaking to us he said, "It is the same with you. You have been given each a different measure of responsibility according to your stage of spiritual growth. Use your gifts and fulfil your responsibilities that you may grow, each according to the measure which is given you."

"You are all in the Way, but you each walk with a different step. So do not look at each other, fearful lest the others are doing more or less than you. Look at yourself and what has been given you to do. Fulfil what is yours in hope; do not bury your gifts because of fear."

∽

As we grew, we began to see the Way which had been obscured for so long. And as we looked at each other, and heard the Master speak to each of us, we began to realize that we had all been spiritual cripples, and that Yeshua was healing us, or rather was guiding us to heal ourselves.

"Do not run from your weaknesses," he would say. "Look squarely at them in meditation, bring them into the Silence also, that you may see them in the Light and find the strength which is in them. For there is no weakness without a finger pointing to strength, and no strength without the possibility of weakness."

"There is no darkness without a light within it, and your light can show you your darkness also."

"Do not fear what is in you, but surround yourself with the light of the Christ-consciousness and nothing can harm you. Descend further into your own hell that you may ascend into heaven. Dispel the darkness which is within you, that all your being may be light. Open the doors to the darkness that the light may stream in."

"All these things will become clear as you enter further into the Silence and Light."

∽

Sometimes, in impatience, one or other of us would ask how long before we could become perfect and stop having to strive. The answer was at first disappointing, until we began to understand. But even then the understanding was imperfect.

"To enter into perfection," he would say, "as the Father is perfect and I am perfect, may take a year or three years or many lifetimes. Each of you has created a different darkness for yourself, and each must learn to enter that darkness fully that all the darkness may become light."

"When your whole being is in the light, so that you can see yourself clearly, and look even into the darkest shadows, then you are close to the Father."

"But you must learn also to love others as I have loved you. When your love is complete, then you will be complete."

"Do not suppose that this will be easy. There is darkness and error within you, which you will not want to face, and there are those you will not want to love. These must come with much prayer and meditation, so that the Spirit of the Father may fill you and bring you to Himself."

At other times we would ask him what would happen when we were perfected.

"On this earth you will learn to fulfill all those things which are in you. Look at the gifts the Father has given you. Can you heal, can you speak, can you express difficult things in words or prophesy? Can you make beautiful or useful things with your hands or minister to the needs of the sick or lonely? Whatever has been given to you, do."

"You must be what you are, fully and in love. When you are perfected, you will be what you are, you will know all that you know, and you will bring all these things to fruit. Then the Father may see that you truly are and know, as He is and knows. Then He will receive you to Himself and you will become One."

"Some of you have a special mission to fulfill which has been given you by the Father. This must be found and fulfilled. The history of our falling away from the Father and of the Father's gracious call to us is full of these special missions, either of words or deeds of love."

"Speak your truth, therefore, as a messenger of God, and show forth your love as a child of God. In this way also you will be filled to running over and the Kingdom of God will come on the earth."

One day a rich man came to Yeshua and said, "Master, I would like to serve you and follow you. What can I do to become as you wish me to be?"

Yeshua replied, "What have you done so far?"

The man explained, "I have followed the Law since I was a boy, I have done as my mother and father wished, I have given myself to charity and good works to help others, I have given a tithe of all I own to the temple and have given even more than that to the poor. This has brought me joy, but there is still emptiness within me. I seek to give all that I am to others, yet cannot escape the guilt I feel."

"You must serve yourself first," replied Yeshua. "All that you have done is good, but you have done it because of the expectation of the world. So it is the world which acts, not you."

"Seek to know yourself, and the springs of your own action and then, when you give, it will be your act, not your father's or mother's. Love yourself and you will know how to love others; find the light and darkness in yourself and you will be able to understand others; seek the Spirit of the Father within you and you will act out of the spirit of the Law, rather than from the letter."

"The great secret is no longer a secret or the possession of a few: turn within to the vast world of mind and Spirit which you share with the Father, and you will then see clearly to act in the world which He has created for you."

"For, if all that is within you is in darkness, how will you be able to act, except by the dim light of the world? Seek the inner light, and then the acts of charity and piety which you do will be a true reflection of you. Then you will be fulfilled."

That man became a devoted follower of Yeshua and was much help to us all in years to come. We would meet often in his house and from that house went forth charity and love to all the surrounding families in times of need.

⌐

For three years, Yeshua was with us, and he taught us many things. The others, remembering these sayings, seem to have forgotten much of the practice of the Prayer of Silence he taught us. But for me, at any rate, the Inner Way was most important. What he led us into became more important than what he said, finally, for in the Inner Way there was guidance provided, even without the written or spoken word.

Thus, every day, I could come to the Christ within and ask guidance, and He would give it. Even for the small things, I could ask and He would, like a friend, help and guide.

I asked Yeshua of this and he said, "You are indeed fortunate, for it is the Father who has shown this to you, and He leads you through the Christ. Continue in your search, for the Father is very close."

But I did not understand fully, and continued still to act in many things on the basis of what my fears and hopes told me. While Yeshua was with us I did not fully follow the voice of the Christ within.

CHAPTER TWO

~

THE DEATH

WE DID NOT WANT HIM TO DIE!

Yet how can I write this part of the story? It is our shame! It is my torment! And who will believe, after all these years?

But this secret has been locked up in my heart for too long.

Why should he die? We all told him of the danger. And we had seen others die for lesser teachings than his.

He had been such a comfort to us, leading us to life. Now he seemed bent on death, almost suicide. We begged him often not to go again to Jerusalem because we knew of the anger of the Temple authorities. They wished to kill him as much as we wanted him alive.

How had he offended them? By telling them of their hypocrisy. "Whited sepulchres," he called them, and "viper's brood." And they proved that way. They would invite him as a guest to their homes, only to find evidence against him.

When he healed on the Sabbath, even in the name of the Father, they said he broke the Law. When he gave the people food for their souls, they said he was in league with the Devil. But when he said he was the Son of God, then in a violent show, they shouted and tore their garments and said he spoke blasphemy.

"He must die," they shouted in a frenzy.

Calmly he spoke to them, "Will it change anything, even if I die? Will you be closer to God or will my words die? Death is nothing but a door. When you kill my body, I will yet see you and your sin."

"Death, nothing?" they shouted. "The Law says that anyone who blasphemes should be put to death. Yes, we will come close to God by obeying the Law. But you will die in your sin. God Himself will punish you. But we will inflict punishment on punishment before you go."

~

We knew this would come. We knew of the hatred in their hearts which blinded them. So we did not want to go to Jerusalem. They had already driven us out with their threats. Now we were in a safe place across the Jordan, where John used to baptize in the river.

Yeshua's fame spread throughout the countryside and people came to him from far away. He would teach them, then we, his disciples, would teach them in smaller groups. Many learned of the Master and his message in this way, so that he had many followers.

But, as with John the Baptist, so with Yeshua: the Temple authorities also came to listen and condemn. Their followers had begun to come to Yeshua and to forsake the bondage to the Law, so they asked questions to trap him, but his answers only made him more loved and brought scorn on the Pharisees and Sadducees.

They hated but, there in the wilderness, they did not dare touch him, lest the crowd kill them. So they came and listened and returned in anger to Jerusalem.

This time in the wilderness, across the Jordan, was our most fruitful. Here we saw the one we had followed become great. We were proud to be disciples of such a Master. He was sought by all the world. Even the Romans and Greeks came to hear him and some became his followers.

One day, escorted by many soldiers, the wife of the Governor, Pilate, came, bringing her child who had been troubled by a spirit that seized him. She sought healing, but when the boy was healed by the Master, she stayed to hear his words as well. Even some of the soldiers believed.

Ah, what days those were! Even the Romans came to his feet! Could we be blamed for thinking that we were coming into our reward for a few years of sacrifice? We even began to quarrel over who would be greatest in this new kingdom.

"The one who would be great must be servant of all," he told us. So we all sought to be servants so that, when he came into his power, he would give us position and wealth.

He only looked at us and smiled sadly. "You still do not understand," he mused. "How long must I be with you before you will learn? How can I change the current of centuries? It will take many lifetimes to undo the error of ages."

But even when he said his Kingdom was not of this world, we could not believe him. We would say, "Look at the people who have followed you. How can you say your kingdom is not of this world?"

He would reply, "These people follow me into the wilderness, not because they see power and wealth here. Rather, I show them the Kingdom of the heart and they are content."

But we wouldn't believe. Earlier, when we had been empty like these people, we understood, but now our hearts were full and we looked with envy to the kingdoms of this world. How we erred! But we could not see, for our greed and popularity had blinded us.

"Even you will desert me," he said one day. But we could not believe him.

"I will stay with you always," I said to him. "You have given me life. Do you think I would let you be delivered into death?"

In great sadness he said, "You do not understand either life or death. But you will learn. You have been chosen to learn what has been hidden from the foundation of the earth. It will be a great burden for you, until you realize it is the greatest blessing."

However, we were afraid still, and tried to persuade him to stay away from Jerusalem and certain death.

"What is that to you?" he replied. "If I choose to lay down my life, what is that to you? And if I lay it down, I can also take it again. You still do not understand life and death, so you are afraid. I tell you, neither life nor death is as you see it with your eyes. This also you will learn."

From that time he watched the opportunities to go to Jerusalem, "So that you may learn of life and death and the great love of the Father."

We set out from the wilderness and crossed the Jordan, going toward Jerusalem. We walked mainly in silence because we could not believe that Yeshua would actually do this. Surely, he must want to die or else he was planning to set up a kingdom and overthrow the Romans. Yet that didn't seem his way.

He had healed the child of Pilate; perhaps he hoped for protection. Yet, who would protect us, his chief followers?

As we walked closer to Jerusalem, many of his converts from the wilderness dropped away, as if struck by fear. We followed with heavy hearts.

There he was, striding along in the long, grey gown that Martha, wife of Nicodemus, had made. But he was quiet now, as if his mind and Spirit were occupied with things beyond our ability to understand.

We stopped for the midday meal under the meager shade of a tree and some outcroppings of rock. Again, after blessing the food, he was silent. Then, gathering us around him, he asked, "Who do the people say I am?" for there had been much rumor.

We whispered together, then James spoke, "Some say you are John the Baptist come back to life. Some say you are Elijah or one of the prophets, reborn. But mostly they don't know what to say."

Then, looking at us all, he asked, "Who do you say I am?"

We were afraid to say what was in our hearts, for we had discussed this very thing.

Then Peter blurted out, "You are the Christ, the Anointed of God," and put all our hopes and fears into words.

We watched him then and waited, for we thought we would either be struck dead for blasphemy or else he would reveal himself.

Again, he looked at us and, with a certain sorrow, said, "Flesh and blood have not revealed this to you, but the Spirit of the Father, working in you, has revealed this. On this faith I will build my Church."

Then he looked back on the road where a small group of his other followers sat eating.

"You see, all but a few have deserted me. How hard it is to change human hearts. The Father calls out for you to return, yet you will not return."

"If you would turn to Him in faith and learn love and patience and endurance, what bliss He has to offer you. Yet out of all the thousands who flocked to hear me, I have now only twelve left, and a few more at a distance." There was great sadness in his words.

So I spoke to him, "But Master, there are many who secretly follow your words and will come to support you if there is trouble." Even as I said it, I knew it wasn't true, that only we twelve would walk with him into Jerusalem, and I realized the danger.

"Even you twelve will desert me," he replied.

"Oh, no, Master," we all replied, encouraging him. Yet our fear grew within us at his words. What was to come?

Later in the afternoon, as we walked on the road and talked among ourselves of the Kingdom that must surely come, we started quarrelling again over who would have the greatest position in the Kingdom.

Two of the disciples, James and John, asked Yeshua if they could be at his right and left hand when he was lifted up in power.

"You do not know what you ask," he answered with a sad smile on his face. "You desire power, yet you do not know what power really is. Do not judge by looking at the Romans or the Pharisees. What is power to this world is weakness to God, and even God's weakness is greater than all the power of this world."

"You will indeed join me in my Kingdom, but you do not know what that means." Then he turned and continued to walk toward Jerusalem.

"We will stay in Bethany, at the house of Lazarus," he said, as we passed along the road overlooking Jerusalem. Then we stopped for a time, looking out over the city.

Yeshua was strangely silent as he watched the buildings gleam in the sun. Then he began to weep over the city. "Jerusalem, Jerusalem. You who kill the prophets and stone the saints, how I would like to redeem all your sins and lead you to life. As a hen broods over her chicks, so I would gather you under my wings. I offer you life, but you give me death. Zion has become a dungeon and a house of thieves."

"How long will you continue in your darkness? Until your stones have been torn from each other and your timbers burned?"

After a time, he turned to us, saying, "The faith of Abraham has not been kept in Jerusalem. Now Abraham's inheritance will pass to whoever will accept it. The children have rebelled and the stranger will have a share in the inheritance."

So we went on to Bethany, to the house of Lazarus, where we were given food and drink and made comfortable.

There was a special closeness, a special understanding, between Yeshua and Lazarus, as if they shared knowledge or a way of seeing which we did not have. We worried that there was danger so close to Jerusalem. Lazarus seemed to expect us and welcomed the Master as if it were a natural thing that he should return.

Lazarus had changed since coming back from the dead. He no longer feared death and seemed to have seen and heard things in his time in the grave that made this life much less fearful.

The dread of death was still upon us. How could anything good come from the death of our Master? So, while Yeshua and Lazarus spoke of things which must surely bring death to them — about going into Jerusalem, about teaching and healing openly, about challenging the authority of the Pharisees — we talked of how to preserve Yeshua's life and protect him.

Looking back, I can understand the meaning of his words. "Unless a seed fall into the ground and die, it cannot grow." "If you would try to save your life, you will lose it; but if you lose your life for my service, you will save it." "Unless I leave you, how can I be truly with you?" These, and many sayings, he gave us then, but we did not understand.

"You hear my words but do not understand. When the time of life and death comes, then you will understand fully. Do not be dismayed that you do not understand. Words can guide you, but the event will teach you."

For some days, we stayed in Bethany resting, talking and visiting. Martha and her sister, Mary (who had been the prostitute), and other friends of the Master, made us comfortable and shared in our fellowship.

A few days of peace before the events which shook all of Palestine! Those events were to create a burden in me which was to last for many years. Why did I not understand then? Why the weight of this burden which no one would believe and take from me? So I write it, and so I will be condemned for writing it. Yet it was a secret which at first was shared, but now became mine alone.

From Bethany we were sent to get the donkey for the Master to ride into Jerusalem. Some of the old glory of the days in the wilderness returned then. Those who had heard the Lord then, came to line the streets and shout, "Hosanna to the Son of David. Glory to the One who comes in power! Hail our king!"

Our hope returned. Here was popular support and, perhaps, with his powers, we could drive out the Romans, overthrow the Temple government and establish the Kingdom of God here in Jerusalem. Our hearts rose within us and we walked behind the

Master without fear, feeling strength from the shouts of the people.

Yeshua taught them in the Temple, drawing large crowds. Again, as in the wilderness, we twelve were assigned to help in the teaching and explaining, and we felt that truly the Kingdom was coming. It was a happy time.

But there was danger, as well. The Romans became uneasy at the crowds, but for the sake of his child, Pilate allowed the crowds to gather.

The Temple authorities were filled with hatred. Pilate obviously was favoring this man who was attacking their authority directly. He healed on the Sabbath, he called them hypocrites, he said that their traditions were not the Word of God and that people did not have to do as they did. He taught them to pray the Prayer of Silence so that they could come before God's presence without the aid of priest or sacrifice.

Then one day he made a whip of some ropes and drove the money-changers and cattle dealers out of the Temple. "This is the House of God, but you have made it into a den of thieves and cheats," he shouted as he moved among the tables.

Every night we returned to Bethany, but we no longer felt at peace with ourselves. Why did he not act? Where was the glory of the Kingdom we expected? It was not there, and now it looked like Yeshua was provoking the authorities more than they would tolerate.

We began to fear again, especially when we heard rumors of plots against us all. Many of the people had begun to turn away when they heard what Yeshua asked of them. He was not going to give them glory, but required that they love each other, forgive their enemies and remain constant in prayer.

⌒

Triumph began to sour in us and even we began to waver. Some of us argued that we should do something to save the Master from death, others that he should do what he wanted.

"But what if part of our duty as his followers is to protect him?

Will God forgive us for not doing that?" our group asked.

The others answered that he knew God's will better than we did.

So the argument continued without a resolution.

And who is to know if what we did was shame or if it was the will of God for a new covenant with His people. Did Abraham know what would come through him or did Moses expect when he fled from Egypt that he would make those Hebrew slaves into a nation?

It seemed right when we did it, yet we have been condemned as liars by the whole Church. I can only write the experience.

From our discussions arose a small group: Peter, Judas and me. We were all hot-headed to an extent, but cared much for the Master. By ourselves we could not act against all the powers of the Temple, but we laid our plans.

The man, Joseph, from Arimathea, we persuaded to join with us, since he was in the highest councils of the Temple, yet was a follower of the Master. We had to trust him with our lives in confiding with him, but we needed also to know what was being planned on their side.

When it became obvious that they meant to have him put to death, we conspired to save Yeshua and have another put in his place.

There was a man, Saul, from Galilee, who was part of the events of Yeshua's life. He was about the same age and looked very much like him. This Saul had complete faith in the Master except, like us, he did not think Yeshua should die. So he took it upon himself to be the scapegoat, to take the abuse which would have been given to Yeshua. Saul did not think he would die, but he was such a Zealot that he would accept that too.

His only comment was, "I have seen many of my fellows die on crosses. Am I, then, too weak to do that for the life of the Master."

We laid our plans. Yeshua had to be kidnapped and Saul put in his place. The authorities had to be sure to find Saul at a place and time when darkness would hide who he really was.

Joseph and I were to take the Master to Joseph's house for safety, because no one would suspect Yeshua of being in a Pharisee's house. Judas was to make sure that the authorities arrived in time, at the appointed place, to arrest Saul, and Peter was to help deceive the other disciples into thinking that Saul was indeed the Master, by causing any disruption necessary.

And Saul? He was ready. He had received powers of healing from the Master, he had the right accent and he was devoted, even to death. And above all, he knew the Master and his ways and could act the part.

The time would be the day of preparation for the Passover. Every evening we went to the Mount of Olives to pray. That would be the place. Judas went to the authorities and offered to betray Yeshua to them, with some excuse and a demand for money. They accepted.

Then we had to wait for that night. Yeshua had arranged, through Lazarus and his friends, to have a supper prepared for us all in an upper room in Jerusalem. It was dangerous for him to enter Jerusalem now, but he wished to spend the Passover there.

So the plans were carried out. A man carrying a pot of water was to lead us to the place and then, in the evening, Yeshua and the rest of us came quietly through the street. The house was the house of Zebedee and the women had prepared the meal beforehand for us.

When we had all gathered, we locked the doors and came together at table to eat. Yeshua was very heavy of heart as we ate, and said little. We ate also, but knew that he had seen things we had not.

Then he spoke and we listened in troubled silence.

"I have been three years with you, but you still do not understand who I am or where I go. It is hard to give something new to people, even when it will bring life, because they prefer to cling to what they have and are."

"You have all changed. Do you remember those first days when I called you to follow me? Would you go back to your old life?"

"No," we all said.

"So, you have learned something new," he continued, "but you know the pain of that learning. There are some things which will be learned only with greater pain. You still do not understand about life and death. You fear death. Why? Yet look at Lazarus. He does not fear death, and he has died, and risen again. Why then do you fear death?"

"Oh, you of little faith! Will God desert you, even in death, or will I be far from you, even if I die?"

"Unless a seed fall into the ground and die, it will not yield fruit. Why then do you fear my death? Is my body not a husk, from which the soul, freed, can live in fullness?"

"I seek to explain these things to you so that, when I die, you may be filled with life. You say I am the Christ, Son of God, but you fear you will lose me if I die. Have you lost the Father because He does not have a body? No! You have Him within you."

"Do you still not understand? When the time comes, then you will understand. I will not desert you even in death, but you will desert me. There are those here who would betray me, yet you do not know what betrayal is."

We were troubled at this. Peter and Judas looked at me, but how could saving his life be betrayal?

We began to ask, "Is it I, Lord," because we did not understand.

"One of you who dips your bread in the cup with me, will betray me."

"I will never betray you," protested Peter, "I will always remain loyal."

"I tell you, Peter; you will betray me three times before the cock crows, although you do not know the manner of your betrayal."

None of us dared ask him again about betrayal.

As the meal drew to a close, Judas rose to do what we planned. "I must go about some business in the city, but will return," he said to Yeshua in excuse.

"What you have to do, do quickly, then," replied Yeshua gently.

When the door was locked again, Yeshua stood up and, lifting the cup before him, said, "This is the new covenant in my blood. Drink you all of it."

After we had all drunk, wondering what this could mean, he picked up the bread and said, "This is my body, given for you. Eat of this that you may have eternal life."

And when we had all eaten, he said, "Do this always in remembrance of me that you may eat and drink to the salvation of your souls."

Then he laid aside his robe and, tying a towel around his waist, he brought the pitcher and basin to wash our feet.

"There was no one to wash your feet when you arrived, weary from your journey," he said. "I will wash them for you."

We were much moved by this, but when he came to Peter, Peter said, "I will never let you wash my feet. You are the Master."

Yeshua looked at Peter and said, "If I do not wash you, you can have no part in me."

To which Peter quickly replied, "Wash not only my feet, then, but my hands and face as well."

When he came to me and began washing my feet, he looked at me squarely and said, "Your pride must be washed from you, Thomas."

He put away the basin, put his robe on and looked again at us. "You wonder at what I have done here," he said. "If I, who you call Master and Anointed of God, am ready to wash your feet, how much more should you be willing to wash each other's feet. If the Father seeks to serve you, can you not humble yourselves to serve others? Whoever seeks to be greatest in my kingdom must be the servant of all."

"What more can I teach you than I have already taught? I go to prepare a place for you, that where I am, you may be also. And I will come again to take you to myself. Do not be dismayed when I say I must go, for how can I be with you unless I go. You do not understand these words now, but you will understand."

"For, in the fullness of time, all things will be changed and the earth will be made new. Then I will come again to you to prepare a way for my coming to the earth."

"In those days, mountains will fall on each other and waves will cover the dry land. For the stench of human corruption will come before God, and He will destroy their corruptions and their pride and bring to nothing their terrible engines of war."

"But do not be afraid, even if you see the mountains cast into the sea, because all who turn to me in those days, I will draw to myself."

"You have a mighty task before you before those days come. If I cannot teach you in this life, how can you hope to teach the world and yourselves except in many lifetimes. Do not then look for my coming here or there, but continue to work, knowing that you bring the whole creation nearer to God by your efforts."

"Do not feel guilt because you fail. All have betrayed the Father, yet the Father loves them and seeks to draw them back to Himself. Work without guilt, seeking the Light and loving one another."

Then, after singing some hymns, and after prayer together for the last time, we left one by one to go by cover of darkness to the Mount of Olives for prayer and meditation. Peter went with the rest as we had planned and I went to the place we had appointed to meet Saul and Joseph and one of Joseph's trusted servants.

This was the last opportunity we had to save Yeshua, and we knew that, so we moved with silence and purpose. Nothing but death would stop us in this.

They were there at the appointed place and after a time we went to the Mount, skirting under the trees, keeping to the shadows. The Master was apart from the rest and, as we watched, he prayed in great agony of spirit, "Let this cup pass from me, yet not my will but Yours be done." These words seemed to be torn from him, for otherwise he sat perfectly still before the Father.

We watched our chance, and when the other disciples were asleep, we went by stealth and, in silence, grabbed the Master. He did not know who had seized him, but as was his practice, he did not struggle, but accepted whatever was to come to him at our hands.

We removed his cloak and put on another which we had brought. Then, quickly taking him away, we left Saul to put on the cloak and to face the agony of whatever was to come. I never saw him again alive, although I saw his body and had to deal with it. We went quickly under the trees and by a long route to Joseph's house.

What happened in the Garden we heard only by report. That Judas came with the men of the High Priest and betrayed into their hands, Saul, who in the dark they could not see except by stature and cloak. Judas knew and played the part well. Peter created a disturbance by cutting the ear of the servant of the High Priest, but Saul, using the gift the Master had given him, healed the ear, and using the Master's words said, "He who lives by the sword will die by the sword."

We did not see the trial of Saul, but we heard of Peter's words which have been widely reported, "I do not know the man." He did not, for this was not the Master, but he began to waver in his purpose. In the firelight, and after some abuse and beating, Saul indeed began to become indistinguishable from the Master. Yet for the sake of Yeshua, he held to his purpose, and often, to keep from being detected, spoke nothing when questioned.

And indeed, Saul was a courageous and holy man, who would give up his life for our Lord, who would sacrifice himself as the Passover lamb that the Firstborn might live.

As we took Yeshua through the streets, he thought we were from the Pharisees, since Joseph had on the robes of a Pharisee. He expected at any time to be taken into their councils. When we came to the house of Joseph, he was much surprised that this secret follower of his should be in league with the party of the Pharisees.

But when we were inside and lights were brought into an inner chamber and he saw who we were, he could hardly believe what had happened.

"Now you are safe," we said, "you need not die and you can continue your ministry after all the turmoil has passed over." We told him then of our plan, of Saul and his great devotion, of the risk to ourselves, of Judas and his heroic act in going even among the Temple authorities.

We were proud of our plan which had worked so well and had brought the Master out of danger. We looked for praise but were met with pity.

"You still do not understand," he said finally in exasperation. "You think by putting another in my place, to change the purposes of the Father? It was revealed to me that I must die. I had thought that death would be by stoning at the hands of the Temple authorities or on a cross at the hands of the Romans. Little did I expect to come into the hands of my own disciples."

"Why do you fear death? Why do you seek to rescue me from death? Death is nothing. It is the curtain between our flesh and our Spirit. How would death put an end to my ministry? Rather it would free my Spirit to minister to others in Spirit."

"You are still men of such little faith. What is death to the Father, or to those called by the Father? I tell you, many of my followers will face a death worse than stoning or a cross without holding back. Life must be lived in faith, and you must live your death also in faith."

"Now the people think I am on trial, but they will not see in Saul, the spirit they would have seen in me, for I would have spoken to them face to face of their hypocrisy and hatred and fear, and they would be convicted before my death. Saul is a good man, a Seeker, and not to be condemned. Yet he seeks death as a solution to the mysteries of life. He must learn to find the meaning in life. For even death is life, the life of the Spirit."

"And what do you hope to achieve by saving my life? Will you command my ministry as well? No. Even the evil within me could not control me. I do the will of the Father. His will as revealed to me was that I must die. I did not know the way of my death, but now I know."

"You have not saved my life for you have no power over life or death. What is death to me? Have I not taught you not to fear those who could kill the body, but to avoid those who can kill the soul? Do you then seek to kill my soul which is in accord with the will of the Father?"

We had not seen such anger in him before, except when he spoke to those who sought to bind souls in laws and rules. Now we sat stunned. His pity had become anger, We had looked for praise for our actions.

So I spoke to him with tears, "Master, Lord. We meant only to help. We thought also we were doing the will of the Father. We saw you threatened and feared to have you taken from us. Lord, how could we live if you were gone? We do not understand your anger. Perhaps we do not understand anything. Help us, then. Help us to understand."

Joseph and I sat there in silence with him, not knowing, now, what to do. Could we now take him and betray him to the authorities? We could not.

Even more difficult, could he turn himself over in Saul's place? How could we have put him in such a position? How? How? There were now only questions.

After a long period of silence, he spoke again, this time quietly and with concern, "You have tried to do what you thought best, and perhaps what you did was at the leading of the Father. Where are Peter and Judas? Did they not help also?"

Joseph answered with a heavy heart, "Peter is with the others to avert suspicion that Saul has taken your place. You know how he can talk. Judas we have not seen, but he was to meet us here when he could get away."

Then, after more silence, Joseph said, "If this does not work out, Judas will have the greatest condemnation. He betrayed. Yet his part at the time was most glorious and dangerous, to walk into the camp of the enemy. What will become of us all?"

Again, the Master looked on us with compassion, finding now in silence what was in our hearts. We had acted from love, yet now we seemed lost.

"Do not fear," he said. "What you have done may also be the will of the Father. There are greater things involved in my life and death than one man can comprehend. I have been sent as the bearer of a New Covenant, but mankind is not ready to accept all my words. I have preached love, yet they have wanted at least some hatred. I have preached forgiveness, yet they have wanted to judge at least a little. I have taught liberation, yet they wish to remain captive."

"Perhaps they also would not believe a death which was not violent. These are people of violence, so they seek a death of violence."

"Let me pray now to find the new direction from the Father. Join me also in this Silence."

We sat then in that room, raising up our Spirits into the white light of the Father, into the love and peace which He had given us within. After the turmoil, it was beautiful to come again in silence to the Father, while our Master communed to find his place in these events.

After a time, he called us gently to ourselves and explained what he had found.

"As I have told you before, I have been sent into the world to free people from fear and hatred and greed and all those things which place limits upon you. But what I have introduced to you will take many lifetimes to complete. People cannot even accept my words of peace, so how would they accept a death in peace?"

"They seek a sign, a humiliation, a fearful death because they have no sign, they feel humiliated and they fear death. If I were to go to them now and say, 'There will be no violent death, but I will teach you about death so that you need not fear,' they would not believe me. They would proclaim Saul the Messiah and follow him.

"You have been entrusted with the secret of my death, but my rising will be shared by many. In the fullness of time, you will come to reveal the manner and meaning of my death, and to prepare for my coming again."

"But before that time, you will be born again many times that you may learn of the degradation and glory, the hatred and love and the fear and hope of life. You must learn much before those days, that you may have the courage to speak my words without fear."

"Do not doubt that as you try to speak these words, many will hate you. They would prefer the death on the cross to the manner in which I shall die. They are violent, lost souls, so they seek their god as a reflection of themselves. They fear death, so let their god die a fearful death. For some, this may be a triumph, if they can see love within the fear. But for many it will be a stumbling block until they are ready for the love and peace I have come to proclaim."

"Wait patiently for that time. It will be made clear to you in that lifetime by your training and your life experience. You will be drawn to the Church, yet repelled by it: you will know its truth but also its self-deception. Many in those days will have the same feeling and they will leave the Church or work within it to find the truth."

"The truth, as I have taught you, is in the Father. It is to be found by cultivating within yourselves, love and patience and honesty and longsuffering. The Way is prayer and meditation. The Father Himself will teach you and embrace you with His Love. I am the Way to lead you to Him."

Then he was silent and we dared not speak, for his words had burned into our hearts and the fear of what was to come was great upon us.

Joseph left the room to arrange the affairs of the house, for it was nearly morning.

After a time, Yeshua spoke again to me, "I must lay down my life that I may take it again. I can lay it down of my own will and the power that is within me. And though my body be dead, I can take it again."

"You do not understand this for your knowledge is far from God, yet you will come to know it. All people will know and believe. But now you think of death as a wall beyond which you cannot see. You are afraid because you think you enter Sheol, the place of shades and darkness. But that is not so."

"The soul can take on the body and lay it down again. But how can you believe this until you have seen?"

"I lay down my life for you and take it again that you may believe. You, Thomas, are open to all beliefs, since you have traveled much, so this truth I leave with you alone. It will be a heavy burden, but it will bring life, also. The other disciples are so immersed in the old Law that they cannot see these things."

"They have not heard the words of the prophet that 'I desire not sacrifice but mercy and love and a contrite heart.' You can carry what will happen here, although it will break the lives of many."

"Say farewell to me now, Thomas, that you may see me again. I must go to the Father and my Spirit will rest on Saul also as he follows his own journey of pain."

He lay down on one of the couches in the small back room and, when I realized that he would die, and that I was alone with him now, I fell on my knees and pleaded with him not to leave. Holding his hand, I wept to think he would go from us in spite of all our care.

He looked again at me with love and compassion and pity filling his eyes and, laying his hand on my shoulder, said, "Do not fear, for I will come again."

Then he closed his eyes and was still. The Spirit rose from his body and was gone. I felt the loneliness, the absence descend, and there I was, alone with the body which had been the Master, but which now was lifeless and growing cold in the dim morning light.

~

Desolation! I still did not understand the meaning of what he said, but feared now only for myself and what we had done.

If this body was found, and also that Saul was an impostor, we would all be tried by the Romans for murder and for conspiring to deceive the authorities by bringing an innocent man to trial.

We could not reveal what had happened or we would be lost, and how could we hide what had happened?

All these thoughts went wildly through my mind as I watched alone in that room, waiting for Joseph to come back.

After a time there was a knock at the door. It was the servant.

"Do not come in now," I said, "the Master is sleeping. But call Joseph and send some food for when he awakes."

His footsteps went quietly down the hall and then Joseph came again.

"Come in," I said, closing the door quickly behind him. "He is dead."

"No!" replied Joseph with sudden fear. "No. He only sleeps. He could not be dead."

He went quickly to the couch and touched his face, which by now was quite cold. Startled, he drew his hand back and stood away from me. "You did it," he said.

Again, that feeling of being utterly alone! "No, no!" I pleaded. "He said he must die, that he must lay down his life. Then he died. No! I did not do it! How could I? There are no marks on his body. And I would not, I would not!"

And this time Joseph held me, for it was too much for me to bear, and I sobbed from the depths of my soul. All now was desolation, all our hopes, all our love, all our plans of living with the Master. All, all was darkness and fear.

Then gradually, as the sun rose into the window and the fury of my hopelessness spent itself, the room settled again into itself and I sat silently in a chair which Joseph moved over for me.

"It's alright, it's alright," he said, soothing. "We will find a way. We will find a way."

But he did not know, either, what to do. "There have been reports," he continued after a time, and I realized that there was a world beyond these walls. "Saul has been tried before the High Priest and has now been taken before Herod. He will have to come before Pilate also, if he is to be put to death. I have asked Agatha, the servant of Pilate's wife, to intervene on his behalf. Agatha does not know it is not the Master, but Pilate's own child was healed by Yeshua, so he should listen. That must be our hope."

"But the Master is dead," I pointed out. "We may be able to save Saul, but the Master is dead. And you know Saul. He actively seeks death by his behavior. He thinks the Messiah should die on a cross, so he will seek a cross. Joseph, does he also think he may be the Messiah?"

"I don't know."

"But Saul told us the Christ, the Anointed One, was made, not born to be the Christ. Does he wish to make himself the Christ?"

"Yeshua told us we could all be the Christ," Joseph said. "Maybe he wishes to be as he was told."

"Maybe. But what then?"

"At least we will try to save his life. Why should two men die because of our foolishness? We will try, and we must wait. I will have reports."

—

The morning stretched long before us. We covered the body as if it were asleep. We slept ourselves, but Joseph had to go about his business also, so I was left with the body to watch, to doze, to eat a little, to pray.

Around noon, the brilliant sun became dim, as if by clouds, but not clouds. The air became chill and wet and the lightning struck far off. It was becoming a strange day, and the fear came upon me again.

The words of the Master, before he died, of death and the body and the Spirit, took hold of me and the terror grew as I watched from the narrow window.

"They will crucify him!" burst in Joseph. "They have taken him to be crucified! All is lost now. How can they not discover what we have done?"

"But what of Agatha?" I asked in fear.

"The people were too strong for his death. Pilate would have let him go, but the crowd shouted, 'Crucify him.' They even accused Pilate of not being a friend of Caesar. They must have known that

Pilate was out of favor, for at those words Pilate called for a basin and washed his hands of guilt. Even his wife's entreaties would not help."

"Then we are lost," I said, as we sat and gazed at the body on the couch, lying there as if asleep.

We sat for some time in silence, feeling the strangeness of the day and the growing storm.

"He told me we could give up our life and then take it again," I said. "When I was alone with him — he said that."

"Nonsense," replied Joseph. "You are babbling now. Only God can give life and take it again."

"No. He said we could learn the power. It is within us to do this."

"That is blasphemy, Thomas. Do not speak these words in my hearing again. Only God can give life. Are you mad to speak like that? The events of today must have turned your head!"

Again silence. Then Joseph suddenly stood up. "I can get the body!" he said. "They cannot leave the body there over the Sabbath and they will not give it to the followers of Yeshua. But me they will trust because I am of the party of the Pharisees. Yes, they will trust me and I have a tomb in the garden which I had cut out for myself. We can still save ourselves! The Temple authorities do not want the body and so we can get it."

"But then we will have two bodies," I objected.

"Yes, but then, also, we can control what happens to each. I have influence you do not know of, Thomas. Wait here still a little longer. If Judas or Peter comes, meet them downstairs. I have left orders for none of the servants to disturb you here."

Then he was gone.

⌒

Peter and Judas were supposed to contact us here, but they hadn't done it.

As the sky grew darker, both Judas and Peter came to the house and the servant called me quietly from the door. I must have had a wild look because, when I came into the room where Peter and

Judas waited, they looked in alarm at me. Then they began to accuse.

"You did not put Saul in the Master's place," they said first. "You did not take the Master from the Garden." I could not believe what they said.

"But he is upstairs," I said. "His body is upstairs."

"What madness is this," Judas said. "When I betrayed him he seemed in the dark to be Saul. But he was not. I have seen him since and he is the Master. Yeshua is on the cross! We put him there! What have we done? You did not fulfill your part of the bargain!"

"But I did," I protested in amazement. "We brought him here." And I told them the whole story as best I could.

"You lie," said Peter in a quiet fury. "You lie. I have seen him on the cross, and it is surely the Master. He even spoke to John and his mother and the other Mary. It is him, Thomas, yet you would put the blame of your error onto us. I wash my hands of this thing, Thomas. I will have nothing to do with your plans. You failed in your part of the bargain. Let his death be on your head."

"But the body is upstairs," I protested again. "Come and see."

Peter wouldn't. "What have I to do with bodies? You would only draw me deeper into your sin. From the time the Master called you in the beginning, I knew there would be trouble. Unorthodox Jew! Seeking truth in Greek and Egyptian religion — dressed in foreign garb — I will have no more of you. You have killed our Lord!"

When he had left, I turned to Judas. He was heavy with grief. "Come and see," I said to him, and he followed to the other room.

He gazed without surprise at the body, as if all life had left him. I told him of the Master's words to try to comfort him, but he would not be comforted.

"Then we are lost," he said, "Then we are lost," over and over in a monotone. "If this is the Master we are lost: if that man on the cross is the Master, then we are lost. Why, Thomas? Why did we do this? We thought to bring glory, but now we are lost."

"No!" I said. "No. We are not lost. He said he would take up his life again."

"This is too big for words, Thomas. This is too big for us. Look at the sky. Where is the sun? We have even blackened the sun, Thomas. We are lost. Yahweh will bring an end to us as in the days of Noah. We have brought on the end!"

Then, seizing his purse, he said, "This! This! They will say it was because of this! Did I do this for money! Didn't we plan together for this thing? What has happened, Thomas? Even Peter doesn't believe. Thomas, they will say I did it for money." He began to sob. "I did it for love, Thomas. I did it for love. Do you remember how we were going to live together in joy, all of us? That was our plan. I did it for love, Thomas, didn't I?" he pleaded.

"Yes, Judas, for love. Not for money. For love. It will be alright. Joseph has gone to make arrangements. It will be alright."

"No," he said, pulling away. "No. How can Joseph make arrangements to drive off the end of the earth? It is me! I hold the money! I betrayed! It is my guilt! Mine! Mine!"

Before I could restrain him, he had gone out the door and down the passage. As they said after, in his madness he had gone to the High Priest with the money, trying to buy back the life of his Master. They only laughed at this follower of the 'King of the Jews.' Then he went outside of Jerusalem and fell on his sword as the Romans do in defeat. Mad! Mad!

The day itself became mad. Darkness descended on the city at a time when it should have been light. No ordinary darkness was this, but a groping darkness, as if the light had been withdrawn from the world. Much lightning and thunder rocked the houses and the earth shook beneath us. Many people ran into the streets, thinking an earthquake had struck, but I had to stay inside with the body.

From the street I heard reports of the dead rising from their tombs and walking in the countryside. There was much terror and panic. It seemed, indeed, that the world would be destroyed, but I stayed. I could not leave the body of my Lord. It was all I had left.

About the ninth hour, when the noise of the skies and the trembling of the earth were at their greatest, a cry came from the direction of the Temple. The cry was picked up and passed down the streets. "The curtain of the Temple is torn! The Veil of the Holy of Holies has been torn in two!"

Great fear struck the listeners. They could not know what all this meant. The terror within my own heart grew and the need to stay there with the body. It was like a force drawing me to stay at that one still point in the mad world.

As night fell, and the earth became still again, people began to move back into their houses. I could only pick up snatches of conversation. It seemed that the "Teacher from Galilee was dead." So Saul was dead and Yeshua was dead. Little did I know the grizzly part I would play in this event in the evening coming on.

Sometime later in the evening, Joseph arrived with the body from the cross. It was bruised and beaten and mutilated. When we asked Saul to take part in this acting we did not realize how real it would be for all of us. Here now was mute reminder of how terribly real it had been for him.

"We have to be careful," Joseph whispered as soon as the servants had left the body in the next room. "The Romans have allowed me to take the body, but they have set a guard at the door of the house and mean to check the body when we take it to the grave. There they will seal it in the tomb. We can't be too careful or we will end up like Saul."

"The women have prepared spices," he continued after a pause, "and I have grave cloths. They are sending someone who knows Yeshua to check the body before it is put in the tomb. If we are to wrap the body of Yeshua, we will have to do some mutilating."

"No!" I almost shouted, but caught myself just in time. "No," I whispered again in desperation, "We can't."

"If we two are to live, and if we would put Yeshua's body in the tomb, we must do it. The soldiers are ready to carry out our bodies if anything is wrong!" retorted Joseph.

Then he continued. "There are doors connecting these two rooms, so we can change the bodies. But I must stay here with this one for now and wash it, in case anyone enters. You, Thomas, will have to make the cuts in the body in the other room. Look closely at this one, so you know what to do."

I could not believe what he told me. I? To mutilate the body of the Master? Had I not sat all that day to protect it? How could I lay such violent hands on him? It would be like murder, or worse than murder!

For a little, I sat with my hands over my face, until the sound of feet in the hall brought me to myself.

The centurion in charge of the soldiers entered to see what progress we had made.

"We don't want to wait all night just for your burial customs," he said brusquely. "Hurry up. Even soldiers have to return home and eat."

"Yes sir. We will hurry. But can I arrange to give you some food?" asked Joseph. He called in a servant and instructed him to get food for the soldiers while they waited.

"I'll be back again to check," the centurion said, "Those are my orders." Then, looking at me and my distress, he said, "He was a good man. I was at the cross and saw him die. We don't get many who die like that. Who is he anyway?"

But without waiting for an answer, he left to feed his men.

"Now you must go," Joseph said to me, after he had closed the door carefully.

With much fear, I examined the body of Saul and noted the wounds. Joseph gave me some instruments and showed me a small door in a cupboard joining our rooms.

There was the body, untouched, whole, on the couch. Suddenly, in frenzy, I began to beat the body with all my might. In silent fury, all my fear and anger erupted and what I did I know not. The hollow thud is in my ear still.

Then the holes for nails and spear — only in madness could I do this deed. Only with anger and fear and a terrible frustration could

I bring myself to pierce the soft flesh.

This was worse than crucifixion. I had crucified myself — more than myself! In that dark room, what deeds of darkness had I done? How could I face the Sabbath morning, doing this on the Sabbath night? Would not God strike me dead?

But somehow, in a daze, I finished my task and sat back exhausted. I had made those marks in the Master's hands and feet and side. Not the Romans now. Why was I so cursed? Would it not have been better to die at once than to see this at my own hands?

There was no time to mourn. Joseph entered by the main door and stood aghast at my handiwork. Then he moved again and said the soldiers were checking regularly. When they had finished their next check we could switch the bodies.

That also was accomplished and when next they came to check, they looked at Yeshua for a moment and commented how we Jews knew how to fix up a body. But the marks were there and they left.

Then we put the spices and the cloth and took the body, sorrowing, to the tomb at the end of the garden. We laid it on the shelf inside and watched the soldiers roll the stone and seal it.

They set a guard there and warned us not to come into the garden again that night on pain of death. Then they took us to the door and let us into the house.

"Saul's body?" I whispered.

"I have family tombs below the house," said Joseph. "We will prepare the body and put it there."

Then, when that was done, we cleaned up the rooms with care and each fell into a deep and troubled sleep. What had happened that day was burned into my soul. This I would never forget for eternity.

When I awoke, late on the Sabbath morning, I looked out into sunshine. The day was alive as if nothing had happened. Being the Sabbath, it was quiet in the street, and only the sound of birds could be heard and the occasional barking of dogs.

A great peace had come over me, too, and I sat then as the Master had taught, entering the Prayer of Silence, surrounding myself in the light of the Father, and I felt the weight of the day before lifted. My hands, which had done those deeds, were still whole, and my Spirit seemed delivered of a great weight. How could this be? For I was alone in this now among the Twelve. Peter refused to believe. He thought only that I had failed and that we had betrayed the Lord. Judas had left in panic and madness. I alone must tell my story, and who would believe?

They had all seen the events of the day before: I had seen only the room and the body. How would they believe now — that it was Saul and not Yeshua that they saw? Again they would condemn me as an outsider, as a Greek or Egyptian rather than a Jew. They would give me no part in the body of the Christ. Little did they know!

It was finished, now, anyway. Perhaps we would all go our way and only remember this time as a mistake. But something remained, and that peace I felt in the prayers he taught us, in the Silence and Light, would go with me always.

After I had eaten a little and said farewell to Joseph, we embraced and I left the house and the city to wander for a time away from these events. No longer could I stay with these people who despised me. What poisons Peter would spread I knew not. They would even think that because I had not been with them during the trial and crucifixion, that I had deserted the Lord. I was with him all the time! Me! I did not leave his side! But they will not believe!

CHAPTER THREE

THE INTERIM

THE ROADS WERE QUIET ON THIS SABBATH. A GOOD JEW WOULD not walk as I walked that day, but now I was no longer a good Jew: I did not know what I was. Something had changed within me. I had seen death which was not death and violence which was not violence, and I had betrayed and was betrayed. Yet I felt no condemnation, and the Law did not tell me about all this. I was free of the Law now in a way I did not understand, so I walked north toward Galilee, forgetting how far I was allowed to walk on a Sabbath.

Yet what had happened weighed heavily on me, so that I did not walk with my usual stride. I watched the path with its dust and pebbles, dung and footprints. Many people had passed this way only the day before: now on the Sabbath it was quiet. Even the Romans had orders not to travel too far unless they had to, so they would not add to the strain of occupying Jewish lands by breaking our customs.

The sun was warm all that day, rising on my right hand, and making the arc of the sky all day. As Jerusalem receded in the hills, and I walked farther north, the events of the days before began to seem like a dream. What really had happened? We had tried to save Yeshua from death but he had laid down his own life. And I had been left so long with a body which was no longer the house of his soul. I had even mutilated that body and then helped prepare it for burial. It was dead! I myself had plunged the knife into its heart and seen the flow of blood and water, even after all those hours.

If the body had not been dead, I had killed it! It was a murder and not a murder, a betrayal and not a betrayal. Yeshua himself had said that I would betray him, yet he said also that I would carry from this experience, truths that had been hidden since the founding of the earth.

What, then, was the meaning of this? And I was alone. Peter denied that we had even taken Yeshua and put Saul in his place. "It was Yeshua on the cross," he said with full conviction. Judas had gone mad and who knew what he might do in the violence of his despair. And Joseph? I could not look into his mind, but he didn't seem to understand very much. He was faithful in his way, but out of ignorance. He knew the ways of the world, but how much did he know of the ways of the Spirit? How much did any of us know of the ways of the Spirit?

So I was alone.

As the day grew on to evening, however, and I sat by the road for my evening meal and entered, for a while, the Prayer of Silence, it seemed I was no longer alone.

Then a voice came to my spiritual ear, "Thomas, Thomas."

I answered, "Yes Lord, your servant hears," remembering the boy Samuel in the Temple.

"Why do you sorrow, Thomas, and why are you afraid of being alone? Am I not sufficient for you?"

"Who are you, Lord?" I asked.

"I am the one who died but who always lives. I am the Christ who became a man so that I could draw you to the Father."

"I have been watching you, Thomas, all these hours, and your sorrow is very deep. Because your sorrow has been deep, your joy will be great. You have been watching over a body and have worried about your body. Do you not see that my Spirit left the body and is free, and that your Spirit, in the body, can be free also?"

"Would you like to learn of life and death, Thomas?"

"Yes, Master," I replied with my inner voice. It was suddenly such ecstasy to speak again with the Master, and now he was closer to me than he had ever been.

"I am dead, yet you see there is no death. You mutilated the body with your own hands, yet I am not mutilated. While I was in the body, I fed and clothed the body and learned, while in the body, to draw nearer to the Father."

"When I entered the body, I forgot the glory of what I had been. Then I struggled back to the perception of glory, by traveling in many lands and learning the paths of many people. Before I gave up the body, I had learned again of the glory to which the soul can come, so I was not afraid of death, but welcomed it."

"But I can take up my body again, if I wish. Death is nothing but leaving the body. It is a door, a way."

"Birth is a greater death, because it is a door from the glory of the soul to the limits of the body."

"Do not think that you have only one death or one birth. You are born many times and die many times. You live many lives that your soul may draw closer to the Father."

"If you die in ignorance, you have added ignorance to the soul. If you die in love you have drawn nearer to the Father as to others. If you hate your brother, you hate God who is in your brother, but if you love your brother or sister you have drawn closer to the Father who is in all."

"Have the same mind within you which is in me, and when you die, it will not be a death but a door opening into the light of your soul. If you die in your sin, you will have to enter the darkness of your soul to learn from it."

"You carry within yourself the death you will die, for you cannot escape from yourself."

"Judas and Saul are also here with me that they may receive instruction. Judas took his life in violence and will have to learn of violence. Saul sought death at the hands of others and will have to learn to accept his own death."

"You, Thomas, feared death, so you even mutilated the body of one you love in order to avoid death. What have you made your life but death and the memory of death? So your life itself has become a death to you."

"Do not seek death and do not try to avoid it if it is necessary. Learn to accept life or death as a gift from the Father to draw you to Himself. If you try to save your life you will lose it, but if you are willing to lose it to follow my Way, you will gain life and the presence of the Father."

"Do not fear life or death. Live now, for only in the present moment will you find me. Look around you at the glory of the hills and the sky. Look at the food which is laid before you. What is the past but a dream and the future but a mist? Live now because you have life and I am with you."

"I am closer now than when in the body. I am released from bondage: release yourself also from bondage to what has happened and eat what is before you."

At that, I opened my eyes and looked around. Much time had passed and it was dark. The stars were overhead and the dark lines of the hills stretched into blackness. Yet I sat now without fear and ate in peace, listening in peace to the night sounds and feeling a warmth growing from within.

This was a different night now, seen with different eyes, and I savored the light breeze and the simple taste of bread and wine. "This is my body, this is my blood," I remembered. All of the world seemed now his body and blood — the life which he had given me.

Would the others believe? It didn't matter now, although I wanted to lead them also into peace.

For five days I wandered north, sitting often in quiet places to enter the Silence and to commune with the Christ. I began to see how his death had been necessary so he could rise in our hearts.

The guilt that had weighed me down was lifted so that even with what I had done, I saw that there is indeed no condemnation with Christ. I was free!

It is hard to express the joy of that time. The sun seemed to shine brighter and all the flowers and grass were like friends. Even the night was not fearsome, and I slept always out of doors knowing that neither thief nor wild animal would harm me.

Fear, which had ruled me in the past, began to melt away, until I could act and think and feel freely. People seeing me then must have thought me mad, but I was intoxicated with the presence of the Master.

So I knew that the death had been no death. It was merely a door opening, and I was no longer afraid even of death.

Then the time came to return to Jerusalem again. I knew that I must return to tell my story to whoever would listen.

In the Silence, the Master spoke to me, "You must tell your story. Some will believe: others will not. You will even be driven from the congregation of believers. But speak your truth strongly and sow the seed."

"Do not be dismayed even if those who disbelieve receive my Spirit. I must work with incomplete people to bring them to completion. Many will follow the way of the cross and will believe still in sacrifice, even though the prophets have said that I require not sacrifice, but love and mercy."

"So they think that Yeshua had to die as a blood sacrifice, that his love and mercy were not sufficient."

"I tell you that love and mercy are sufficient. The violence of sacrifice breaks that bond. But some will find love and mercy even in the cross and so will find fulfillment."

"Tell your story, then, and I will guide you. You will carry the burden of this story for many lifetimes, until the time is ripe to tell it again. Then many will believe you and turn to me."

So I turned south through Samaria and walked with strength toward Jerusalem. I did not know what I would find when I came to Jerusalem. Would they, too, have seen the Master?

Much to my surprise, when I arrived, they greeted me, asking where I had been.

Then Peter, with some animosity, said, "We have seen the Master, Thomas. I was the first of the Twelve to see him."

I replied that I had seen him also, in my heart, and had spoken to him.

"No," he replied, "we have really seen him, in the flesh. We saw him eating bread before us. And the tomb was empty. I was the first to see him."

"Mary was first," objected one of the women. "She saw the Master first and came and told us. But you would not believe, Peter."

"I was the first of the Twelve," he replied.

All this was strange to me. I had walked with the Master in peace and now here was bickering already over seeing the Master in the flesh. Why the flesh? And I had mutilated the flesh with my own hands. Was this body of the Master or of Saul? I would know if I saw the body.

"I cannot believe you," I said at length to Peter. "Unless I can touch the hands and feet and put my hand on the wound in his side, I cannot believe."

It was not necessary to have the body, too. The Spirit was sufficient.

Many then condemned me and called me the Doubter because I would not believe their words. I did not tell my story to them then, because I thought they would reject me completely. So I stayed with them and tried to discuss what had happened as if that was what had really happened.

They spoke much of the crucifixion and sought the Scriptures to find prophecies of that event. Some spoke saying that the man they had seen die hardly seemed like the Master. Others said he must have been in much pain and was different.

Peter silenced them and, glancing at me, said that whoever

doubted the crucifixion and the resurrection was damned and could have no part in the Fellowship.

What was this Fellowship, I wondered, where already some began to lord it over others? What did this resurrection mean when it brought discord rather than harmony to the Fellowship.

The women were kept at a distance, even though Mary Magdalene had been the first to see Yeshua, according to their accounts. I was excluded and Peter began to lord it over all of us.

Could the Christ use this disunited fellowship for his purposes?

Then a few days later we were gathered together when Yeshua appeared in our midst. It was him. This was not the body of Saul, but of the Master.

He looked at me with love and said, "Do you not believe that the body can rise also, Thomas? Come, put your finger on the wounds of my hands and feet and see the wound in my side and believe this also."

I looked in dismay and saw that these were the prints I had made with my hands. He had taken up the body again! Not only had I seen him in my heart, but here in the flesh I saw him too.

I fell on my knees and, holding his feet, I wept with such joy as I had not felt before.

Then he raised me up and embraced me and said, "Many believe I am alive because they see me with their eyes." Then looking directly at me he said, "Blessed are those who have believed even without seeing. Theirs is the greater reward."

Then he embraced me again, said a few more words to us all, and left.

"See, you should have believed," said Peter. "But you have always been a doubter."

"I believed he was alive before I even heard your story," I replied. "I believed he was alive without seeing."

"In the Spirit, maybe," Peter replied. "We all believed that. But how much greater in the flesh! You should have believed. But you and your foreign ideas! You never believe anything we tell you."

"Are you the Master then," I retorted, "that I should believe your words? The Master spoke to me in the Spirit before I came back to Jerusalem. What have I to do with bodies?"

"You seem to have much to do with bodies," he replied with a knowing look, and turned away.

From that time on, I sought, in vain, for a place among the Twelve. I belonged only because I had been one of those who were chosen by Yeshua. But now we began to fall into disagreement.

Peter wished to impose his authority because he felt that he should be the leader. He was the first of the Twelve, he said, to see the risen Christ. That must mean that he was chosen to lead, he reasoned.

Some followed him in that.

By the same reasoning, some claimed that, since Mary Magdalene had been the first person to see the Savior, she should lead.

"She was not one of the Twelve," Peter countered.

"But Yeshua had followers we did not even know of," said Levi, "How can we claim to be the only ones who can lead. And besides, Mary was closer in spirit to the Master than any of us."

Several people resented this closeness and so opposed Mary. Peter again was chief among these.

When I told my story, there was much opposition. Peter would not support me and told the others not to trust a doubter. He said he had nothing to do with it.

"I did not doubt that Christ lived," I replied, trying to defend myself. "I had spoken with him in the Spirit before coming back to Jerusalem. I just didn't think it was necessary to have the body as a sign. I knew that body too. I knew the marks I put there. I wanted to make sure it was the right body!"

Some believed. But we were a small group. The larger group wanted to be instructed in a new law, and Peter gave them that.

So there was much disagreement in the Fellowship, and even hatred began to grow. Yeshua began to appear among us more frequently and he spoke often of love, saying, "People will know you are my followers in that you love one another. Do not hate, but love."

To some, this statement seemed to mean that there was a company of the elect and that they alone showed themselves followers of Yeshua by loving themselves. Others they excluded.

"If you cannot love us," they said, "you are no part of the Christ."

There were other differences among us as well. The party which followed Peter began to ignore the Prayer of Silence which the Master had taught us. Peter had always been disturbed by what he saw in himself during these prayers, and he sought now to find support for its abolition.

"Now that Christ has risen, we have no more need for this sort of prayer," he said. "Now we can address God with our words and there is no need for this silence. The Christ will take our words before the Father and intercede for us there. Christ can bring our needs before the Father."

But we objected strongly. "We can ourselves come into the presence of the Father in the Prayer of Silence. Why do you seek to create divisions between the Father and the Seeker? Do we need a priest to come between us and God; do we need Yeshua as a messenger carrying our words? This is not what he taught. We are all the children of God; we are all the Christ, the Word of the Father, if we will only recognize it. Why do you seek to lord it over us, when we are all equal in Christ?"

"We must seek the Christ-nature within ourselves," we argued, "but you seek to make this whole message of salvation a matter of messengers taking prayers from us to God. Is Yeshua just a messenger boy for us? Is he now our slave in the realms of Spirit? What do you try to do to the Way — make it a new bondage?"

They would not listen, because they began to see that in their way they could gain power over others. So they started to set people in authority over others. They even appointed a Council to decide on matters of belief.

"We are establishing the Kingdom on earth," they said, but to us who followed the Way of the Inner Silence and measured the Kingdom by the love and harmony we felt with those around us, this seemed the worst sort of bondage.

The divisions had their effect on us as well. I sought guidance from Christ in prayer to know why these divisions must be.

"Your experience has been different from that of others," He said to me in Spirit. "Not all people can have the same experience because all see with different eyes. You see with the eyes of the Spirit, so you grow in the Spirit. These others are afraid to have the Spirit grow, and to have their eyes opened."

"Yet my message must be kept alive over many generations until I come again. The Inner Way will now attract only a few, and you must devote yourself to strengthening the Way. But there are others who can come to me only with their outer eyes."

"These people will grow over many lifetimes to be able to enter the Silence. Now they need to hear my words with their worldly ear and see me with the eyes of the body so that they may believe at least part of what I have brought."

"The physical man seeks power, and those who are followers of what they can see of me in the physical, will also seek power. But even this power may be necessary that my words may survive."

"The time will come when the powers of the earth will crumble to dust and the senses will be confounded — then the fullness of the Spirit will be made known. You are the guardian of the Way of the Spirit, but it will be a burden, rather than a glory, until my coming again."

"Do not judge the others, then. Do not condemn Peter. Their way is necessary too. They seek power, but they also seek to serve me as far as they see. Their power may serve themselves, but it will also serve me. They will draw many to my words, even if only with the senses of the body."

"And I will pour out my Spirit on them also, so that they may feel in the body what the greater glories of the Spirit could be."

"Do not envy them because I show myself bodily to them. They will only believe what is in the body. You have seen me in the Spirit and so have come closer to the Kingdom."

"But you hate, Thomas, and you envy, and you feel rejected by the Fellowship. You, too, must learn, even though you are of the Spirit. What is this hatred and envy and rejection? This you must understand to draw closer to me."

"So do not judge the others. Peter has betrayed me in some ways; so have you. Peter is far from the Kingdom: so are you. I came now that you might start to seek for my Spirit within you. This search will take many lifetimes. You will fall into error many times, yet you will rise again into a new life. In the fullness of time, I will come again and lead you all to myself."

"Then will the earth itself be born again into a New Earth. Yet the birth pangs of the new age will be great and the earth will be shaken to its foundations that all evil may be taken from her, and those who remain with her will be able to seek me in peace. Seek the strength of the Spirit for those times."

"In those days, you will be there again. But so also will Peter and the rest of the Twelve, Saul, Mary Magdalene and the other women. You will all have learned much and will be drawn to each other, that as you have helped to bring in this Age, you may also help to bring in the next."

"Learn not to hate, then, even when you are hated by others of the Fellowship. You all have your part to play: do what is set out for you without fear or envy or hatred. Let the others do what I have given them to do. If they, too, are blind, have pity on their blindness, for hatred and fear and animosity come from blindness."

"The Kingdom comes through love and patience and a seeking of the Christ-nature within. Let not worry or envy or hatred or slander take you from the path which leads to Life."

When I reported these words to others of our Fellowship, they were glad. There is no one who is right, but only the coming closer to the Christ. So we sought ways to love, even to love those who spoke ill of us. No longer did we enter into argument with Peter, but we let our love shine forth and graciously invited others to look at our truth.

We looked also to see what things of the Spirit of Christ we could encourage in others, and so built up the Fellowship. We refused seats on the Council, saying we were not worthy to judge the beliefs of others, and continued to serve in the ways we could.

Humility and love and devotion became the centre of our practice. We met together often in the Prayer of Silence and communed with Christ, seeking peace, strength and guidance for our life and work.

We tried to speak of what we learned, but the ever growing congregation of believers would not hear us.

Many came because they could get free food or because some of the Apostles performed miracles and the people sought healing. But our message had been discredited, and the new believers were warned not to join us.

So, although our numbers increased, the increase was slow. We did not offer wonders or instant salvation. We preached forgiveness and the Inner Way.

But we did not break away from the other followers, either. We practiced the Prayer of Silence and tried to show love within the congregation.

~

Without the discipline of prayer and meditation and without the inner guidance, the Church began to break into factions early in its life, so that some wanted to follow a new law, some said no law could bind them and they could do anything they wanted to. Some said they must all sell their property and give to the poor, and others wished to keep their property. Some said the non-believer would be cast into a fiery hell, while others claimed there was no such place as hell in the Jewish scriptures and that it was a pagan belief.

There was much debate in those early days and much animosity, so that each group would remember, or even make up, sayings of Yeshua to support their ideas. There were thus many accounts of his life, and many collections of his sayings, all struggling for supremacy.

I suppose we appeared as merely one more of these fighting groups, but because we claimed to speak in our meditations to the living Christ, they said we deceived ourselves. They would accept no authority except their own and they would not even try to come to the Christ as we did in our Inner Way.

They wished to know the Christ by what they could remember of his teachings, not by his presence with them.

So they remembered fondly those times when Yeshua appeared before us in the flesh after his resurrection, but they would not seek him in the Spirit, saying that faith was belief and that they needed only to believe and that was counted to them as faith.

We, of our fellowship, did not accept that all of Christ's teaching had stopped with his death, so as he spoke to us in Spirit, we recorded his words for guidance.

Much of this instruction we wrote down and used in our teaching. We too, then, had a collection of teachings, but not only what had been remembered. We also wrote down those teachings which the Spirit showed to us.

But of more importance was the inner teaching which the Christ gave to each one of us as we progressed on the Way.

There was disagreement among us about the Christ, so we sought guidance and received the message about the Christ:

"Do not think of the Christ as one person who lived so and so many years ago. There is no one person who is the Christ. Christ is the Spirit of God in the whole realm of human life, spiritual and physical, and cannot be confined to a body. To say that Christ died, then, is nonsense. The Spirit of God never dies, nor does it come within the power of human beings. The man or woman who is filled with the Spirit of Christ must obey the laws of the body and die, and the body can come within the power of hate and fear, but the Christ can never die."

"You wonder how people can die the most cruel of deaths rather than deny the Christ. That is because they understand the law of the body and the life of the Christ. To deny the Christ would be death of the soul and all that the soul has accomplished in this life. That is death indeed! But if the body dies, what is that? Fear those who have power to destroy the soul, rather than those who can destroy the body. Many bodies can be created, but the soul must find its way to Christ."

When I asked, "Was Yeshua, then, the Christ?" he replied, "Yes and no. I was in Yeshua, bringing the world back to myself, but no body could express fully what I am. Yeshua himself had to become aware of his mission, because he was not always aware, although, from an early age, he had a sense of his mission."

"So also, you must all become aware of the Divine spark within you which can lead you to discover the Christ within."

"There are too many people who think that when Yeshua lived, the world was suddenly changed. They even make up stories about how he was the second Adam, and work out formulas about sacrifices and appeasing the anger of god. That is not God."

"The Christ does not put spells on the earth, like a giant magician. He does not force people to see him in themselves. Rather, he created an image of himself, in Yeshua — loving, sympathetic, compassionate, slow to anger and willing to forgive — so that people, looking on him, might recognize in themselves the qualities of the Christ they see in Yeshua, and thus turn inward to find the Christ within themselves."

"But those who are afraid to look within say that the drama was all external, that the act of the Christ in Yeshua was only what they could see outside themselves, and they try to impose their view on others, even to the point of persecuting those who follow the Inner Way. Those who see only the outer, cannot bear to look within, and they call their hatred the zeal for their god."

"Do not fear them because, although they claim to be religious, they really have control only in the realms of the body. They cannot control the Spirit. The Spirit is free to move so that the soul might learn and grow. Stay away from the religious who will not look within, because they are like worms which would eat the beautiful leaves of your soul to feed their bloated sense of power and righteousness. They appear white and fat and holy because they have gorged themselves on the freedom of others, and their followers serve them as if they were their gods."

"Christ is not a man or a woman; Christ is not contained in your laws and doctrines; Christ is not contained in Yeshua or in the Scriptures. Christ is over all beliefs and all laws, over all religions and all peoples, over the whole earth. I AM. I am also within each one of you if you will only turn to me in the Inner Way."

There was much talk of evil and sin and Satan among some of the Fellowship, so we asked for guidance, since many were becoming slaves of guilt and fear because of this. We were taught:

"The Way is not easy, yet it leads to life. When you first look within, you will find much darkness. That is because you have not invited my light. If you look closely at the darkness and ask things to come out of the darkness, you will find that your whole life is in that darkness. Can you not see that your life needs to be brought into the light?"

"Do not judge what is in the darkness of your soul as if it were evil. Do not judge yourself because of what is in your darkness. Do not fear what comes from the darkness. Pay attention to what you see. Remember that the ignorance which brings darkness can also take quite simple things and turn them into quite fearful monsters. Look at the monster you perceive, in the light I provide, and it will gradually cease to be frightening."

"You are not fighting against evil as if it were a force in itself. When you see what appears evil, you will know that it has been created by the ignorant among you, or by your own ignorance of the potential of life. Do not fear the evil appearance because that only gives it strength from your belief. Rather, acknowledge its presence and ask me or it where it comes from. An inner voice will answer, and if asked, will explain how to get rid of it."

"Remember, it is from ignorance and fear that you create evil, and it is through my light that you will be able to examine it with the inner eye and perceive its cause."

"Call upon me for light each time you enter the darkness of your life, and I will provide light to illumine one thing at a time, until your soul is full of light. So one day you may find light for a memory of dark deeds, or for an action which comes from the darkness of belief or ideas or fears. Look at what comes from the darkness, with the light which I provide, and soon you will find that your life is not ruled by darkness, but by light."

"Master," I replied, "I have always been afraid of the idea of eternal punishment and the devil who comes out of darkness to possess my soul. Why should I look into the darkness?"

He replied, "You give power to the numerous devils within you by keeping them in darkness. When you know them in my light, they will no longer be devils. Close your eyes and tell me what eternal punishment looks like," he said.

I closed my eyes and saw myself on a peaceful hillside with a stream before me in the valley. Christ stood beside me. Then as I watched, a cloud came across the sun and the hillside became dark. As I watched, Christ himself began to change and to stand back. The ground opened in cracks and smoke began to rise. Then huge claws reached up from the depths and began to tear away the land on which I stood.

When I turned to Christ, he had become like a devil himself, with dark cloak and clouded face. With terror in my mind, I cried out to him, "Who are you really? You have been my guide and now you bring me to this. Have you come only to bring me to eternal damnation?"

In great terror, I drew back and did not know where to turn and I did not dare to open my eyes for fear I should find myself in a hell such as the pagans spoke of.

Then the scene began to clear, and the Inner Way became again peaceful, and Christ returned to his accustomed place.

"I am the Christ," he said within, "but you imposed your fears upon me. You fear I may be leading you astray, so you make me into a devil. There is no eternal punishment awaiting you, except what you create for yourself, and that is not eternal. If your life is darkness and fear, then your lot will be in darkness and fear, but if you turn to me for light, you will rise above the darkness into the light of inner understanding, and your lot will be the light of my

Spirit for eternity."

"He who dies in darkness of the soul will not be completely lost, but he will have to be born again into the flesh until he finds that light which I can give. He who kills himself escapes nothing, because his soul will have to be born again to find light. That in itself can be a hell, because he will have to face again that which prompted his suicide the first time."

"Pursue the light which I can give, so that you do not have to live in darkness. The light will dawn each day into your soul if you come to me each day for that light."

"Follow the way of understanding so that you might be able to act from light and love rather than from darkness and fear. Your life will begin to reflect the light within so that your deeds will be an expression of my work within you. Show forth my light when you receive it."

"Do not hide my light from others through false modesty. If you fear to act, that also is darkness, and you should bring that fear to my light in your meditations. Keep no fear from the light, for you will have to face all of your darkness."

"Sometimes it will be hard to look into the darkness of your soul, because there is much pain and fear and regret there. It is not always easy to burst the bounds we have set for ourselves, or to enter again the pain of the past. But I will be with you and will show you the Way, and you will know that I am there, and this will become something more precious to you than any possession, and you will pursue my light because it is life and relief from the pain of your soul."

"The time will come when the light within you will become greater than the darkness, and you will then begin to see things with clarity and understanding. For a time you may want to withdraw from the world, to break those bonds of habit and fear which bound you to the prison of your self. Withdraw where it seems right and stay where it seems right. Trust the Inner Voice in this, because the Inner Voice will begin to speak to you. From a man or woman of darkness you will have become a soul of light, which can find its own way through life."

"And, after that, there is a Higher Way which leads beyond the laws of the body, where you will perceive the souls themselves, dancing before the glory of God. You will pray and bodies and minds will be healed; you will love and the hearts of others will be drawn to you; you will open your mouth and the voice of Christ will speak; you will enter into my light and the fears of life and death will possess you no more."

"Do not suppose that your body must die before you can enter fully into my light. Of what value would it be to say that only after death will you overcome the fear of life and death? That would be the worst kind of cruelty."

"No. I seek those now who would enter my light. I seek those now who would bring themselves and their darkness to my light so that they may grow to full stature as my children, my brothers and sisters. I seek those who would pledge themselves to pursue my truth and my light in this life so that they may show my love and their love fully to the world."

("And you, who read these words, do not think that they are a fiction. They are written by a human hand like yours, from a life which was full of darkness like yours, yet I speak through the words as I can speak through the lives of all who follow these words to find my light.")

"Taste, and then you will know that I am good, for how will you know if the food is good, if you stand back from the table while others eat with joy?"

At another time he spoke about the importance of the day and what it brings.

"Happy are those who can accept each day as it comes, knowing that the Father has given this day in which to live. Do not worry about the morrow, what you shall eat, what you shall wear, where you will live. The Father who gives you the day to live in will also provide the means for living."

"Do not think that wealth will give you security against the changes that tomorrow can bring, or that a fortress will protect you against your fears. The only fortress which will protect against the inner fears is a fortress of the Spirit, and the only wealth that will not rust and vanish is wealth of the Spirit."

"All the things you accumulate to protect yourself in the future cannot keep you from the fear which made you accumulate them. It is fear which is your problem and not the future, and the fear you have is the fear of being alone, with no real help. So you cling to whatever seems to provide security against the aloneness which the future might bring."

"But I offer you a different way. Follow my words and you will have life without fear in the present and companions and love and wealth without measure in the future."

"Has not the Father of all given you the day? Live then for the day which has been given you. The Father knows your needs and, if you live the day in harmony with Him, He will supply all your needs."

"You find this hard to accept because you have not fully tried it. You would keep a small or large reserve of yourself or your money in case your faith does not work. What kind of faith is that?"

"But that is to be expected because, from a life of fear for the future and of longing for the things of this world, it is hard to give up all worry. So we will have to do this in steps, as a child learns to walk. The child does not stand up and run without first crawling."

"You must learn to crawl in faith before you can walk in faith!"

"Look within your life to see what fears you have of the future. Close your eyes and explore your idea of the future and what it holds for you. Take the biggest problem which you find which keeps you from walking. Now, say to yourself in your mind that what you see there will not happen — that, in fact, the opposite of what you fear will happen. So if you fear failure, success will come; if you fear hate, love will come; if you fear rejection, acceptance will come. Whatever the fear is in your mind, meditate on the possibility that the opposite will come. Continue to meditate on this opposite every day in your time of meditation and it will gradually come to pass. Live each day in the expectation of this fulfillment and God, who has given the day, will give also the fulfillment."

"When you have rid yourself of one fear, then you will have greater faith to rid yourself of others: you will gradually stand and walk in faith."

"Do not tell me that this is impossible and that the world is not that way. Have you not made your world miserable by thinking in one way? Try to expect something different from the day and the day will give it, as it has given you misery, when you expected misery. You make your own world, and you alone can change it."

"Taste and know that my words are good."

"Sometimes you will desire things that are not good for you and, when they come, you will blame the Father. Do not blame and do not judge yourself. Rather learn. The day has given you the fulfillment of many unwholesome wishes, merely because you expected them to come. How much more will the Father be willing to give to you good things if you ask Him?"

"So, if your wish brings greater distress, examine your wish. Do not blame the Father. It is your wish and your belief which brings you distress, but it is the distress which can teach you about your belief. If you have distress, change your belief, but change it in meditation, bringing your distress before the Father who can instruct you."

"Although many of you seek distress itself, thinking that it is a sign of holiness and wholeness, the Father does not wish suffering for you. Do not seek distress: it will seek you if you are not whole. Distress and suffering are not blessings, except as they point you to the Father, and the Father can show you which beliefs to change to bring that peace and wholeness which He gives. Suffering does not sanctify and cleanse: only you in meditation with the Father can sanctify and cleanse. Suffering is merely a sign that all is not right, and if you suffer, you must take the responsibility for changing your inner life."

"The Father never forces and He does not punish. You create

your own force and your own punishment. The Father does have a purpose for each one of you, though, and until you turn to Him in meditation, in quietness and trust, you will feel the conflict within you which seeks to bring you to harmony with the Father's will."

"There is no hell, neither does the Father have an eternal punishment for anyone, except the punishment you create for yourself. So, do not worry that you will be cast into hell if you are evil. Rather, know that you create your own evil and suffering and hatred now and in time to come by the beliefs you practice. The Father does not punish; you punish yourselves."

"But the Father wishes to deliver you from your prisons now and in the times to come, if you will only turn to Him. The Father wishes your well-being, your joy, your pleasure, your love, your fulfilment. So, if you fear hell and death, know that you have prepared your own place, and that the Father wishes to deliver you from the ignorance which causes you to believe such things and to create such things for yourself."

"The people of old said that God was a jealous judge and that he would punish, because those people were afraid to take responsibility for their own beliefs and actions. They thought that they would surely not punish themselves, so they had a god who would do it for them. Yet it was they who brought their own doom and created the place where they would go."

"I tell you that the Father is not a judge that He does not condemn and does not punish. Do you think the Father would throw you into an arena, only to watch with glee as you failed to live up to quite arbitrary laws, and then would condemn you for not achieving that of which you are completely ignorant? What kind of Heavenly Father has been created by the churches who preach that God will punish with fire. They do not know that fire is not to punish but to cleanse, but because they fear to be cleansed of their sin and the absurdity of their beliefs, they think fire is hell and cleansing is punishment."

"The Father cleanses so that you may be free. What man with a stinking shirt does not know that no one will come near him until he takes it off and washes it? So, when the Father cleanses you of the filth and ignorance within, you will have love and the companionship of others without reserve. Who wants to be with a man who stinks, except others who smell the same and have had their senses stopped up with their own infirmity? Seek the sweet smell of the soul which has been cleansed by the Father, sometimes with fire, rather than the stink of ignorance."

"There are many in the Churches who think that evil comes from the realms of darkness, and they fear to face the darkness within for fear some sort of devil will possess them."

"There are no devils, except the ones you create for yourselves, yet some of those have great power because you continue to give them authority by recognizing them. If you would withdraw your energy from them, they would cease to exist."

"Those who are religious believe in devils because they have hidden so much of themselves in darkness and the darkness has power over them. Bring your darkness to me and there will be no more devils to contend with. Accept the darkness within and you will be able to turn it to light with my help."

"The religious think they must always walk in the light and so feel guilt when they wander into the darkness of their own souls. They cannot accept this darkness, so call it a devil and thereby give the darkness power over themselves."

"Do not turn from darkness or flee from your personal devils. Rather, face them in meditation, knowing that there the Father can give you the strength of His light. Look at your darkness in all its terror and ugliness and take responsibility for even the greatest ugliness you see within. Do not feel guilt or horror at yourself but count yourself fortunate that, together with the Father, you can look on the horror of yourself and learn from it."

"So, together with the Father in meditation, look on the greatest horror or fear or guilt or anxiety within you, and watching, as from a safe place, let the image of your horror or your devil do whatever it will. Is it murder or cruelty or rape or violence or some lesser fear — let it play its course before your inner eye and, without judging, learn from it and ask the Father to cleanse it from you."

"If you have long tried to deny your darkness, it will break out with greater strength, and you will need greater serenity to view it and let it follow through its violence. When it has spent itself before your inner eye, and the fury of its acting has calmed, then you are closer to truth and an understanding of its meaning. Ask the Father or the guide He has sent you, what this means, and they will instruct you."

"If the darkness is great within you because you have been fearful for a long time, the cleansing will take a longer time and the pain will be greater, but do not think this is hell. It is, rather, the deliverance from that hell which you have created for yourself. If you are religious and think yourself holy and better than others, your darkness may be much greater than that of the prostitute or thief. They already know their darkness and can start to seek the light. The religious will have to come to know their darkness before they can see the light on the other side."

"But the religious have an advantage too, for, having read the Scriptures, they have a map to guide them in the darkness and the light. So, all people who would seek truth and freedom should read their Scriptures and those of others. There are many Scriptures and many paths to the One Truth, as there are many nations of people and many individuals in those nations."

"The Father does not provide one highway into which everyone must crowd. Rather, he provides a narrow path for each person, so that the road may be suited to each pair of feet. Do not, therefore, say that everyone should follow your path, since the soft earth there may be thorns to the feet of other travelers."

"Rather, walk your own inner paths which the Father shows you, and share with each other your insights and new discoveries, in case they have a message for the others on their paths. All your paths lead to the Father, but some of them must go in different ways. So, some Followers will be walking through their darkness while others will be walking in light. Neither one is better nor worse than the other: you are just on different parts of the path."

"Put condemnation and guilt and accusation and self-righteousness far from you. But if you still condemn others or feel guilt or consider yourself better than others, these are areas of darkness within you. Examine them in meditation, let the violence of your guilt or condemnation play itself out before your eyes, and again, when it has spent its fury, you can discover from yourself and your guide what to learn from it."

"Always put what you have learned into practice. Do not think that you are better than someone else just because the Father has given you a task to do. He has tasks for everyone else as well, and no task is greater or lesser than the other: they all are to help establish the Kingdom."

Another time he said, "I will speak to you of faith."

"Faith is not belief, but beliefs upon which you act. Those who have only beliefs have nothing, because they are less than air. The beliefs of many of the religious are merely the doctrines of scholars and theologians, empty wind blowing from the lungs. Such beliefs come from nowhere and go nowhere and are the product of mere speculations and the spinning of words. Stay far from the theologians who do not act to test their beliefs."

"Faith shows itself in action, but do not think that all the action of faith is external. As you walk the Inner Way, you must act in faith to an even greater extent than walking the outer way. The world of the senses can be touched and seen and smelled: what faith is required to give bread to the hungry and clothes to the naked? That should arise out of your common humanity, yet many people do not even have that simple faith to act on their perceptions in the world. How much harder it is, then, to show faith in the inner life."

"If you believe that all are brothers and sisters, then act on that belief and share what you have with those who are less fortunate than yourself. They are your brothers and sisters. If you believe that all are your brothers and sisters, then you must forgive your enemies because, although they may have harmed you, you are all children of the one Father, and deserve love and forgiveness."

"If you believe all are the children of God, do not condemn the man or woman who goes astray, but bring them again to the Father who does not condemn."

"Many people say with words that all are brothers and sisters, children of the One God, but I have yet to see the faith which makes those words a reality. Only a few are willing to act, even on those simple beliefs, because they are afraid of the change that will bring."

"How much more difficult it is, then, for people to turn to me who they have never seen. Many people say, 'I believe in Christ,' but for them I am merely the wind of the theologian. Their belief is not faith because they do not act on their belief. If you can not love your brother or sister, who you see, how can you love me?"

"But it is difficult also to say, 'Love others,' if you are full of fear and hatred and anxiety. How then will you enter into a life of faith?"

"You cannot love others until you first love yourself, and you cannot see me until you have first seen yourself."

"I am within each one of you, yet you cannot see my face because you are afraid to look on the beauty and terror of your own inner face."

"I am within you and you are within me. Learn that saying!"

"The road to faith in all actions is the inner road, because it is from within that all actions come."

"Again, try something small to begin with, so that you may crawl before you walk in faith. Close your eyes in meditation and think of something you would like to happen, something you would like to be able to do. Since this is a beginning, do not choose anything too difficult or you will become discouraged."

"Hold that hope in your mind and see in your mind's eye how that hope would be put into action. Faith is shown in action! Meditate in your time of prayer each day on the actions which will make the hope a reality. When you feel strong enough, act on your hope, believing fully that what you want to happen, will happen.

Do not doubt."

"How many times have you believed that a thing would not happen and it did not? That was reverse faith!"

"Believe, and act upon that belief in faith and prayer, and you will be surprised by the result."

"So also, you believe that your enemy is your brother or sister. Take the hatred from your mind in your time of meditation and, visualizing your enemy in your mind's eye, send love and light to him or her. Do this for a few days and you will find that the hatred and fear have turned into the hope of love and trust."

"Now act. Go to your enemy and try to reason in love. When you have developed strength in this, you will be able to come to your enemy in love, even if he should strike you on the other side. When that happens, the hatred is no longer yours. He must deal with his own hatred, for you are free of that bondage."

"If you cannot give to the poor, meditate on your own fear which makes you cling to your material possessions. If you cannot forgive, meditate on the need you have to gain revenge. In all things, strive to remove the walls within you which separate you from others."

"These are easy things and quickly mastered, if you are honest with yourself. Do not try to blame others for any failure in this area, but accept your own limitations and turn them to strengths through meditation."

"From these will flow other gifts of faith: the ability to heal others from your own wholeness, the ability to travel and to see in the Spirit, the gift of prophecy and knowledge, the gifts of peace and serenity, but above all the gift of love. These things and many more will flow from your beliefs acted upon in faith."

"You will also come to know me, each in a different way, through faith. I am the power within you, moving you to life and fulfillment. Act on that faith, and you will grow in mind, body, heart and Spirit. Meditate on my active and powerful presence within you, and you will grow and open to the light of the Father."

"I am in you and you are in me. We can transform the world, through our power and love."

"Faith is freedom to act. You have closed yourself into a small room with your fears and unacted desires. In there, you tremble with fear and hope lest someone should open the door and you would be free. Faith is freedom, but those who fear the world, also fear freedom. Do not fear to open the door of your small room and to step forth because, stretched before you, the world is wondrous and new, and the powers of faith will raise you to love and joy and light and peace."

"Do not be afraid. Act in faith."

When we were discussing one day the beliefs of the other groups of Christians, and how they spoke of hell and damnation, the Spirit of Christ again came upon me and spoke these words:

"There are many levels of spiritual reality. Do not imagine that God is so simple that he creates only earth and heaven and hell. There are many mansions in my Father's house and you can find your way from one, to another, to another with my guidance."

"And do not think that you are a simple soul being judged for doing right and wrong. What is right and what is wrong? If you cannot agree on that question, how will you be judged by the Father who does not even require that of you?"

"Each one of you has something different to learn. Some of you being pious, must learn to love those with no piety. Some of you being violent must learn the ends of violence. Some of you being tied to the desires of the body must learn the limits and the beauty of the body. If each of you is to learn a different thing, how can you be governed by the same rules?"

"Let this only be your guide, that you love the Lord your God with all your heart, mind, soul and body, and love your neighbor as yourself. Within that love, you can learn all that the Father requires from you."

"So, you can enter into the mansions of our Father, growing steadily in your own peculiar understanding."

"Do not be surprised if your inner Guide asks you to break some of the rules which have been taught by the people around you.

Often you have to break their rules, and reject their doctrines, to enter into the mansions of the Father."

"Do people tell you that the body is evil? I tell you it is the temple of God, and the desires of the body are the bounty of God. Love the Lord and others and yourself with the body."

"Do people teach that the mind is the most spiritual faculty? I tell you that the mind and the body and the heart and the soul are all equal in this life, and you must learn to bring them into harmony."

"Do people tell you that the emotions of the heart are to be feared? I tell you that the heart, balanced by the others, can lead you to fullness of love in the world."

"There are many false doctrines of the soul. As you move through the mansions of the Father, and see the rich rewards and the abilities and understandings of them, you will know that the soul is always new. It is created yet it, too, creates. It can know great joy and great sorrow. It can see the light of the Father and the darkness of the Father. It can rise up high and descend to the depths. It can know the greatest ignorance and the most sublime knowledge. It can be less than dust and greater than the angels."

"The Father has given freedom to the soul so that His creation may be perfected by the creature itself. So rise up in your freedom and find the bounty which the Father has for you. Why stay in the small room of your religion when the mansions of Spirit are all open to you?"

Since the centre of our life together was prayer, Christ would continue to teach us about prayer from time to time.

"When you pray, do not use a lot of words, and do not say your prayers to impress others with your piety. Those come only from your outward self and have only the fulfillment which comes from your outward self. Turn, rather, to the inner Self in prayer. You do not need many words because God knows already what you need and is there waiting to help. In prayer, meditate on the thing which is of concern to you, whether sickness in yourself or someone else, difficulties of any sort, fears, joys or thankfulness. Meditate on these things, and the answer will come."

"There is another kind of prayer, as well, which will give you growth. Meditate on the Scriptures, on a passage or a person or an event. Or meditate on my words. The meaning will be made clear to you."

"You cannot do someone else's praying for them. Each person must do his own praying, because the answer must come to the individual. It is possible, when you are gathered together, however, for the leader to lead the others in prayer. This prayer brings the meditations of all present onto one concern, but all must assent to the prayer. In this prayer, again, do not use many words, but guide with few words and much silence the concerns of the faithful. This kind of prayer is good for strengthening the fellowship."

When there was a movement among us to deny the body and to spend all our time in prayer and meditation, the Spirit taught us:

"Many of the religious among you scorn the body and think that its functions are low and filthy. Do not be deceived by these people, because you know in your heart how important the body and its desires are for you. What husband or wife does not know of the desires of the body which make them one, and what man or woman also knows the power which can draw them together even to a lack of fulfillment."

"And those who scorn the body, how will you act out all those good intentions of the mind, without the body, for what is good to you except the actions of the body?"

"Some say that we are conceived in sin because of the sin of Adam and Eve. They think that the full knowing of the woman and the man is sin and that their nakedness is their sin. But I tell you that the nakedness of man and woman is the beauty of God, and the shame and guilt are themselves the sin. Lose your shame and guilt and you will become, again, like the first creation of God."

"You think it impossible that you can become again like the

innocent creation of God? Then listen to this story."

"There was once a man, upright and strong before God, who married a beautiful woman. The woman, however, was not all mind and could not live only on the stuff of the mind. The husband was surprised and shocked that his wife would have desires of the body and would desire him. He wanted only the things of the Spirit."

"So, although he loved her, he put her away from himself, hoping thereby to save his soul."

"No one would come near her after that, thinking that, if such a good man had put her away, she must indeed be evil. So, in process of time, to support herself, she became a harlot and shared her desires with those others who had been denied the needs of the body."

"After many years, the husband found that his soul was as dry as a desert where there is no life. He sought for water and companionship of the Spirit, but could find none. So, seeking solace, he took to frequenting the houses of the harlots, until he came at last to the house of his wife."

"There he found such a sweetness of body and Spirit that he took her again as his wife, and the desert blossomed as after rain."

"I tell you, he who would have a great soul must have love and compassion for the things of this life, but he who has love only for this life or the other will not find his soul."

We recalled an important event from the times when Yeshua walked among us, because it spoke of our bodies and Spirits as well.

One day, when we were in Jerusalem, the Pharisees and others who lived only by the letter of the law, brought before Yeshua a woman who was beautiful and, having been caught in the act of adultery, had been stripped to the waist to reveal her shame to others.

"The Law of Moses tells us that those caught in adultery should be stoned to death. This woman we caught in the very act and her shame is revealed. Should we stone her?"

Yeshua looked at the woman, crouched on the ground, with her nakedness revealed. "Stand up," he said to her, "and face your accusers."

Then he said to the men who had brought her, "Look on her! Is there any man among you who does not feel the wish in his heart to do the same act with her? She is a beautiful woman. Let him who is without sin cast the first stone."

There was much hesitation, the woman standing before the men, as the stones dropped one by one. When the accusers left, Yeshua turned again to the woman and said, "You may clothe yourself again. No one has condemned you. Neither do I."

Then he turned to us and said, "Any man who has looked on a woman with lust, has already committed adultery with her in his heart. Do not judge the woman if the same desire is in your own heart, because then we would all be stoned to death."

"What is your name?" he asked the woman.

"Mary — of Magdala."

"Go and sin no more," he said.

"I will not sin, but I cannot go. You have already taught me much and I would learn more. My life was darkness, but now I see light in your face. You have saved my life. Perhaps you can teach me how to control my great desire."

"Why would you control it?" he asked.

"Because I know it is evil, yet I do the act with many men and cannot help myself. So I act, yet am full of guilt for acting. And my pleasure is my pain, my joy is my guilt."

"You have already learned much, I see. What more would you learn?"

"I would learn not to have this desire."

"Yet I see that the desire is strong upon you and you do not really want to lose it. Your words tell me you want to lose it, but you do not, in your heart, wish to lose it. Why, then, do you tell me you want to lose it?"

"The desire comes from fear, yet I do not know what fear it is."

"Then you wish to be free of the fear?"

"The fear is like a devil which possesses me, and I go out seeking men to assuage the fear. Deliver me from this devil."

Yeshua looked long at her face and then asked her to sit on one of the stones nearby. "By your clothes and hair I see you are a wealthy woman. You have made much money from this fear of yours. Do you also want to be delivered of the money?"

"Lord, even if it takes all my money, deliver me from this fear. What is money to me now who was almost stoned to death? Take all my money."

Again Yeshua looked at her and said, "If I take your money, I will be acting. You must act. Sell your goods, keeping only a little for your needs, give to the poor, and then follow me."

Fear entered her eyes then and the beauty of her face receded. "How will I live without money?"

"Do not worry about that. Money has become your devil, and to escape it you must learn to trust God. Trust yourself also."

Peter said, when Yeshua invited Mary to be one of us, "Master, must we have this woman in our midst? She is a sinner. How can we share our authority with her?"

Yeshua replied, "Peter, Peter. I saw your eyes when she stood naked before us, and you longed for her in the way of the flesh. Why then would you say she is a sinner, and thus condemn yourself? Do you, then, throw the first stone? Look into your own heart, Peter."

"And why do you say, 'Must we share our authority with her?' What authority do you share? Do you not receive your authority from the Father? Has He not shared with you? You do not share your authority! The Father shares His with you and with her and with many you do not know. So beware, lest you claim more for yourself than is yours!"

Then, speaking to all of us, he said, "When you meet together, let not one of you be always the great one, the speaker or the teacher or the prophet. Each time you meet, draw lots to see who should speak and who should read and who should perform the sacred duties. For you are all children of the one Father, and you have all received the breathing in of the Spirit according to your capacity."

"You, who would be truly great, be the servant of all, yet not in such a way as to make a show of your servanthood. Rather, show yourself humble by being willing to take the public tasks as well as the menial tasks. So there will be no menials and no great ones among you, but you will each have a measure of humility and a measure of greatness."

"Neither must you say, 'this task is for a man, that for a woman; this task is for a slave, that for the freeborn; this task is for the rich, that for the poor.' Rather, share all tasks equally so that all may grow equally in the spiritual life. God, who sees all things, will assign to each the task which is appropriate."

"There is no authority but God's authority, and that He shares with whom he will, sinner or saint."

⁓

[I need to interject something here which has developed since this text was written in the early 1980's. Today, October 24, 2006, I drove some friends to the airport. When I was coming home, I had a sense of a tremendous rage erupting in myself. I knew the anger did not arise from my own consciousness, so entered meditation and became aware that it was Judas Thomas trying to get my attention for something very important regarding the text of this book — something he had left out twenty years earlier. I finally allowed him to write in my journal what follows in quotation marks.

But before I do that, I should explain something of which I have become aware over the last twenty years and more, since the text of the Gospel was written.

The story which Yeshua tells above, about the righteous man and his wife, who becomes a prostitute, followed by the account of Mary from Magdala being accused by the priests of committing adultery, is actually a hidden account of Yeshua's own marriage. I think it was encoded in this way because, at the time I wrote it, my still conservative beliefs would not allow me to write what was actually going on here. The messenger can only bring a message for which he is ready.

Magdala was a prosperous fishing village not far from Yeshua's own home in Nazareth. In spite of the unsavory sexual reputation of the village and its people, Yeshua had wed Mary out of love. However, after the marriage, Mary's desire for sexual closeness came into severe conflict with the Essene sexual beliefs with which he had been raised. He had "put away" his wife, as any good Essene would have under similar circumstances. It is not clear if they were divorced or merely separated, but it seems they were not divorced.

There were many prostitutes in Israel, including Rahab the harlot hero. Having sexual relations with a prostitute was not a sin punishable by death. But the temple authorities specifically brought Mary to Yeshua because she had been his wife and may not have been divorced. She would then have technically been committing adultery all those years. The authorities wanted to see what he would do to his own wife who had committed adultery.

They expected condemnation from this Essene Rabbi, who was also an heir to David's throne, but they found only love. Notice what Yeshua says: "Let him who is without sin cast the first stone." Yeshua does not cast a stone, and so admits his own blame in the whole matter. His attitude to sexuality and the relation between men and women changed drastically after this event.

Many of the conservative Essenes (especially the leaders of the movement) feared sexuality and were allowed to indulge in sex only for procreation. Through the above experience, Yeshua learned about the importance of the sexual relations between men and women, the importance of the family and the need to find fulfillment in the body — something the Essenes refused to do. A number of the teachings in The Thomas Book *reflect Yeshua's realization about the importance of sexuality.*

If you have wondered why there were so many "prostitutes and sinners" among Yeshua's followers, it was because they were Mary's friends who knew that Yeshua would not condemn them.

Some of this relationship is preserved in other texts. In "The Gospel of Philip" in The Nag Hammadi Library, *Philip writes, "And the companion of the [Savior is] Mary Magdalene. [But Christ loved] her more than [all] the disciples [and used to] kiss her [often] on the mouth.*

The rest of [the disciples were offended] by it [and expressed disapproval]."

In "The Gospel of Mary," in the same collection of manuscripts, Peter says to Mary Magdalene, "We know that the Savior loved you more than the rest of women. Tell us the words of the Savior which you remember — which you know (but we do not nor have we heard them)." Reflected here is the tradition that Mary Magdalene was the chief disciple and knew spiritual secrets which Yeshua had told her and no one else. Notice that she is not just the chief disciple, however. We are told that he "loved" her. Even Peter, who was promoted as the chief disciple by the orthodox branch of the church, is seen asking Mary, the woman Jesus loved, for instruction.

This whole tradition of the relationship between Mary Magdalene and Yeshua was covered up for centuries in order to promote a completely different idea of Yeshua's message. Judas Thomas obviously wanted the truth to be told. It is against this background that Thomas' comments can be understood, and he insists that I include them here.

There is another dynamic at work here as well. Thomas did not express his anger when I was writing the Gospel in the 1980's. However, as he wrote this passage, I sensed his bitterness against the other disciples who refused to accept him, against "Saul and his superior, condescending, Zealot ways," against "Peter and the other lapsed Essenes who thought they were so superior."

Then Thomas' words begin, and although I am reluctant to record his actual words here, for fear of offending some readers, I must include the uncharacteristic swearing that came with them, to illustrate just how angry he was. The swear words used here are expressive of anger in 21st century English, and he uses those to translate his rage into words we can understand. He also refers in his comments to the book of Hosea the prophet, and these words are eminently appropriate in referring to the relationship between Yeshua and Mary Magdalene or between Hosea and his wife. Hosea had been instructed to marry a harlot in order to illustrate prophetically something about the relationship between God and the nation of Israel.

Thomas writes: "The anger is against the f——ing early Christians and their f——ing bickering and condemnations. I am furious at James the Righteous, as they called him, because he undercut everything his brother Yeshua tried to do and turned the nascent church back to being an Essene, strict morality organization. Anyone like me, who held heterodox ideas like Yeshua's, was excluded."

"The Essenes and the Zealots and their 'righteousness'! And James, 'the brother of our Lord,' as they called him, to give him and his Essene ways legitimacy (not realizing I was the closest brother) destroyed everything Yeshua stood for. James hated what Yeshua was doing, admitting all of us riff-raff to his kingdom. James wanted to be a Teacher of Righteousness. He couldn't stand what Yeshua was doing. James wanted a Messiah who would rule this world and hated it that Yeshua, the real heir to David's throne, threw it all away and told us to look for the Kingdom within us. James would have loved to be king, to overthrow the Romans, to have a pure Jewish state following all the laws and forcing everyone else to do the same."

"Yeshua's Jewishness had compassion. He was like Amos, calling for justice and mercy. He drew teachings from the Therapeutae of Egypt, Jews who sought the power of God to heal all of life. Yeshua had experienced exclusion himself. There had been rumors that his birth was not quite righteous, that his mother had been pregnant before her marriage, that she herself was attracted to her husband and to sex in what, to the Essenes, seemed an unseemly manner. She was not allowed to live in the strict Essene community because they did not want ' her kind of pollution' to infect the others."

"Then Yeshua had reunited with Mary Magdalene, his wife whom he had divorced. Unlike the Essenes and James, who feared sex, Yeshua now found fulfillment in his love with Mary."

"It was so beautiful. All of us who were outcastes were welcomed in by Yeshua's love. But James shut the door again and tried to create a new bondage of morality, of Essene exclusiveness. This is why I had to speak today, as you get these books ready for publication. The anger and bitterness you felt were the only way I could get your attention so you would have to write."

"Please include this in The Thomas Book because it would be so *incomplete without it. You can leave out the personal parts which you will have to resolve in your present life, but you have to put Saul in there. His Zealot, boastful superiority was insufferable. I had sugar-coated that. And James drove away so many people who had been drawn into the fellowship by Yeshua. It was such a struggle between love and a self-righteous Righteousness."*

[There was a pause here so I asked, "Thomas?"]

Thomas began to write again, "I think that's enough. I think I can rest in peace now. The whole story has been told, or enough of it. Make sure you tell about Yeshua and Mary, though. The Essenes destroyed family by forbidding sex. Yet, after Yeshua found Mary again, he had such joy. It was beautiful. It was like Hosea of old, except the union of Yeshua and Mary was like the loving union in Hosea's prophecy of a forgiving God (who had himself learned of his errors) and his bride, the holy New Jerusalem coming like a bride to her husband. Mary and Jerusalem, driven from their husbands by harshness and judgment and brought back by love."

"Include that. Polish it a bit, if you want, because I have written in anger and that destroys style."

"This is so important. It is the sinners who find God — not those who already think they are deserving. That is so important."

"And add also — we, who came to Yeshua, came because he accepted us, even when we were not holy or righteous. His other brothers and the Essenes were offended because they thought we were unworthy. Yet, after Yeshua's death and his coming to us again, many of his followers who wanted to be respectable, those who had been offended at our shortcomings, tried to rehabilitate us in the eyes of the people. Oh God! They even felt they had to rehabilitate his mother and Mary Magdalene. So they made us into perfect saints for the sake of their reputation. They would not accept us as ordinary men and women who had found the love of God through Yeshua. This is so important. If you make saints of us, if you make perfect people of us, then you do not see how you, being imperfect, can come to God. Yet, we were imperfect and were accepted. All must come from where they are. You do not have to be righteous. This is so important and has been so distorted. Write this."

When I spoke to God about all of this, the Inner Divine Voice replied, "You see, Thomas could not rest without setting that right and you could not hear except through the welling up of his anger. Now you can let it go. But make sure you include this in the book, to set right a tremendous wrong in the transmission of Yeshua's message."

[And now we can continue with the main story.]

⌐

At another time he spoke to us of the Inner Way and the growth of wholeness.

"After a time you will be given a symbol on which to meditate. Do not try to force the symbol to come. Do not assume that you have not succeeded if you do not have the symbol. The symbol will be given to you in the course of time, and when it has been given, you will know."

"You may not, at first, recognize the symbol. It may be an object or a shape or a word. It may seem strange and meaningless at first, but it will serve two purposes. First, it will lead you to the deeper reality you seek, and then, or at the same time, it will be the centre of your spiritual power. So, if you would heal someone, you need only meditate on the symbol. It is a symbol of your wholeness, and you can then transfer the power of wholeness to the person who is sick."

"But you must become whole."

"Do not try to interpret the symbol with the intellect. Absorb it with the whole being. It has been given precisely because it will take you beyond the familiar world of your ideas and prejudices, if you do not put up the wall of the intellect."

"As you move into the Kingdom which is within you, no earthly guide will be able to show you the Way. You can give each other encouragement within the fellowship, but you must walk the inner path with a guide I will send you. It may be that I myself will come to guide you, but since you do not know what I look like, I will appear in a way you can understand. I will be an inner voice to you, or it may be that I will send one of my messengers and co-workers to be your guide."

"In the Inner Kingdom, the Inner Way, you are never without a guide, if you will call upon my name and seek me out."

—

Also, about sickness and the life in the Inner Way, Yeshua said to us, "Do not be afraid of the demons and worries and illnesses that plague you. You are greater than they are. But do not be content to think yourself greater: act on that thought."

"Illness and worries have their own life which you have given them. Could you be ill if your body had not provided the house for the illness, or could you worry if the mind had not given lodging?"

"You cannot just drive them away as if they came from somewhere else. You have given them life! Do not cringe before them as if they were an affliction from the universe, then, but get to know them as a part of yourself. I tell you, you will have to change before they will cease to exist."

Someone asked, "How can we do all this, seeing that we are not prophets?"

Yeshua replied, "Remember that the Kingdom of Wholeness which you seek is not outside you: it is within. Illness is also within. Illness is a sign to you that the Kingdom of Wholeness is not established within you."

"Wholeness comes through prayer. Not the prayer of loud words, as I have explained, but the prayer of quietness and acceptance. Still the voices of the body and mind, therefore, and then ask the inner voice of quietness about your illnesses of mind and body. Start by asking about the most troublesome. You might even address the illness itself, asking it why it has come, how you have allowed it to stay and grow, how you can get rid of it. You must find out what there is about you that has permitted it to stay."

"This may take many days or years, as you begin to discover what it is within you which allows the illness to stay. Within your prayers, then, for the morning and evening, remember the illness within you, and be ready for the Spirit to show you the changes you must make in your life to bring wholeness of mind and body."

"Remember not to neglect the spiritual journey you are making, as you concentrate on the body. They are one, Spirit and body, in this life. So you must grow well in Spirit, mind and body. Do not think of one as better or worse than the other: they are one."

"If, while in prayer, you see something in the inner kingdom which frightens you, do not run away, but call on my help and I will be there to interpret for you. What you see in the inner kingdom cannot hurt you if I am there to interpret and guide. There are many beings within you who you do not understand with the earth mind, because they are not of the earth. Do not let them have power over you, but call on me and I will be with you. The saying is true, 'Yea though I walk through the Valley of the Shadow of Death, I will fear no evil, for Thou art with me.' I will be with you even in the thick darkness of the soul, and will show you the way to light."

"Do not only listen to my words, but do what I say. How will you know the inner life unless you practice faithfully the discipline of the Prayer of Silence?"

One day, one member of our Fellowship complained that he tried to follow the Way, but always fell into error again.

Christ instructed us, "You will fall back into the error of the world, because you are of the world. But you are also of Truth and you will be brought back to Me by Truth. So, when you fall, as you must, do not fear and do not feel guilt. Look rather in the inward person at what caused you to fall back into the world, and learn from it, for the world is not evil. Rather, it is a place to learn."

"But if you run away from your errors, and do not examine them, how will you learn?"

Within the Fellowship of the Way I was consulted often, since I had been part of the events of the life and death and resurrection of Yeshua. So, although we encouraged all members to take their place, I had a certain prominence and was a spokesman for our group.

When there was criticism, it was levelled at "Thomas and his followers," even though we were all the followers of the Christ.

When persecution came, I was at the centre, although our peaceful life kept us from the major sufferings. We did not, like the others, openly provoke the authorities but, in quietness, tried to change the world from within.

But our teaching and our practices and our peace and freedom from persecution brought greater condemnation from the other congregations that had sprung up. So, finally, they grew to fear me and drove me out because I saw with different eyes than they. Yeshua, the Nazarene, they said, was as they taught. In those early days of our movement, there was much disagreement and much distrust.

Many things had happened among us which we could not explain. The dead rose; people were healed; we saw visions and heard voices which came from we knew not where. But we were simple people, most of us, and these things which we had not seen even in the Scriptures, shook us deeply. Most of the new followers wanted to see the world the way they had always seen it, except with the shining appeal of religion. But for me, the whole world had changed, and this Man had given me new eyes with which to see.

When I told all this, and much more, to the other Apostles, they merely said that I was deluded and would lead the people astray. "What you propose is too far beyond how our fathers taught us the world and God is. No! Yeshua is the fulfillment of the Law; he does not come to change our world. God loved the world as it is and came to redeem it." And so they would go on, speaking words which, finally, came to mean nothing because the world looked different to me.

They even made up a statement to discredit me, so that no one else would listen to me. "Do not be like Thomas who doubts," they said, "but believe, even without seeing." So they bound the new converts to the lies and half-truths which they had salvaged from all those years of teaching which we had from Yeshua.

"Believe without seeing," they said. "Don't look for evidence, but believe our witness. Don't be like Thomas, the one who doubts."

So they silenced me in Judea where, as I stayed longer and tried to speak of the new way of seeing which Christ taught me, they turned more and more against me and the small band of men and women who followed the Way of Seeing. They would not look for the evidence within, but insisted from the first on the authority of the other Apostles.

Peter, who had seen much of what I had seen, but was not so deeply involved in the darker side of our actions, was the loudest in denouncing me. He it was who carried the story of Christ's resurrection and how I refused to believe until I had seen the prints of the nails and the spear. But he knew why I doubted, too!

He would not tell that part of the story! And later, he seemed to have forgotten that all those things happened. He seemed to recollect none of it, as if he had not even had a hand in it.

So they were again like people without a guide, even after Christ had appeared among us many times. In their councils, they would pray as they had always prayed in the synagogues, piling words on words, and they believed, then, that their words became the words of God. Some could heal, some could speak in tongues, and there was a great pouring out of power. But it looked to me as if they had the Spirit without direction.

Some expected the end of the world, some the coming of Christ to the world. Some expected the return of Eden while some thought the wicked would be destroyed in flames before their eyes. They sold all their goods and brought the money to the Apostles to distribute, but the food and money attracted large crowds of the poor who wanted bread and not the new Way. After not many months, the Church in Jerusalem was reduced to poverty and famine.

What had happened to that glorious vision of the Master, I wondered, as we hid in rooms down the stinking, dark streets of Jerusalem? And even in that darkness, I was an outcaste. "Do not listen to Thomas, the one who doubts," they said. "Be thankful that we are persecuted for the sake of Christ. Remember His cross, always."

CHAPTER FOUR

~

THE JOURNEY

IT WAS DURING THOSE DARK DAYS OF POVERTY AND PERSECUTION that the voice of Christ came to me again:

"Leave Jerusalem and walk to the East, to a land where My words will be accepted, for here in Jerusalem the seed has fallen among brambles. In Jerusalem the seed will grow, but it will be twisted and without light. Walk to the East and I will meet you on the road."

I had become accustomed by then to following the Inner Voice which I knew had come from Christ. So, even though the Apostles taught that the Christ had been taken away into heaven, I listened and, rising in the night, prepared to leave.

The others in the house asked me where I was going at that time of night, especially since the Romans would be abroad.

"I am going to walk the path which Christ shows me," I said.

"We all do that," they taunted, "but you will not follow us. Maybe you are running away from persecution."

More woke and sat up in the half-light of the lamp, the flame flickering for a moment on the shine of faces and rough clothing.

"Your path has brought you already to this darkness," I retorted, "I go to seek the Light."

"But you deny the cross," they said, as they had said so often. "How will you be a follower of the Way if you will not take up your own cross of suffering? We suffer and will enter at last into the Kingdom, as Yeshua suffered and was then allowed into the Kingdom, and as the prisoner crucified with him suffered and entered the Kingdom. You will not suffer with us, but would flee. Go then."

"I will certainly go," I said. "The Christ, who was not crucified, but who rose from death so that you could live in the Light and not in this squalid darkness, will continue to lead me into greater Light. Why do you worship the cross? It only brings you to pain and death. Yeshua did not die on the cross, as you believe, but gave up his life so that we might have life with him. You know my teaching, but you want to suffer instead of having life. Why do you want to crucify in your mind, one who was never crucified? Can you not accept life?"

"We know your teaching, but you are mad," they said. "We do not believe your witness. Peter has denounced you. Go your way. Leave us. We will not listen to your words. And may the Roman legions find you walking the streets at night. Then you will know crucifixion!"

So, following the Inner Voice, I left that house and went quickly through the dark streets of Jerusalem. The night was cool and the stink of the day had settled. I walked quietly in the shadows to stay out of sight of any guards and, taking the alleys, soon came to the wall, at the place where we smuggled people and goods in and out — and so, out to the hills surrounding the city, the holy place of my ancestors, the city of our great King David, sleeping there in the folds of the hills. I would never see that place again. It had killed the prophets and now even the followers of the new Way were twisting and destroying and darkening the Light which had come into the world.

The East held promise. There, on the road, I was to meet the Christ again.

So, I walked East from the city. In the past it would have seemed like desertion, leaving undone a task which seemed to need doing. But I was being called out of that religious squalor and bickering into another path which I did not comprehend. I would go to places I had never been, see faces I had never seen, and learn things of which I had not even the faintest hint. Yet, through the long discipline which Yeshua had taught us, I was ready.

No more would it be new wine into old wineskins: I had become in my meditations capable of holding any wine of the Spirit which was poured into my soul. Sights of the Spirit which would earlier have torn my poor skin to shreds were now fulfilling rather than destructive.

That newness is what I tried to pass on to the converts, that discipline of the Spirit which Yeshua taught us, but discipline was too hard when they expected to be filled from heaven with a wine that would leave their skins intact.

I was discredited because I taught what I had received, that we must prepare ourselves for the coming in of the Spirit, but they all wanted the easy way, to wait passively for the new wine.

It did not take long for their skins to split and tear, and the ruin I had left was of those who were not prepared for the Spirit they called into themselves. They could make no sense of their visions and so waited in stinking wretchedness for their death. If life had not given them insight, they thought a death by persecution would lead them to the Kingdom.

There is much bitterness in my mind about all that, but I must learn from the bitterness. There the sun rises over the hills as I walk with only my staff and a small bundle. Even the thieves on the road would not want what I have, so in my own poverty I am safe. There is peace in the air, away from the brawling habitations of men and women. A few birds sing as I walk toward the rising sun.

"History has already taken its course in this place," the voice said to me. "I tried to teach a new way of living and seeing, but they have gone back to the way of suffering and blood. I offered them wholeness but even those who speak in my name offer doctrine and law. You can do nothing here. If they would not follow me, how will they listen to you, the one they have called "Doubter." Leave them to their blood sacrifices and the worship of a Roman torture instrument. Come, follow me."

"But what is to become of them?" I asked. "Have you left them entirely?"

"I never leave the world entirely, and I do not leave them entirely. There will be those among them who will continue to seek truth and who will be shown the Way as they come to me in constant prayer and meditation. The others are lost already."

I walked for many days toward the East, over rough country and through fertile valleys. I stayed in inns and slept in caves and under trees. As I walked and as I prayed, the memory of the Christ came again to me and the bitterness of my last years in Jerusalem was gradually purged from me.

It was a great comfort to remember again the days when Yeshua was with us, and I learned many things about myself and my own path by remembering.

I remembered the crowds who came to Yeshua, and the hunger with which they listened to his words. I remembered the glory we felt and the fear. All these things ran through my mind with his teachings and his love.

Yeshua healed many people in and around Galilee, so much so, that crowds of people, the sick and the lame, would come out to him as we approached every village, and he looked on them with compassion and healed them.

He said to them at each town, "Is there no one here who can heal you? Where are the religious leaders of this place, those who profess to know of the power of God? Have they not healed you?"

"No," they would reply, "they can only tell us in words of our God, and their words are stern, speaking of laws and condemnation.

But we are already condemned in our bodies to sufferings worse than they describe, so why should we bother with the added burden of the laws?"

"But did not God deliver our ancestors out of slavery in Egypt into freedom?" Yeshua would ask.

"Our priests have laid on us the yoke of slavery again, then," the people would complain.

Yeshua taught us many things concerning healing on these trips.

"These people are slaves indeed. They are the decedents of Abraham and Isaac and Jacob, and they live in the land promised to our forefathers, but they have become slaves again as if they had never been free. Not even those who claim to be close to God can do anything for them, for they also are bound in their laws. The whole of this people is lost because they do not know the mercy of the Father."

"To heal truly, you must deliver the person from slavery to the laws and beliefs which have been imposed upon them. I heal the bodies of these who come to me, and then I teach of the freedom which is theirs. If they follow the Inner Way, they will be immune to the traps of the teachers of the Law. The law of the body and of the world cannot bind the inner being once you have truly started on the Way. Only if you listen to the teachers of the Law, will you fall into their trap and become again slaves to their doctrines."

"But how will this heal them of their diseases?" we asked.

"As long as the Spirit is the slave of those who preach law and morality, it cannot fully inhabit the body and make it whole. The Law forbids so many things and your parents and friends forbid so many things to the body that the Spirit cannot enter and heal the body."

"Then how shall we heal?" we asked.

"You will be given the power to heal the body through the laying on of hands, as you have seen me do. That is easy, and many people will be given this gift. The harder gift of healing the Spirit must be worked for. You will have to spend much time in meditation to learn the healing of the Spirit. Because you will guide others in the healing of the Spirit, you must follow the Way of inner healing first to know the Way. I will guide you if you will walk the Way."

"You will be able to heal the Spirits of others when, in love, you can enter your own life and the lives of others without condemnation. You must be completely free of the Law to look at the lives of others without condemning, and to examine the darkness of your own life without condemning."

"Many of the religious people among you question how I could heal prostitutes and tax collectors and other sinners. I heal because I do not condemn and they come to me for the freedom from condemnation. If you want to cling to your sin, then you are condemned already by yourself; the Father does not condemn you."

"You are condemned already because you have accepted the slavery of the Law. But if you wish to be free and to let the Spirit inhabit the whole body, then nothing you have done will condemn you, because I will deliver you from the bondage of guilt. Much of what you call sin is not sin anyway, when seen through the eyes of the Spirit, and sin is bondage to the laws of the physical nature."

"Much of this you will not understand until you start to walk the Inner Way with me, but then it will be made plain to you. Many of you will fall away from me into the path of the Law, but for those who remain faithful and walk in my Way; much that is dark now will be made plain."

"Do not be afraid of those who arise to tell you that your body will be burned with fire in the last days because you follow my Way. Many will be afraid of my freedom and will follow the Law in a new form, trying to impose their slavery on others. Even they may be healed if they turn to me."

"Like the city of Nineveh, in the days of Jonah, there will be no condemnation if you turn in repentance to the Father."

"Why should the Father condemn when the sinner turns to the Way of love and freedom within, and why should you, like Jonah, condemn others, if the Father has already forgiven them?"

"If you would heal the Spirit of others, then, take the Inner Way, listen to my words, do not condemn yourself, do not condemn others, but show them also the Inner Way of love and freedom. Stay far from the law which condemns: stay far from the slavery of those who think themselves superior because they are religious and holy: walk the path which I will show you, which leads to life."

There was much dissatisfaction among some of Yeshua's followers at these words, and they left him to join those who defended the authority of the Law.

"Let them go," he said, "because they must learn the limits of the Law before they can follow my Way. They imagine that the Law will lead them to life: they must live out their ideas. But you who have seen in your minds the futility of the Law, need not live that idea because you have examined it within and found it lacking. Do not condemn them for not seeing what you see. They have already condemned themselves to the slavery of the Law and will create the suffering appropriate to their bondage."

"You, continue in the Way, and thank the Father that you have been given grace to see both freedom and bondage, health and sickness. So do not condemn your enemy or strike the man who strikes you. What advantage is that to you?"

"No. I say to you, turn the other cheek to him who strikes you and give your staff as a gift to the man who steals your cloak, if you find him, so that they may see the life of freedom which is lived without fear. Those who strike and steal and murder and cheat, those who condemn by the Law and teach others to condemn themselves, these all live by fear, and so they must strike out against others. The sin of the thief and the priest of the Law are the same, because they act out of their fear of capture and their desire for gain."

"Do not live for gain or do anything from fear. If you fear, bring that fear to me in your meditation and I will help you to understand it and be free of it. If you live your life only to gain possessions or position or power or approval, bring that desire to me in meditation and I will help you understand the limits of your desire."

"First, seek the Kingdom of God in the inner being, which is freedom from all slavery, and then you will be able to see the world with new eyes and enter the life of the world with new feet, and the Father will supply your needs without your having to enter the prison of desire, and the Father will give you life which will be free of all fear. Then you can truly do the work of the Father in light and love."

"Do not ask, 'Where will I get the power for all this?' I will give you the power when you enter the Inner Way and trust me."

We did not spend all our time with the crowds, although they became insistent toward the end. Much time we spent quietly in boats or on the hillsides, listening to Yeshua's words, or practicing the discipline of the Way in our minds.

As long as he was with us, though, it was inevitable that the people would come to him, not to us, his disciples. He had to die, to leave us, he told us more often as time went on, or else we would not come into our own.

But we lacked that assurance and authority which he had, so we found it hard to speak his message with the same conviction.

"I am the Way," he replied to our questions, "not the end. Follow me and you will be in the Way. In my Kingdom the road is more important to mortal man than the destination. So why do you worry about where you are going? You cannot determine that anyway, with all your effort, and your effort only makes you a slave to time and your accomplishments. Pay attention to the road you walk, and your destination will be clear."

"But how can we teach these truths to others with your assurance?" we asked.

"I do not teach truths," he replied. "I point you to the Way and tell you the signposts on the Way. Do the same for others. Do not trust in your abilities or certainties to teach others. They also have a mind and a heart and can find their own way. Do not forget that, as I am with you, I will also be with them. I am with you in the flesh, but they will see me in Spirit. So as long as I stay with you in the flesh, you cannot see me in the Spirit. I must therefore leave you so that I can be with you all."

—

At another time, after Yeshua had cast a demon from a woman, he said to us, "Do not think of the devils within her in your usual way. They are real, but you also look at a stone or a tree and say, 'That is real.' I tell you, the devils in her were more real than a stone or a tree: a stone can be thrown away and she could walk around a tree and be on her way, but the devils in her ruled her whole life."

"All people have within them what became a devil for her. Anything that comes from a secret place within you and rules your life is your devil. Come to know the secret places of your life and all devils will flee from you. If the person who is possessed by some darkness is helpless and cannot be taught, then you may have to cast the devils out of them as I did with this woman, but it is better to teach people how to cast the devils out of themselves and thus have the benefits of freedom and insight. So enter your own places of darkness in your time of Silence, and thereby learn to teach others to do the same."

—

A member of the Pharisees asked him one day if he was the Son of God.

Yeshua replied, "You also are a Son of God."

"No! To claim such a thing would be blasphemy. I dare not claim such a title. Do not speak to me of that."

Yeshua looked at him intently, and then spoke. "You sense within yourself how close to God you are, but you are afraid to step closer. Was not Adam a Son of God? And are you not a spark of the Divine Fire? It is easier to be a mortal obeying laws than a portion of the Spirit of God lighting the paths of others. It is not blasphemy you fear, but responsibility. Yet I tell you, the yoke I would lay on you by making you a Son of God is lighter than the yoke of the Law. My yoke will bear you up: the Law can only weigh you down until you fall exhausted in the dust."

—

One day, as I journeyed further to the east and as I looked at the people around me, and wished for their life and their possessions and their place, and was assailed by doubts of what had been given me to do, the Voice spoke to me again in my time of quiet.

"All Nature is my kingdom. You have served me when you live in harmony with my world. When it is said that God loves the world, people think it is only they who are loved: but I love all things which I have made. There is nothing evil in all of my creation, but people have called many things evil. If you do not understand, then you call it evil. Evil is ignorance and is only perceived by those who do not understand what I have made."

"Do not imagine that you can escape from the world or from Nature. You are a part of the Earth, an expression of its consciousness. When you degrade the Earth, then, you degrade yourselves and defile your Mother, for you were taken from the Earth and must return to her."

"Look at the daisies of the field, how God supplies all their needs. They rise up in the morning and die in the evening. They lift their heads to the rain and sun and wind. They live out their allotted time, and then die, so others may take their place. They live to fulfill the purpose that is within them, and they die without regret. God has supplied their wants and he has gathered them again to himself."

"Why do you imagine you are better or more worthy than the flowers? They do what has been required of them, but you do not even do what the Father asks. Are they not more worthy of long life and many days in the sun?"

"You too are part of the Earth. You too rise up in the morning and die in the evening, and God supplies your needs. Do not look at the plants as your enemies or slaves that you may use. They also are your brothers and sisters on this Earth, because you have the same Father."

"Do not say that this animal is unclean or that plant is evil: you are all part of the Garden of the Father. Walk in His ways in the Inner Light and the whole Earth will open its spirit to you. So the land will bear crops for you and you will till the land with love. You will rise up on the land and die that others may take your place, as the plants rise up and die for you and for the Father."

"Open your mind and heart to the Earth as God does. Listen to the bird with love and to the cricket with rejoicing. Open your ears to the plants to hear even their love and their sorrow, and you will live as in a Garden where all things are alive in Light and Spirit praising the Father."

"How different it is to look at your stinking cities and the squalor of your soul. What do you seek, O Man? What great lust has seduced you from the Garden of the Father? What have you accumulated that can weigh against the love and peace you have lost? Look within and see the aching void which swallows all your possessions as if they had never been. Can anything bought with money, fill that emptiness?"

"So, in your hour of darkness and despair, do you look out and say, 'I am better than the daisy?' Or do you look at its brief span of life and wish also for the darkness to close over you? And if the darkness of death closes over the darkness which is already in you, how dark is that?"

"Do you imagine, then, that you can create your world within God's world? Are you also God? But your world is so small, and the power you wield is like a straw in the wind."

"When you grow tired of this game you play, turn again to me; become again a little child running in the grass among the trees. Enter into the light of the Inner Way, away from the darkness of your cruel games of darkness. There, in the quiet, in a garden of light and peace prepared for you, I will meet you, and talk with you, and together we will look at your life of darkness, part by part, and understand how you have taken light and turned it to darkness; how you have taken freedom and made it a prison; how you have transformed love into hate, trust into suspicion, peace into war."

"Come to me, I who dwell within you, that you may find light when all your world is in darkness, that you may find peace, even when your world is all war and cruelty."

"But do not imagine I call you to death. I call you from the world so that with new eyes you may enter again into the world to fulfil that purpose which the Father has for all his children. Enter again into the womb of Light that you may be born in love."

After that my envy stopped and I sought to follow Christ without looking with longing eyes at the people around me who lived often in luxury or in voluptuous style.

Most of the time I was alone on my journey, even though I sometimes walked with a fellow traveler. The loneliness gradually drew me away from the world into what I imagined was the purity of the Spirit. So I dreamed of drawing others into this purity as well. I imagined setting up a school where men and women could learn the new Way and so escape the ravages and torments of the body.

"You will indeed teach," Christ said to me in the Spirit, "but before that happens, you must journey far and see many things and you will remember my words and receive my instruction. And do not imagine that you will become great through your teaching. You will be hated and scorned by many, but you will also lead many to me, and I will be in them, drawing them to myself."

Then I recalled things which happened while he was with us and these memories spoke to me of my own dreams of teaching the Way.

We said to Him, after he had taught us much and some new followers had come to us, "You have taught us many truths, Master, and we see the spiritual kingdom plainly. Can we not instruct these new followers who have come to you?"

He thought for some time and then replied, "You see much, and you must teach what you have learned, so that others may see and hear clearly as well. It is good that you should want to pass on to others what you have seen of the Kingdom."

Then, turning to all of us, he said, "The new follower, because he has been liberated from his blindness, thinks that he sees all light, when in reality he has come from blindness only into the night. He can distinguish forms and grope his way around, but let him not think he has all wisdom."

"Those who have walked farther on the Way see more clearly as dawn approaches, so that they may say to those behind them, 'Take heart, for the day comes.' But let not the person in the darkness of spiritual beginnings nor the one approaching the dawn think that they have seen Truth, face to face."

"When the dawn comes and the morning mist rises, you will see the Kingdom spread before you like a fruitful valley with all things brighter than the sun. Then you will know that God is in all things and you live in God. You will know that every blade of grass and every hair of your head and every bird that flies is in God and God is in all. When you have seen this and know this in your heart, then you can speak with authority, for you know that God is in you and you are in God."

"Encourage each other, then. Share your visions, interpret, change your old ways to enable you to see more. Remember that in the Kingdom of the Spirit, the child is wiser than the most learned people of the world. Share, then, in humility, not calling one another 'Teacher,' or 'Master,' but 'Brother' and 'Sister,' for you all walk together."

"Remember, also, that the one who thinks he has become great in the Kingdom, thereby becomes least. Even those in the light can fall back into the darkness, and they will have to learn even from the children among you."

Then he turned to us and cautioned us, "Do not presume to teach. There is no special knowledge of the Kingdom, no laws and doctrines which must be learned in that way. Rather, guide others in the methods of prayer and meditation which I have showed you, and in the silence of meditation those who have responsibility for you on the spiritual plane will show you which way to go. Guide rather than teach, so that every person will know the experience of the Kingdom and not just the words of the vanity of the mind which thinks it knows, but is spiritually naked."

Again, to us, he said, "You can guide others, but be ready to learn from the experiences of others, even the most humble. So when you gather together, let those with a special revelation or those in greatest need speak. Others can interpret or seek to guide. Question each other about what has been given you, so that you all will have more. Test all visions and guidance to make sure it is really from me."

"Meditate in quietness and share in the gathering of the faithful, so that the Kingdom may be within you and among you. Share equally in the gathering, letting all speak. You are not heard for your many words, either in prayer or in the fellowship of others."

One day, while Yeshua was teaching in Jerusalem, some of the learned men asked him how he dared to teach what were his own words. "Are not all truths and all knowledge contained in the Scriptures, and should not all teaching be an exposition of the truths of Scripture?" they asked.

Yeshua replied, "There is no knowledge in Scripture and there is no truth. Knowledge and truth are within you, and only those who have traveled the Way within will find knowledge and truth. You seek to separate the truth within, from yourself, so that you do not have to take responsibility for it. So you look in the Scriptures and find there a mirror whereby you can see yourself reflected, then you say the mirror image is truth. Why not look within, using the Scriptures as a guide?"

"But are we, who have devoted our lives to the study of the Scripture, speaking only falsehood?" they objected.

"It is not falsehood. I do not speak against the Scriptures, for they can be made to speak truth or falsehood, as you know from your many schools of interpretation. You use the Scriptures as objects to be studied, words to be pursued, so you must come to disagreements."

"Look at the Scriptures, rather, as evidence that the Father can be present in human experience, then seek the experience of the presence of God in your life."

"Of what benefit is it to you to win one of your interminable

arguments? Have you come any closer to God? Why then would
you seek to multiply arguments by coming to me to seek yet another
interpretation? I will not enter into your sifting of the fine points
of the Law. Rather, forget the quarrelling and the fighting over the
laws, and come to know the Father who gives laws and frees from
the burden of laws. Truth is in the Father, who can send you many
more Scriptures if that were needful."

"You will become a leader," he said to me in my time of quietness
one night in a cave I had found to sleep in. "But, to be a leader in
the Way is to draw out of yourself all that is dark and all that sepa-
rates you from God, from the Earth, and from people. To be a
leader, you must go over the paths yourself first."

Then I again remembered Yeshua's words while he was with us
in the body. He said many things against the practices of the religious leaders while he taught. Some of the leaders took his remarks
to heart and tried to change their ways, but others were angry.

"Why do you constantly criticize us?" they asked. "Do you
expect us to feel kindly toward you or your teaching, if you behave
in this way?"

"Whether you feel kindly or not is not my concern," he replied.
"If you will not follow my words, like some of your brethren, kindliness does not matter. You are not angry at me but at yourselves,
because you know in your hearts that my words are correct but you
will not change. Your anger is really toward yourself."

"For this evening's prayers, if you can so far examine yourselves,
sit in quietness and then look at yourself as if you were someone
else. Do not feel afraid of what you see or condemn what you see,
for there is no condemnation in the Inner Way. Rather, see yourself
as the love of the Father sees you, and if repentance or joy or relief
or pain or love are in order, feel these things about the person you
see. What needs changing, change; what needs strengthening,
strengthen; what needs forgiveness, forgive; what needs praise,
praise. Do not condemn, since the Father has not condemned, but
know yourself as the Father knows you."

"Do this for a few days and then return to me and ask me again why I criticize you. You will then not need to ask the question, because the criticism I give will no longer affect you. Taste, and know that it is good."

Then he said further to the leaders of the people, "Do not call anyone on this earth 'Teacher,' because you thereby put them above yourself. And do not accept great titles for yourself, lest you fall into pride. The people of this world give glory to the great and think they themselves are small. I tell you, you are all both great and small, teacher and learner. Everyone has something to teach and even the greatest master has something to learn. Do not then put up divisions among yourselves, but all must be equal, teacher and learner taking their turns as the Spirit moves."

"But you must respect those who have gone far in the Way, whether they are old or young, for they can speak to you of where you are going, and can bring back tales of the lands of the Spirit which lie beyond."

"Respect and listen, then, but do not say to yourself, 'He or she is so far advanced that I can never get there.' You also are in the Way, you are a child of God, you are enveloped in His love, and all are equal."

"Be always willing to learn, and if you make a mistake, what is that? All make mistakes, but all can walk, still, in the Way."

Then he went further to explain the aim of our search. "Do not be dismayed if you feel within yourself that you are the Christ. This is not blasphemy. I will pour my Spirit out on those who truly seek me and they will speak to me in the Inner Way, and I will confirm that they are Christ. They will be in me and I in them, and their mission will be to carry my Spirit to the world. They will be the Christ acting in the world."

"So, if someone claims to be the Christ, understand their words in this way, and accept their ministry. But test their ministry as well, because anyone may say the words, 'I am Christ,' but only those who are filled with my Spirit will act the words."

"But remember that the body has laws which must be fulfilled, and the soul of the Seeker in the Way has its own task. My Spirit will give an added life to the Seeker, powers of the Spirit and authority in various realms of consciousness, but the soul and the body of the Seeker must find their law as well."

"So, do not say, 'Christ is weak,' because those who seek are weak. Rather, see how the weakness of the Seeker can become strength, if you turn fully to me."

As I walked along the roads, through so many strange lands, and heard the voices of so many strange tongues, I felt that I was indeed going to some destiny of which I could know nothing. Doubts began to grow in my mind, but for some time I did not bring these doubts into my time of meditation, but put them somewhere in a dark place of the mind and tried not to look at them.

How was I to carry out the will of the Father in a place where I did not know the language or the customs? Perhaps they would kill me for speaking of other gods than theirs, or perhaps they would drive me out to some other place or think I was mad.

I had been in strange lands before, so I could survive, and there was usually someone in any city who knew Greek or Latin, so I could communicate. There had been much travel, and many people had gone to Greece or Egypt to learn, or had gone to Rome on business, so that I was not looked upon as strange, as long as I remained in the compass of the Roman influence. But the Spirit seemed to be leading me farther to the East than I would have liked to go.

In the Roman world, my rationality was accepted, and they understood my words, as long as I phrased them in ways that the mind could accept without suggesting the necessity of moving also into the Spirit. But as I went to the east, the tone of the lives and expectations of people seemed to change, and I ran into ideas and feelings which were not familiar in the Roman world, but which had some similarities to the things Yeshua had taught us.

Now, beside the road on a morning, it was not uncommon to see people sitting in meditation, as we had done when with Yeshua.

When I sat thus in meditation, people no longer asked what I was doing, as they had done closer to Jerusalem. Was I walking into a world which had already heard the message of the Christ, I wondered?

But there were differences as well. They seemed not so concerned with the love of their neighbor as Yeshua had taught. They entered into the Silence also, but from talking to them, it seemed they sought to have no guide, to have nothing within. This I could not understand yet.

Why did they seek nothing within, when the Christ taught me to find the Way within?

These were all questions I wrestled with in that dark corner of myself which I did not bring into my Silence. Then, one night, as I was sitting by the road and doing my meditations, the inner voice of the Christ came to me again and said, "Thomas, you must now learn much of what sages of the East have learned long ago. Have you not heard that there were wise men from the East at my birth, and that they knew of the plan which the Father has for His world? So also you can learn from the wisdom of the East. They have not the whole of the knowledge of the Father, but they have come closer than any, to the sort of knowledge which can lead to salvation."

"You wonder why the Scriptures say that the Children of Israel are the chosen ones. The Father chose them to carry the burden and blessing of His Word, and they have carried part of His truth. But no one people has the whole truth, and no one nation can come to God. Rather, the Father has given it to many nations to strive, each on one part of the plan, that in the latter days of this age, all peoples, working together, might come finally to the Father and His love."

"You wonder at this, because the leaders of your people teach that they have all truth, and the Greeks and Egyptians teach that they have the truth. You know in your own experience that no one has the whole truth, so you have been travelling in many lands to find the truth. You must travel farther, but now I will guide you, and will show you the ways you must go."

"Do not think that the Way is simple, because then you think the Father is simpleminded. The Father has made you and all of humankind higher than the angels, and you have the potential within you to be one with all that the Father has made. Yet you have fallen far from the Father, and your soul has come into the flesh to redeem what is fallen, and to bring it again into the Light of the Father. The body, which is darkness, must be brought into the Light, that the body may itself be Light."

"You do not understand this now, because so far you have only gone into the darkness of your soul and body, and have not seen the vision of the Light which is the Father. When you have purged yourself of the dross of the body, and the darkness of the heart and the blindness of the mind and the rebelliousness of the soul, then you will enter into the full Light of the Father."

I said to Him in the Spirit, "But how will I do what you ask me to do? I do not know the wisdom of the East nor do I know how to purge myself of the things you speak of."

Then he spoke again, "You have been keeping doubts and questions secret from me. But all things are known to me and you can keep no secrets. So the secrets are only secrets to yourself. You doubt what the future will hold because you do not think I know the purpose for your life and your soul. You look into the unknown and wonder what can possibly have possessed you to come all this way on a journey into an unfamiliar land. But you are not alone! I am with you."

"And you do not trust my guidance either. Have I not brought you far since that first day when I met you in the wilderness and asked you to follow me? Have I not brought you rebirth and the baptism of the Spirit? Have you not given up your lower nature so that you could move into spiritual realms with purity? Now you are caught between the world of the flesh and the world of the Spirit and it is quite natural to have fears of where you are going. What is in this land of Spirit and how will you live there if you have found it so hard to live in the land of the flesh?"

"Do not fear, although you may wonder. Wait. Cleanse your

body and mind. Direct your attention in meditation to the Light of the Father and speak to me, asking for guidance in the Way. As you do these things, you will gradually find that the body is less important to you, because it is cleansed and cannot bother you, and the Spirit will be drawn upward to the Light of the Father."

"In your journey, you will come to the edge of the abyss which lies beyond the five senses, and you will fear to cross it. It is as large as the universe and as narrow as the eye of a needle. When you become aware of this abyss, do not fear to enter it, but call upon my name and then enter. I will guide you, for I am the abyss, and I am the Way, and I am the needle's eye, and you cannot come to the Father but by me."

"I can draw you to myself, and through me, you can go to the Father to live always in the Light. But now the time has come for you to enter into the abyss. So in the next few days, cleanse the body by eating little and drinking much water or the juice of fruits. Bathe regularly in the water and breathe of the air which the Father has given to all of His creatures. So the body will be cleansed of its dross and can be like a new wineskin for the wine of the Spirit."

"Cleanse your heart, also, of all hatred and envy and lust and anger, that you may radiate my love to others. Walk with patience and with concern for the needs and wants of others. But do not seek to show yourself great or generous or pious. Rather be humble and submit to the discipline of purity."

"Cleanse the mind also, that it may not hold onto any ideas of this earth or of the religions of this earth. All religions are partial and they see only in part. So the mind should not be tied to them or feel compelled to believe what they teach. That way is only more bondage. Rather, direct the mind to thoughts of the Light of the Father, and in your meditations, see in the mind's eye the Light which surrounds you and is in you and is at the centre of your soul. Hold the Light in your mind."

"Thus, cleansing on the physical plane, the body, the heart and the mind, you will be able to bring all three into the Light of the Father. But do not fear that you will have no part of the earth after that. Rather, when you have seen the Light, return again to be servant of the earth and the people on the earth, that like the Father, you may show love to all people."

"Then you will be able to love your enemy, because he will be no longer your enemy, but part of the creation of the Father which you will help to bring again into His Light. If your enemy strike your body, which has been perfected, what is that? What is not perfected cannot injure what has been perfected. What is of the lower nature cannot injure what has been drawn into the Light of the Father."

"This is why I said that you should seek first the Kingdom of God and then all things would be added to you, because when you have entered the Light of the Father, all things will be drawn to you that you need, and all things which are harmful to you will be driven from you. So do not fear, because I lead you to a state where there is no fear and where there is no harm."

"And when the whole creation has been raised into the Light of the Father, then there will be no tears and no sorrow and no suffering, because all will be in the Light, both human and animal, plant and rock, land and sea. And there will be a New Heaven and a New Earth, and the souls of men and women, although neither man nor woman, will live in harmony upon the earth and the dross will be purged away."

"As there is upheaval in you as you approach the transformation, so there will be upheaval in the earth, as it approaches its consummation and its transfiguration. Those who are of the Spirit and who live in faith will not fear the times to come, but those who seek only to live in the dross and to pull their souls into the mud, will fear and tremble and will be drawn into their own hell. But even then, if they turn to me in the Inner Silence, I will come to them swiftly and will deliver them into the Light, that they too may be part of that glory which the Father plans for the children of Light."

"Again, I say, all can enter into the Light. There is not one who needs dwell in the hell of his own darkness. The Father wishes to have all people enter into His Light, but He will not compel. All must come of their own accord and must enter into the Silence and call upon me that I may lead them into the Way."

"Come to me that you may be born into a new life. And when you are born, I will lead you into the baptism of the Spirit which will wash away the darkness of the dross of the material world. Then in time you can enter into the transfiguration of purification. And beyond that you can come to the abyss between the lower and the upper, between the darkness and the Light. Then you will enter the abyss which I am, you will pass through the needle's eye which I am, you will enter into the nothingness which I am and enter into the Light of the Father."

"I will be with you always."

⁓

So I journeyed for many days, seeking the transformations which the Christ spoke of to me, but I did not find the transformation. So I sought much in meditation and strained after the Light and thought on the Father and His glory, and struggled with myself to see why I was not pure enough or loving enough. Yet nothing came.

Then I thought in my mind that perhaps there was no such thing as this transfiguration of purification, and that perhaps I was deceived, and that perhaps the voice which I followed was a lying voice and I had been led astray. And I complained against God that He had brought me out of Jerusalem into this wilderness where I knew no one and where I could find no guidance.

After much struggle and after much suffering in my soul, I turned again to Christ and asked him what it was that I was doing wrong, and I prayed, "Christ, if this voice which I follow is not you, then appear to me, because I can only follow what I hear, and I try to follow you, and call upon your name. So if you are elsewhere, and wish to save me, then come to my aid, or I am wholly lost."

Then I sat and wept that I was all alone in this and that I had no other guide, and that no man seemed able to tell me where to go.

As I sat thus, the word of the Christ came to me again in my inner parts and comforted me. "You feel pain, Thomas, because, although you want the Light of the Father you also do not want to leave behind the things of the earth. You would keep at least one foot in the assurances of the intellect and the philosophies and teachings of the priests and learned men."

"Listen to me carefully, Thomas, for these are the words of life to you. What you love, that you will be. Your love is the centre of your life and being. If you love God wholly, then you will be able to find Him, but if you say you love God and want to hold onto your philosophies, then you will have only your philosophies."

"No ideas, no names, no wealth, no friends can contain the Father, and even to call Him the Father or 'Him' is to limit what God is. God is the All, the Incomprehensible, yet He has made Himself known as the Father, or the Mother, or the Compassionate one, or the Son, or the Christ. So you start by following Yeshua, or the Christ, or the Father, but you must progress gradually, as the Spirit gives you strength, to a love of the One, the Light."

"But do not seek ideas or names. Your love is the centre of your life. Seek to love all of the creation; then you will be able to come closer to a love of God. For if you hate what He has created, how can you love Him?"

So I sought in myself all those things which I hated or all those things which I tried to put away from myself. I thought to myself that I had been free of all hatred, but as I looked within I found that there were many things which I had denied or forgotten in my attempt to come to the Christ. So I had to accept them again to myself: I had to understand them. I could not condemn anything.

It seemed strange to me that our traditions had taught us to put all things of the earth away from us to come close to God, but now I had to reclaim them in a different light. No longer was I attached to them: no longer did I find security in them, but I had to accept them as part of myself and raise them with me to the Father.

This was often painful, and as I remembered things from the past and tried to accept them as part of myself, I often wept in my time of meditation for what I had been and for the love which others had given to me and for what I had failed to do which could have changed so much in my life and the lives of others. And I repented for what I had done, and saw the beauty in the lives of others, even the most despised, and I saw others as perhaps God sees them, as struggling people, fighting within their pain and bewildered within their darkness.

I said to the Christ one evening, "Why must all this suffering be? Can I not bring all these people to you that they may be healed and come into your glory?"

But he said to me, "I would that all people would come to me and be saved. But no one can bring them. They must come themselves. Only what you achieve by your own will and your own act are yours. No one can bring you your salvation. Even I cannot bring you your salvation."

Then I asked why so many people remained in darkness when they could come to the Christ.

And he answered me, "Because they do not wish to see and they do not wish to hear. We have sent to them the prophets and great men and women of the Spirit to show them the way, but they would not hear. We have sent them Light in their inner being, but they would not look within, so enamoured were they of the darkness in which they live. We have even sent Yeshua that they might see the Love of the Father, but they would not listen, and they pervert even what has been given them and turn it into hatred and bigotry and lust for power."

"If all people, this instant, were to come to me, I would receive them and present them before the Father, and they would be saved from their darkness. But they wish to cling to the darkness and will not trust even one who comes from the dead."

"When can I come before the Father?" I asked, for now I felt the longing to go beyond the darkness of my soul into the Light of which he spoke.

"You can go very soon," he said to me. "But do not decide what it will be like for you."

So I waited that night, in patience, to be taken before the Father, and the next morning I waited again. I expected a great flash of light or that I would be ushered into a great light, or that my body would be transformed. But I waited in vain, for nothing happened.

Then, in my inner self, I thought of the gulf which Christ spoke of and the needle's eye, and I imagined these things in my mind and tried to move through the needle's eye, but could not. Then, in my despair, I felt I was at the bottom of a dry well and that all around me was trash and filth.

Then, in my mind's eye, I saw a man like me come into the pit and ask how to find the Lord. And I said to him, "You will have to climb that ladder over there."

So he began to climb, until he was far in the air and had come to the top of the ladder. But there was nowhere else to go. Then I realized I was the man at the top of the ladder, and I could go no farther. But when I thought of climbing down again, I looked below me and found that the bottom of the ladder went so far out of sight that there was no way I could descend.

Then a voice came to me saying, "Let go of the ladder and jump."

Then, in fear, I held on all the harder. "Let go of the ladder and jump," the voice said again, and this time it sounded like the voice of the Christ.

So I let go, but my feet would not come free. Then I struggled to get my feet from the ladder, but they would not come.

"Cut the ladder off below you, then," the voice said.

So I cut the ladder off, and the ladder I had climbed up tumbled down and I remained in the air. The small bit of ladder I held also fell, and the hands of the one with the voice bore me upward and brought me to a land of softness.

Then I saw before me a road, as it were, going through the clouds, and following the road I came to a great gulf with no bridge, but in the middle of the gulf was a needle with an eye much smaller than myself.

Thinking that I had to squeeze through the eye of the needle to find the Light, I quickly imagined that I had gotten through and that I had come to a great light. But I was unhappy and seemed to be absorbed into large masses of bodies of light. And I struggled to escape from this mass of bodies, feeling that I did not want to come to this place.

Then the voice came again, saying, "Leave your imaginations. Do you think you can force yourself into the Light of the Father? Do you think what you are doing is only a thing of the imagination?"

"I am the Door, and no man comes to the Father but by me. Anyone who forces his way into the Kingdom of the Light is not in the Light, but in the dark of his self-deception. Do not try to force yourself. I will take you when you are ready. And do not try to think in your mind what it will be like. Can your mind grasp what the Father is?"

So, in shame, I waited again on this side of the gulf and saw the needle's eye before me, and felt now that I would wait, for of myself I could do nothing, and all my learning had not taught me how to cross this gulf.

After several days of waiting and coming each morning and evening into this same place, the voice said to me, "Go forward."

And I said, "How will I cross that great gulf and enter the needle's eye?"

And he said, "Go forward."

So I went forward, as I had been instructed, and came to the edge of the great gulf, and it seemed like a great pit before me.

Then the voice said again, "Enter the gulf and walk toward the needle's eye."

So I entered the gulf and found that I could walk across toward the needle's eye.

And the voice said, "Pass through the needle's eye."

So I put my body into the eye of the needle and it went through. Then I put my arms through, and my legs, and my left foot. But my right foot was too big, and I could not get it through.

Then the voice said to me again, "Thomas, you seek to take your rationality with you into the Kingdom of Light."

And I looked and saw that my boot was very dark on my foot, and that it had swelled and would not come through the eye of the needle.

Then the voice said again, "Remove your boot, and take the shoe from your other foot as well."

So I reached down and took off the boot and the shoe, and my foot passed through the eye of the needle.

Then the voice said again, "Do not presume to depend on your own reason in the country ahead. Leave all patterns and all creeds and all doctrines behind, because they see only in part. But in the Kingdom of the Light you will see without clouds obscuring what is before you."

Then I saw a road going into the country before me over what appeared to be the roof of the clouds. And the Christ then came to me and embraced me and said, "I have brought you this far. I am the Way, and I am the Door, and I am the Needle's Eye, but now you must go forward and the Father Himself will teach you."

But I clung to him and said, "But I have grown to love you, and you have guided me out of so much darkness into such glorious light. And you have been like a parent to me, guiding me and showing me love and even showing your anger when that was right. Can I not stay with you here and help you?"

Then, gently, he put me away from him and said, "The Father seeks not that you would love me now, but that I should bring you to the Father and He will show you His love. I show His love to the world that through me many may be drawn to Him, and He may be able to show them the Love which is the centre and the being of all. Go on the road in front of you and you will meet the Father."

So, with many tears, I left the Christ on the road and started forward to see what I would find. I feared the image of the light and the mass of lights I had seen in my imagination, but I walked with the assurance of the Christ still in my ears.

As I walked along this road above the clouds, I began to wonder in what guise I should meet the Father. Would He be a large light, and would I be consumed as by fire when I met Him?

There was some fear and anxiety in me, but now my devotion to the Father led me on. Whatever happened, I would go on. It was the Father I sought.

It seemed to me that I was far above the earth here, and that the land through which I walked was soft like clouds. The road was white and smooth on which I walked and gradually my hesitation passed and I began to look ahead eagerly for whatever I should see.

Then, far off, I saw someone coming toward me, and I hurried my step to meet this person and ask him which way I should go. Then, as I drew nearer, I saw that the person ahead of me was like an old man, but that his face was full of love and welcoming.

I suddenly realized that this was the Father, not as I had thought He would be, but as Yeshua spoke in the story of the son who had gone far from home and returned. And I realized also that I was the son who had left, and that now I was being welcomed home.

So I ran over the path, and with tears in my eyes flung myself into the arms of the Father and wept on His shoulder, and He embraced me and held me to Him and spoke comforting words to me. And I wept the more because I had been so long from home, and I knew now that this was my home. I wanted to fall at His feet, but he held me up and would not let me. And my joy was complete, and I did not know what to say or do, for my heart was full and my mind could only think of silly words, such as a child might use.

And I asked if He were the Father, and if this was the celestial sphere, and if I had really come to Him, or was imagining, and where I had come from, and if this was a dream. And to all my babbling He smiled and laughed and assured me that I was with Him and that this was a greater reality than I had ever known before.

But I felt like a child who had just come to himself, and knew nothing about the world around him. And I could not believe that to come to the Father would be like this, because my mind had told me everything differently. But the feeling of oneness with the Father was so great, and my joy was so full, that I could not contain myself and wept and laughed and embraced Him.

After a time I began to come to myself again, and asked Him if this was indeed the celestial realm, if this was the Kingdom of Light, because all was light around us.

And he said, gently, that it was, and that I had come to Him here, and that we would always be together.

And then I asked Him of the Christ who had guided me to this place, and He said that the Christ was that aspect of Himself which calls out to the people of the world to come to this place and that this place is within each person.

Then I was puzzled and asked how this could be in me.

He said, "Did not Yeshua, who came from Us, say that the Kingdom of God is within you? But you would not believe him, and sought the Kingdom elsewhere. I tell you as your first lesson in this place that where we stand is within you."

"Did you not listen to Yeshua when he told you that he and I are one, and that he wished also for you that you and I could be one? But again the ears of flesh cannot hear that word. Did he not also tell you that you are all sons and daughters of God? But you would not hear."

"Many of your learned men have made Me into a vast light, or into something which is unknowable. But I seek the lost and, like a father, I send out my messengers into all the countryside, seeking those who would come to my feast. But they will not come, for they want the darkness of their own world."

Then, in great longing, he said to me, "I would that they would return to me, but I cannot force them. Any parent knows the same longing, because they cannot force their children to be what they want or to accept their love. You are created in my image and in your own world you can find Me."

Then he said again, with pain in his face, "I long that the earth would return to me. All my creation serves me and shares in my love, but the earth has rebelled and the people on the earth have gone far from me, and will not hear my call. I have sent them the prophets and the saints and even my Son to call them to me, but they would not come. I cannot force them, because only what comes of their own will is true, and only those who discover the love which calls them from within can turn to me. But they are too much enamored of the external to look within."

Then he looked at me again with love, and welcomed me to this Kingdom of Light, and took me by the hand and led me farther on the road.

I said to him, as a little child might, "Is the earth then far from here?"

He turned me around then so that I could see where I had come from, for I thought that I must have climbed high above my old ignorance. And I saw the path, and the great gulf with the needle's eye and the path going, not down now, but over flat country to a city far away, with its walls and towers in the distance.

I was astonished, because I felt I had climbed far on my journey, but He explained that all reality is not only on the same plane, but that if I could see aright, I would see that all things were in the same place.

"You have only to open your spiritual eyes to see the spiritual realms which are within you. All possibilities are within you as I am within you and you are within Me. You cannot comprehend this now, but I will lead you farther and you will know all things which are necessary to you."

And I wondered in my mind why I had not been transfigured, and whether others would see a change in me as I continued my journey in the external world. Would my face be shining with light like Moses or would I be able to float through the air?

He looked at me with love and said, "You seek for mighty signs in the outer world when in the inner you have seen so many changes and you have come into the Light. The inner will finally be reflected in the outer, but now you must learn on the inner plane and come to the centre of Love within you before you will find many changes in your outer self."

"You will find greater joy and freedom, and less fear: you will feel love toward your neighbors and will see my Love in all around you.

But do not seek for a sign in the outer world. Signs will come when they are needed."

Then I asked Him, "You do not seem to be what I thought you would be. Are you not more that this? I do not mean to say that I am not satisfied with what You have shown to me, but what else are you?"

"I show you what you can learn from at every stage of the journey, if you come to me with patience. If you force your way, you may see things which are not good for you. So I appear in a form from which you can learn. Could you accept all my glory at once? No. It would destroy you, and I seek not to destroy but to save."

"So, at first, I was just a doubt in your mind which urged you to search for truth. And I was the man Yeshua, teaching you the inner way to me, and I was the living Christ, guiding you to my Kingdom. But even now you could not accept the full glory of my being, so I appear to you as a Father who loves you and seeks to welcome you home. For this is your home, and I am your Father, and my Love is ever seeking you."

"But, to some, I will appear differently, but with love always, bringing you to myself. So I am also a Mother to some and a Friend to some and the burning Light to others. I seek to serve with my Love, not to punish. I am not any one thing which your mind can grasp, but am all things to all people who will turn to Me."

Then I knew that I was indeed but a child in this Kingdom and that I had much to learn. I was only at the beginning of the true journey and was like a babe at the breast, not yet weaned from the spiritual milk on which I had been fed. And I was humble and full of gratitude for the blessing which had been given me. I knew that I was nothing, yet the Father would not let me be nothing. "You are in Me and I in you. How then can you be nothing?" He said to me.

After that experience, I was shown much and guided in many ways, but of those experiences I am not permitted to speak, because each one who comes will have different lessons to learn and it would not be good to speak of my lessons lest others think they too should have the same lessons. Also, the learned and the intelligent would turn the celestial realms into a system and into doctrines and so would enslave those on the physical plane.

"This upper level of heaven is a place of freedom and creativity," the Father told me. "There is no right or wrong here, for all are the ways of Love. Laws are not necessary, for each tries to love as he or she knows best, and their guide is the Love which is the centre of their being. Love is their being."

Then I asked, "Father, can I pass anything else on from this realm?"

And He said, "These things only. That you must not expect others to notice that you have come to Me, but you will be peaceful in your heart and will work for peace in the world. You will have patience and work in love. You will take joy in the things you have to do in the world, however humble. No one will say of you that you shine like the sun or that you are a pious man or woman. Rather, you will know in yourself that you walk with your God, the Father of all."

"In this realm are people of all religions and all creeds, since religion and creed are not a serving of me. It is the action of Love, free from within you, which brings you to me, and that Love at the centre can only be found in the Inner Way."

"Carry also the message to others that I love them and wish their good. Whatever tends to bondage in the self or in others, shun. Whatever tends to true freedom and Love and a respect for My creation, think on those things. For the higher way, come to Me in the Inner Way, and I will guide you to myself. Work diligently in your search."

⁓

As I continued my journey, and as I was brought to this place on the seashore among a people who are dark in skin but who have followed the Light within, I continued to learn many things from the Father.

When I looked around me and saw people who had been searching before I arrived to bring the words of the Christ and the

Father, I began to wonder about the nature of what Christ had given me to do.

The Father said to me one evening in my time of meditation, "You wonder that people other than the Jews have the secrets of the Kingdom as well as you. As you have been instructed before, the secrets of the Kingdom have been given to many people, but to no one in their complete form, so that each, seeking in their own way, may gradually come closer to me, but no one group can say, 'I have the secret and you are excluded.' Indeed, any who say that, have already put themselves outside of the Kingdom, because the Kingdom comes by Love, and Love is a working together. Love is not exclusively for one group."

"In the end of the Age, peoples from all parts of the earth will bring their knowledge together and will find the Inner Way to me by working together. So, read and know what has been given to others, that your knowledge may be complete and you may be able to come to Me, all working together in Love."

So I continue my work among these people and grow to love them in the years I have been here. I learn their language and teach them and learn also from them. And from day to day I learn more from the Father of the celestial which is at the heart of our lives.

Now there is no fear, even though I am in disfavor with the authorities of the temples here. These people also have priests who seek to enslave, and they resent my coming here to teach a way of freedom and love and mercy. So perhaps I, too, will find an end like many of the followers of the Christ before me.

But I do not fear now, and I know that in life or death I will not be separated from the Father who is within.

That is my story of the Christ — not a birth and not a death, but a life which is within us. There is no doctrine and no law, but only the search within and the guidance of the Christ and the Father. What may come at the end of the age I have not been given to know, but it, too, will arise from Love and the fulfilling of the life of Love in the world.

CPSIA information can be obtained
at www.ICGtesting.com
Printed in the USA
BVHW031257030821
613539BV00001B/3